THE YOUNG PARENTHOOD PROGRAM

D1736586

THE YOUNG PARENTHOOD PROGRAM | A GUIDE TO HELPING YOUNG MOTHERS AND FATHERS BECOME EFFECTIVE CO-PARENTS

**Paul Florsheim
and the Young Parenthood
Program Team**

OXFORD
UNIVERSITY PRESS

UNIVERSITY PRESS

Oxford University Press is a department of the University of Oxford.
It furthers the University's objective of excellence in research, scholarship,
and education by publishing worldwide.

Oxford   New York
Auckland   Cape Town   Dar es Salaam   Hong Kong   Karachi
Kuala Lumpur   Madrid   Melbourne   Mexico City   Nairobi
New Delhi   Shanghai   Taipei   Toronto

With offices in
Argentina   Austria   Brazil   Chile   Czech Republic   France   Greece
Guatemala   Hungary   Italy   Japan   Poland   Portugal   Singapore
South Korea   Switzerland   Thailand   Turkey   Ukraine   Vietnam

Oxford is a registered trademark of Oxford University Press
in the UK and certain other countries.

Published in the United States of America by
Oxford University Press
198 Madison Avenue, New York, NY 10016

Library of Congress Cataloging-in-Publication Data
The young parenthood program / edited by Paul Florscheim.
     pages cm
ISBN 978–0–19–930947–4
1. Teenage parents—United States.   2. Teenage pregnancy—United States.   I. Florscheim, Paul.
HQ759.64.Y68 2014
362.7′8740973—dc23
2013035296

9 8 7 6 5 4 3 2 1
Printed in the United States of America
on acid-free paper

CONTENTS

ACKNOWLEDGMENTS

The book is dedicated to Daniel Offer (1929–2013) who was a wonderful mentor and a pioneer in the field of adolescent development.

This guide was written with input from the members of the Young Parenthood Program Team, which includes Jason Burrow-Sanchez, Mary Fisher, Kayla Flores, Tim Fowles, Sarah Heavin, Sheri Johnson, Megan Howard, Cristina Hudak, Amy Kirby, Laura McArthur, Rocio Paredes-Mora, Trina Salm Ward, and Selena Webb-Ebo. Creating the Young Parenthood Program has been a team effort that has benefited from multiple perspectives.

Over the years, the Young Parenthood Program and related research has been funded by The Centers for Disease Control, The National Institute of Mental Health, and the Office of Adolescent Pregnancy Prevention Programs. We are grateful for this support.

We greatly appreciate the openness and goodwill of the young men and women who participated in the young parenthood research studies and the focus groups in Chicago, Salt Lake City, and Milwaukee. We wish to thank the following stakeholders and local experts in Milwaukee, Wisconsin who provided guidance for adapting the Young Parenthood Program for use with African-American youth in Milwaukee: Darryl Davidson, City of Milwaukee Health Department; Jill Denson, Milwaukee Health Services, Inc.; Gerry Howze, Pearls for Teen Girls; Tashiba Johnson, New Concept Self-Development Center; Patricia McManus, Black Health Coalition of Wisconsin; Terence Ray, Milwaukee Fatherhood Initiative; Dawn Shelton-Williams, Aurora Family Services; Ramel Smith, Children's Hospital of Wisconsin; and Don Sykes, Milwaukee Area Workforce Investment Board.

We also appreciate the effort and expertise of Lorraine Lathen, from Jump at the Sun Consultants, who facilitated our focus groups and expert panel forum, as well as provided us valuable feedback and insight. We are forever grateful for the support of Alicia Richmond Scott and Cassandra Chess from the Office of Adolescent Pregnancy Programs, who have supported this work and the lives of pregnant and parenting adolescents. Finally, a special thank you to Carolyn Bucior, whose feedback and skillful editing was essential to the completion of this book.

All proceeds distributed to the authors are donated to the Healthy Teen Network, which advocates for the health of young parents and their children.

THE YOUNG PARENTHOOD PROGRAM

BEYOND SINGLE MOTHERS AND ABSENT FATHERS

1

YOUNG FAMILIES AT RISK

IN RECENT YEARS, THE RATE OF TEENAGE PARENTHOOD diminished substantially from 62 births per 1,000 youth in 1991 to 34 per 1,000 youth in 2010, which suggests that the current generation of adolescents is more careful about sex than the previous generation. This decrease, which is mostly attributable to the dissemination of effective sex education programs and the wider distribution of contraceptives, is a public health success story worth applauding (Santelli & Kirby, 2010). Yet despite this success, some of the larger social issues that we hoped to prevent by reducing adolescent childbirth—such as high rates of single mothers and absent fathers, chronic poverty, and unstable family relationships—have not improved in the general population (Census Bureau, 2012). One of the reasons for this is that as the rate of teen childbirth decreased, the rate of babies born to young unwed parents in their early to mid twenties increased dramatically.

In 2012, the United States Census Bureau reported that more than 4 out of 10 babies were born to unwed parents (Census Bureau, 2013), which means the rate of children born to unwed parents has more than quadrupled since 1960 when just 1 in 20 babies were born to unwed parents. The percentage of unwed mothers and fathers is highest among young (under 25) economically disadvantaged (living under the "poverty line") minorities (African American and Latino), but the trend is spreading throughout the population. For example, among women between the ages of 20 and 24, the number of babies born to unwed parents is more than 6 out of 10, averaged across ethnicity and socioeconomic status (SES). Experts and policy makers concerned about the welfare of children had thought that preventing unsafe sex among adolescents and reducing the rate of teen childbirth would help create a more stable family life for economically and socially disadvantaged populations. This was a reasonable assumption because the children of adolescent parents were (and still are) among our most vulnerable. However, as society's gender roles and social norms loosened over time, young men and women began to have children without bothering to get married. Ironically, the same cohorts of young men and women that were being more careful about sex in their teenage years were having babies outside of marriage as young adults. Some of the problems we had sought to fix with "sex education" became broader and more profound. This upward trend in unwed childbirth in young adults suggests that our society—as a whole—is undergoing a monumental shift in how we define and construct our family lives (Furstenberg, 2011).

Previous generations of men and women, born in the 1950 and 1960s, struggled with the failure of marriage (first their parents' and then their own) to meet the high expectations of family life. Consequently, the subsequent generations were left without much guidance about what holds a family together. Whatever the reasons for the shift away from marriage, there is little doubt that there is a great deal at stake. Marriage has been a socializing force in most societies, including our own, anchoring families and organizing kinship groups.

As an institution, marriage has given structure and meaning to our commitments and helped protect the best interests of our children, who thrive when provided with a stable and secure home environment. The legal and religious basis of marriage helps to ensure cooperation and collaboration through the most trying moments of our lives. It has kept us at the table, quite literally, negotiating the day-to-day tasks: getting the kids to school, figuring out what to have for dinner and who should make it, deliberating about which bill to pay and which one to put off, and hopefully giving each other a little love and compassion along the way.

Many social scientists (and social pundits) have suggested that without the anchor of marriage, our society is adrift and heading for disaster (Murray, 2012; Popenoe, 2005; Popenoe & Whitehead, 2002). In addition to holding families together, or perhaps because of this, marriage decreases stress, supports health and psychological wellness, dampens the effect of economic downturns on families, and increases the benefits of economic prosperity. The research has consistently found that marriage is good for us (Amato, 2001; Kiecolt-Glaser & Newton, 2001; Robles et al., 2013). Most notably, children growing up with their married parents fare much better in almost every aspect of their development when compared with children growing up in single-parent families (Amato, 2008). It is also the case that adult men and women are healthier when married, presumably because we benefit from the security and stability that marriage provides (Newman & Roberts, 2013).

If we were to assume that most children with unwed parents are being raised by their single mothers, then the long-term impact of this shift could be quite bad, leading to significant hardship. Children in single mother–headed households are at increased risk for a range of negative developmental outcomes. They are more likely to drop out of school, get into trouble with the law, and report clinically significant levels of depression and anxiety than children growing up in two-parent households (Amato, 2005; MacLanahan & Sandefuer, 1994; Scharte & Bolte, 2012). These risks are partly attributed to the strain and stress associated with poverty, as single mothers are much more likely to be poor and live in impoverished neighborhoods (Brown, 2012). But the risks are also attributable to the absence of fathers, who add stability and security to their children's lives even when their primary contribution to parenting is indirect through the support they provide to the child's mother (Carlson, 2011; Lamb, 2010).

In addition to the social and financial disadvantages associated with single parenthood, there are also psychological disadvantages. One of the consequences of the shift away from the traditional, two-parent family structure is that many children lack the opportunity to see men and women—their fathers and mothers—struggle to negotiate and compromise with each other or grow and learn from each other (Lamb, 2010). If we believe that fathers and mothers occupy distinct psychological roles in a child's life, then it makes sense that children growing up with only one parent will find it more difficult to create a coherent sense of self (Pleck, 2010). These children know less about how to engage and sustain intimate relationships or find compromise, which will make it more difficult for them to establish stable environments for their own children when that time arrives (Amato et al., 2006). Perhaps most importantly, families—however they are defined—provide us with a sense of security and belonging and identity. Single parents can provide their children with these fundamental elements of our humanity but when there is strife between a child's mother and father, the split between them threatens to undermine the integrity of those elements.

Although it is not likely that we are going to turn back the clock to 1960, something needs to be done to address this problem of unstable families. Some have suggested that the problem must be addressed at the broadest level by adjusting our economy so that two-parent families can thrive and creating policies that promote marriage (Moynihan et al., 2004; Murray, 2012; Smeeding et al., 2011). This may be the case, but those political and economic solutions seem distant, abstract and elusive. The goal of this book is more modest and specific, up close and personal. We hope the program described in the following chapters will help young parents provide their children with a sense of belonging, connection and support regardless of what happens between them as a couple. This book is not about trying to save the institution of marriage or about declaring that marriage is dead; it is about providing young co-parenting couples with some tools for creating stability and security.

The point here is simple: Not all children born to unwed mothers are growing up without their fathers or living in unstable homes. Although most unwed fathers do not reside with their child's mother, many participate in child rearing and provide some financial and emotional support to the child's mother (Amato, 2005; Carlson et al., 2008). And there is evidence that children whose nonresident fathers stay involved are psychologically healthier than children whose fathers are truly absent (Amato, 2005; Carlson et al., 2008; McLanahan & Beck, 2010). One obvious question that emerges from the research on nonresident fathers is why do some men disappear? Are the absent fathers just heartless or too self-absorbed to be concerned with the well-being of their children? After almost 20 years of studying young fathers, I believe that only a small proportion fall into these unfortunate categories, at least at the outset of parenthood. Most young fathers are just woefully unprepared for the tremendous work of parenthood and not up to the interpersonal challenge of co-parenting. Do some men stay involved with their children outside the context of marriage?. Broadly speaking, evidence suggests that sustained paternal involvement is closely linked to the quality of a co-parenting couple's relationship (Carlson et al., 2008; Dubowitz et al., 2001).

It is difficult to zero in on a percentage of unwed and nonresidential fathers who remain actively involved with their children because the US Census does not track nonresident father involvement. Although family researchers have found that the rates vary with age and socioeconomic circumstances, it can be estimated that roughly half of nonresidential fathers stay involved and about half disappear (Carlson et al., 2008; Cheadle et al., 2010). In our own research—in which we followed young parents across the transition to parenthood—we found that about 25% of young fathers co-reside with their partners through the first two years of their child's life; about 25% remain romantically involved with their child's mother but live in a separate household; about 25% are not romantically involved after two years but co-parent in some fashion; and 25% are no longer involved by the end of the first year. These rough estimates are based on interviews conducted with young fathers who were willing to meet with us in the first place at least once. We estimate that about 20% to 30% percent of the young expectant fathers we tried to recruit into our research—through their pregnant "partners"—had already disengaged.

Although unwed parenthood has not caught us by surprise (the rate has been creeping up for decades), social service and mental health professionals have not developed a constructive, forward-looking plan for responding to this change in our social structure. This is not to say that nothing has been done to address the "problem" of single motherhood. To be sure, there are several excellent programs that address the needs of young single mothers and their children (Harris & Franklin, 2012). Some of these programs focus on establishing social and economic security (such as Temporary Assistance for Needy Families); others focus on providing parenting support (such as the Nurse Family Partnership Program). Most assume that father involvement is minimal or not relevant to child rearing or fathers will not participate in parenting programs (Carlson & McLanahan, 2006). The lack of attention given to fathers or "couples" raises the next obvious question; is it possible to support the development of positive "co-parenting" between young unwed mothers and fathers who want to work together to raise their child? We think it is worth trying.

In the chapters that follow, we describe an approach for helping young couples learn to work together to raise their children. *The Young Parenthood Program: A Guide to Helping Young Mothers and Fathers Become Effective Co-Parents* provides a crash course on how to facilitate the development of fundamental co-parenting skills among young couples who are expecting a baby. Most adults would agree that young women and men should do everything possible to avoid getting pregnant until they are mature enough to take on the responsibility of supporting and raising a child. Yet, despite what adults say and do, many young couples get pregnant and have babies anyway, often with high hopes for their co-parenting relationship and a strong determination to become good parents. When this happens, what is the appropriate response? We believe that as mental health and public health professionals, we have a responsibility to help young mothers and fathers meet these challenges of parenthood. This book presents a new approach to supporting young parents that draws on three important resources: (1) decades of research and theory on healthy adolescent development (Brown & Prinstein, 2011); (2) time-tested principles and evidence-based practices of couples therapy (Gurman, 2008); and (3) the high hopes and good intentions of young expectant fathers and mothers.

USING THE YPP GUIDE

The first four chapters of this book, including this one, provide some background to orient you—who we presume to be a mental health practitioner—to the general Young Parenthood Program (YPP) approach. Chapters 5 through 10 cover the core elements of the program; these chapters read like a clinical manual or a practitioner's guide because that is their intended purpose. Prior to practicing YPP, it is important for you develop a solid understanding of the philosophy and the concrete steps involved in administering the program. The final chapters are intended to help the reader adjust the model to meet the particular needs of his or her practice and the populations served.

The guide is intended to be a resource for training counselors new to the program and to be used as a reference once training is complete. It is also intended to help counselors adhere to the program's structure, goals, and spirit. Counselors delivering the YPP should be guided by the same set of principles, follow the same intervention format, approach couples with the same relational intent, and undertake the same major activities to ensure that the program's effectiveness can be adequately assessed. As a YPP counselor, you should carefully study the entire guide prior to meeting your first YPP couple. Once initial training is complete, the guide should help you address case-specific issues. Review the guide in preparation for specific sessions and then check back to determine if program goals are being met. Throughout the guide, we take a strength-based approach to common co-parenting issues but also cover potential problems you (and your participants) might encounter along the way. Although the guide will help you address many of the issues and problems presented by young co-parenting couples, it is likely that you will be asked to respond to some other issues that are not covered.

The idea of doing co-parenting counseling with young expectant parents is new, so it is quite possible that you will encounter clinical challenges we have not considered. When faced with such challenges, it is wise to consult with your supervisors and/or colleagues who can help you think through how to best respond. On the other hand, we cover a great deal of territory in this guide and you should not feel compelled to use all of it with every couple. You may not encounter all of the issues we present, and you should focus your attention those issues that seem most relevant to the populations you work with on a regular basis.

This guide is accompanied by a toolbox of worksheets, intended to help you work with couples around specific issues. Some of these tools are borrowed and adapted from other couple and parenting programs. Carefully review the toolbox materials prior to work with each couple. Select only those tools that are relevant to each couple. Although you probably will not use all the materials for all couples, it is important to be familiar with them and know how to use them. The materials in the toolbox can be used in a flexible manner so long as YPP's goals are maintained. A table describing the worksheets in the toolbox is provided at the end of Chapter 7 (Table 7.3).

KEY TERMS

Co-parenting: The relationship between two or more adults that focuses on taking care of the physical, social, and emotional needs of their children to support their health and positive development. Co-parenting involves the sharing and/or dividing of parental roles and responsibilities.

Co-parenting alliance: The cooperative and collaborative element of the co-parenting relationship. An alliance implies that all parties are committed to working together toward a common goal. The co-parenting alliance is distinct from other elements of the co-parents' relationship. For example, it is possible for two co-parents—a mother and father—to have negative, hurt feelings about their partner based on their failed romance, but still maintain a positive co-parenting alliance.

For a more detailed description of co-parenting see:

Feinberg, M. E. (2003). The internal structure and ecological context of co-parenting: A framework for research and intervention. *Parenting: Science and Practice, 3*(2), 95–131.

Feinberg, M. E., & Sakuma, K. (2011). Co-parenting interventions for expecting parents. In J. P. McHale, & K. M. Lindahl (Eds.), *Coparenting: A conceptual and clinical examination of family systems*. Washington, DC: American Psychological Association.

---

2 INTRODUCTION TO THE YOUNG PARENTHOOD PROGRAM

RESEARCH BACKGROUND

OUR WORK ON THE YOUNG PARENTHOOD PROGRAM started in the 1990s when we conducted a series of studies to examine the role of co-parenting relationships on the parenting outcomes of young mothers and fathers. When we began this work, young fathers were generally regarded as irrelevant to parenting because they were not expected to stay around (Carlson & McLanahan, 2006; Easterbrooks et al., 2007; Fagan & Palkovitz, 2007). There was a clear bias against young fathers—the partners of pregnant and parenting teens—based on the assumption that were destined to become deadbeat dads, not worth the clinician's time and effort (Lerman, 1993). One of our initial goals was to test the alternative hypothesis that most of these young men wanted to become good fathers and good partners (Florsheim & Smith, 2005; Florsheim et al., 2003).

We quickly learned that the best way to find young expectant fathers was to work through their partners—the pregnant adolescent who could be identified and approached through prenatal clinics and school programs for pregnant and parenting teenagers. Recruiting fathers was not easy. We worked hard to convince these pregnant teenagers to invite, cajole, or drag their partners into our offices. We have been successful in recruiting approximately 60% of the young expectant fathers we identified. The vast majority of these young fathers were highly invested in "being there" for their children and hopeful about staying together with their child's mother.

In the first set of young parenthood studies, we found that the quality of the young father's relationship with his partner helped predict how well he functioned as a parent, including *whether* he stayed involved with his children and the *quality* of his involvement as a father. For example, if the relationship with the young mother was hostile, he was at greater risk for becoming disengaged. Also, fathers who were hostile toward their partners during the pregnancy were more likely to be harsh and punitive with their children a couple years later. This pattern was also the case for young mothers, but the strength of the connection between partner relations and parenting relations was not as strong. As expected, her relationship with her parents was also an important factor in how she functioned as a mother.

Young men with troubled histories—substance abuse, school failure, and poor relations with their parents—had a more difficult adjustment to parenthood and were less positively engaged as co-parents. However, having a supportive partner often ameliorated the negative effects of an adverse developmental history on parental functioning for young fathers (Florsheim & Ngu, 2006). In fact, we found that those young men whose partners were observed to be interpersonally skilled became more positively engaged as fathers. More specifically, we found that some fathers seemed to be learning about how to be more positively engaged as a parent...from their partners.

Encouraged by these findings, we developed the Young Parenthood Program (YPP), drawing heavily on the theoretical and clinical writings of several experts in marital counseling (Cowan & Cowan, 1995; Gottman, 1999; Mikelincer et al., 2002) and experts in the interpersonal development of adolescents (Collins, 2002; Furman & Shaffer, 2003). In our initial tests of YPP, we hypothesized that by helping young parents maintain a positive co-parenting relationship we could support the development of positive parent-child relations (Shultz, Cowan, & Cowan, 2006). The research on YPP is ongoing but initial findings of two randomized clinical trials have been promising. For example, results indicate that the program helped to reduce or prevent intimate partner violence between co-parenting partners (Florsheim et al., 2011). More recently, we demonstrated that young fathers who were randomly assigned to participate in YPP were more likely to stay positively engaged with their co-parenting partners and more likely to become warm, nurturing dads than young fathers who were randomly assigned to a control group (Florsheim et al., 2012). So far the program seems to be working; with a relatively minimal level of professional guidance and support, young expectant fathers and mothers are able to develop the skills they need to maintain a constructive, co-parenting relationship and engage more positively with their children.

CO-PARENTING APPROACH

The Young Parenthood Program is a brief intervention designed to help young parents develop the skills to co-parent. The premise of YPP is that with a relatively modest amount of support across the transition to parenthood, many young couples can develop the skills they need to maintain constructive co-parenting relationships. We define co-parenting as the process through which two parents work together to provide for the social, emotional, and physical needs of their child (Feinberg, 2003; Feinberg & Kan, 2008). In this clinical guide, we apply the term "co-parenting" to the relationship between the biological mother and father of the child, regardless of whether or not they are romantically involved.[1]

Like marital therapy, YPP is couples-focused; we believe that in order to facilitate the rapid development of positive co-parenting skills, we need to work directly with couples. Unlike programs that isolate mothers and fathers into gender-specific groups, YPP invites a couple into the same room at the same time to learn and practice new communication skills. As described in the following chapters, the model is systematic and structured but also flexible and designed to be tailored to the needs of each couple. The program is brief (10 to 14 sessions) to keep costs low, but long and intense enough to provide a clinically useful "dose" of relationship skill building.

One of the primary goals of the Young Parenthood Program is to keep fathers involved in co-parenting and help them develop a sense of their competence and value as fathers. Why focus on the young father? One reason is that without a concerted effort to include fathers in co-parenting and help them develop their identities as fathers, the trend toward father disengagement will continue and might increase. Young women are socialized into the motherhood role from early in their lives, presumably because of their biological role in reproduction. When a young woman finds out she is pregnant, both maternal instinct and gender role

[1] The YPP focuses explicitly on the quality of the co-parenting relationship between biological parents, regardless of their relationship status. A co-parenting-like relationship may exist between a young mother and her mother, or a father and his new partner, or any number of other co-parenting configurations. The Young Parenthood Program is not designed to address the co-parenting concerns within these other co-parenting dyads. These relationships require a somewhat different approach from what is offered in this guide.

socialization kick into high gear. Additionally, there is often an outpouring of support and assistance from her family, her school, and her doctor to help prepare her for the responsibility of childrearing. No matter what happens to her relationship with the father, the mother's identity is likely to remain intact. By contrast, a young man's identity as a father and the role he plays in his child's life tends to be dependent on how his relationship with the child's mother pans out over time. He is unlikely to receive much support in this role from outside sources, including his own family. If the relationship with his partner sours, his connection to his child and his sense of identity as a father often suffers. As such, the YPP is intended to shore up outside sources of support and provide some of that support directly.

It is important to note that just keeping fathers involved with their children is not sufficient. The relationship between co-parents can be either a protective factor or a risk factor for children, depending on how they engage with one another. When co-parents are negatively engaged, their hostility affects the overall family environment and often spills over onto their relationships with their children (Grych & Fincham, 2001). However, positive relations between the couple can also "spill over" onto the parent-child relationship, contributing to the child's sense of security. The primary goal of YPP is to help young co-parenting couples develop the capacity to support each other in the best interests of their children. We see the prenatal period—when young expectant fathers and mothers are highly motivated to work together—as a window of opportunity for helping them learn to become constructive, positive co-parents (Carlson & McLanahan, 2006).

Why focus on co-parenting? Most programs for young mothers and fathers focus on helping the single parent improve his or her (mostly her) parenting skills. Our efforts to work with the mother and father together is based on presumption that parenting is a fundamentally social and collaborative enterprise (Cowan et al., 2010; Feinberg, 2002). Our focus on co-parenting is intended to optimize the value of a primary, naturally occurring support system: the co-parenting couple (Hawkins & Fackrell, 2010).

There are many ways to define the co-parenting relationship. The specific model that we propose in this book—which focuses on the biological father and mother—is only one of several possible models of co-parenting (McHale & Lindall, 2011). In many societies mothers cooperate with each other or with a group of maternal elders to raise the children, often without much input from the fathers (Hrdy, 2009). This more communal model of co-parenting is an equally valid and viable approach. Indeed, some might argue that this female centric model is more appropriate in some cultural contexts.

Of course, different approaches to co-parenting are not mutually exclusive. A young mother's relationship with her child's father can be seen as complementary to the support she receives from her mother or sister or aunt. The co-parenting couple—young mother and father—can grow and learn from supportive grandmothers and other mentors, even males. There are many possible co-parenting configurations; many naturally occurring family structures (Hrdy, 2009). So why focus on the young couple?

Without arguing *against* other cooperative family arrangements, we believe that the potential value of the young co-parenting couple—the biological father and mother—has been underestimated and overlooked. The YPP model is designed to include the biological father primarily because our research strongly suggests that (a) young fathers want to contribute to the well-being of their children; (b) the quality of the couples co-parenting relationship is a strong predicator of paternal functioning, which means that fathers depend on their relationship with mothers; and (c) with minimal support, biological fathers are likely to remain engaged in co-parenting. Generally, we believe that the biological connection between a father and his child is a compelling and under-utilized resource.

THEORETICAL COMPONENTS OF THE YPP

The Young Parenthood Program is designed to help young expectant couples manage the intense interpersonal challenges of pregnancy and early parenthood. It draws from the principles of attachment theory to help couples develop their capacity for creating an emotionally secure environment for their child (Cowan & Cowan, 2002; Cowan et al., 2004; Englund et al., 2011). Its general approach also draws from the principles of family systems theory and social learning theory and is based on the following assumptions:

(1) Participants are more likely to stay engaged in the program when they are encouraged and when there is a clear focus on the link between *their* behavior, *their* co-parenting relationship, and *their* child's development.

(2) Interpersonal learning is most likely to occur under conditions that promote support and respect (Lerner et al., 2006). Counselors should create these conditions through demonstration and by redirecting nonsupportive and disrespectful behavior.

(3) Relatively small changes in a participant's interpersonal process can open the door to significant individual growth (Hatton, Conger, Larsen-Rife, & Ontai, 2010). Counselors should work to facilitate incremental learning and commend couples on even the smallest interpersonal successes.

(4) The most efficient way to facilitate interpersonal development is to work directly within the context of significant relationships (Gottman, Gottman, & Shapiro, 2010). Although some didactic instruction may be appropriate for some couples, most learning and growth occur through action (e.g., the demonstration, testing and practice of new skills).

The Young Parenthood Program consists of two components: co-parenting counseling and care coordination services, described briefly below:

Co-parenting counseling: Co-parenting counseling facilitates positive communication skills and interpersonal competencies between at-risk co-parenting individuals (Solmeyer et al., 2012). These skills and competencies are defined as the capacity to: express warm feelings, provide support and reassurance, regulate hostility and de-escalate conflict, state personal needs and feelings clearly and tactfully, listen reflectively and empathically, and repair relationship damage (Christenson & Jacobson, 2000; Gottman & Gottman, 1999). These fundamental components are drawn from research literature on couples and family counseling (Gurman, 2008). The counseling component should be administered by a master's level counselor or social worker (or trainee).

Care coordination services: We recommend that young parents be given access to a care coordinator or case manager, as most need help with pressing life stressors related to school, work, legal issues, housing, and so on.

They often need help developing self-advocacy and coping skills to meet the challenges of parenthood (Rapp & Goscha, 2004). The YPP care coordinator approach is based on an "active" case management model that teaches participants communication skills to help them advocate for themselves and their families and increase their access to resources. As a whole, YPP is intended to help young parents take care of each other and work together to make sure their children grow up in a safe and secure social environment.

The Young Parenthood Program can be offered in various settings and may be an especially good fit for those programs that already serve pregnant and parenting populations such as high schools/junior colleges, prenatal clinics, and adolescent health centers. A setting's own policies, procedures, and standards may require some adjustments to the practice of YPP as presented throughout this guide. Counselors, supervisors, and administrators will have to consider their required standards and available resources as they determine how to deliver YPP with the most fidelity possible.

THE THREE PRINCIPLES OF THE YPP CO-PARENTING COUNSELING

In this section, we address three basic principles that guide effective co-parenting counseling. First, all YPP counseling should be tailored to the developmental capacities of the co-parenting couple; counselor activities should facilitate that couple's interpersonal development. Second, counselors should focus on individual and relationship strengths in order to support a positive connection between the co-parents. Third, counselors should help young parents understand and recognize the association between their *relationship* (and how they treat each other) and the health and well-being of their child. These three principles should be emphasized and re-emphasized.

PRINCIPLE 1: THE YPP IS DEVELOPMENTALLY FOCUSED

The transition to parenthood is a developmental process that is influenced by the developmental status of each parent (Belsky & Pensky, 1988; Miller-Johnson et al., 1999; Ngu & Florsheim, 2011). When working with young couples, it is useful to remember the unique developmental challenges of early adolescence, mid-adolescence, and later adolescence/young adulthood. Unlike adult parents, young parents often feel stretched between two stages of development. On the one hand, many young parents are immersed in the world of adolescence and struggling with typical concerns about self-image, peer relations, sports and competition, and becoming more independent. On the other hand, young parents are suddenly faced with adult-level responsibilities and commitments. Straddling these two worlds can be confusing and overwhelming.

Under normal circumstances, counselors would not necessarily provide adolescents or young adults with couple's therapy. Typically, when young people are having relationship problems, they are expected to "live and learn" and move on to new relationships. Almost by definition, these early romantic relationships are unstable and impermanent. By contrast, adult parents are expected to have achieved the capacity for making long-term commitments. They are also expected to successfully engage in a number of other rather complex social and emotional challenges, such as learning to accurately read their infant's cues; manage their frustration, anxiety, and aggression; and provide their infant with a sustained level of warmth and comfort. Some adolescents and young adults may be able to rise to the challenges of parenthood on their own, but many need additional support. The Young Parenthood Program helps these young parents "speed up" their interpersonal developmental process and acquire these skills.

The effort to speed up development can be particularly difficult for younger adolescents (14 to 16 years old), who may not have the cognitive or emotional capacity to manage the intensity of new parenting and the co-parenting relationship. For example, many younger couples will not know how to talk with their partners about personal issues or seek support when needed. The success of co-parent counseling will depend on how effectively the counselor adapts the intervention process to meet the particular developmental level of each parent. For example, this adaptation could include inviting the young couple's parents to participate in the intervention process, providing support, and offering their insights regarding the challenges of parenthood.

WHAT IS ADOLESCENCE? WHAT IS EARLY ADULTHOOD?

Anyone reading this clinical guide about working with young parents is likely to have some well-developed ideas about how to define adolescence and early adulthood. Nonetheless, our shared understanding of this period of life has changed rapidly over the past 30 years because of advances in the neurosciences and rapid changes in social norms that guide development. Clarification of what these terms mean is important because they appear with great frequency throughout this book and the concepts are central to the topic of providing co-parenting counseling to young couples.

Adolescence is derived from Latin term that means "to grow up." It has been traditionally defined as coinciding with the teenage years, but more recently it has been suggested that adolescence may extend from as early as 10 years and as late as 26 years when the brain is thought to reach "maturity." Whatever the specific parameters of adolescence as a developmental stage, it is widely regarded as a period of transition between childhood and adulthood, during which exploration, experimentation, and some instability is to be expected. Highly responsible 12-year-olds can become reckless 14-year-olds. Risk-taking behavior increases, but so does the capacity for formal reasoning, autonomous behavior, and social engagement. During this phase, young people develop an identity, which means that they develop a core, durable sense of self (*Who am I? What do I value and believe?*) and a sense of their place in the world.

Early adulthood is the phase of life that follows adolescence and ends in the early thirties. The primary tasks of this developmental phase are to (a) form intimate, enduring and stable relationships; (b) acquire the skills needed to take care of oneself and others; and (c) commit to specific constructive social roles, including the role of parenthood.

Although some young people may need (and want) structure and guidance, like most adolescents they are motivated to be independent, take care of their own needs, and make decisions for themselves. Young parents may feel uncomfortable receiving help or advice from others and it is important to couch your support and guidance in a way that does not diminish their autonomy. For example, before making a suggestion, ask if they are open to your perspective. This will give the participant a greater sense of control in the relationship and increase his or her receptivity. It is not unusual for young people to initially appear dismissive of adult input only to reconsider it later, when they are able to decide—on their own—whether it makes sense for them.

Although adolescents are not expected to have well-developed relationship and parenting skills, it is important to avoid assuming they are completely deficient simply because they are young and inexperienced. Despite their age, some adolescent parents have strong interpersonal skills and are capable of functioning well as co-parents (Breen & McLean, 2010). Some are able to draw upon the support of extended family in ways that help ensure that the child is cared for and healthy. In fact, some young men and women who appear to be at very high risk for problems with parenting surprise everyone with their capacity for change and growth (Florsheim & Moore, 2012; Florsheim & Ngu, 2006).

PRINCIPLE 2: THE YPP ENDORSES A STRENGTHS-BASED APPROACH

Young people are most likely to respond positively to an approach that emphasizes their strengths and will feel appreciated by counselors who are able to see their "unrealized" or potential strengths. Many expectant fathers and mothers feel very unsuccessful in their lives and doubt their ability to meet the challenges of adulthood and parenting (Arcinue & Prince, 2009). Although it is not helpful to deny a person's difficulties or challenges, it is essential to help your participants use their strengths to cope and manage whatever challenges they face. When working with young people who are clearly in trouble, your credibility as a counselor (rather than a cheerleader) will depend on your ability to convey that although you see their negative traits, you consider their strengths to be their most important characteristics.

For example, a young man who has an aggressive, argumentative style—which creates conflict with teachers, parents, police, and his partner—will benefit from an approach that helps him redirect that energy toward constructive goals. Often, such young men have strong moral convictions; they feel they are defending what is right or their personal integrity. In such a case, lead with a statement about how you admire the young man's willingness to stand up for himself and his beliefs and point out that he can use this strength—this sense of protectiveness—by channeling it toward taking care of his child. . . . if he can stay out of trouble.

The more you convey that you see the "good" in participants (without denying their problems) the more effective you will be in helping them develop their skills. In this way, you can build their self-esteem, facilitate the therapeutic alliance, and most importantly, help them understand that they possess the raw material for becoming a good parent and co-parent. When young men and women identify and engage their innate (and possibly hidden) strengths, they are likely to feel encouraged and even excited about the possibility of interpersonal growth.

In addition to helping individuals build upon their strengths, YPP teaches partners to see the positive traits in each other, which helps them respond more patiently and empathically to each other and accept each other's flaws and limitations. If one partner is feeling like a failure, it usually helps if the other partner points out past successes, or offers a reminder of the courage and strength already displayed. For example, if a young mother is upset with the amount of time the father spends playing soccer, the father will be more likely to listen to her complaints (and requests) if she is able to clearly state what she values about him, including his investment in soccer. This strength-based approach increases the likelihood that the couple will leave the sessions feeling more positively about themselves, each other and you.

PRINCIPLE 3: POSITIVE CO-PARENTING SUPPORTS POSITIVE PARENTING

There is a strong association between a positive (or at least civil) co-parenting relationship, positive parenting behavior, and healthy child development (Grych, 2002). The capacity for expressing warmth and acceptance toward one's co-parenting partner can be transformed into the capacity for nurturing a fussy infant or encouraging a frustrated child, for example. You can help by verbally connecting the couple's relationship issues to parenting issues. For example, if one partner compliments the other, use that moment to underscore the impact of complimenting young children and explaining the value of positive reinforcement.

If a pregnant adolescent listens carefully to her partner and responds empathically, fold in a discussion of how being attuned to each other's feelings is good practice for becoming sensitive to their infant's feelings, whose "language" will be completely nonverbal. Conversely, it is important to address the connection between negativity in between partners and the parent-child relationship, explaining that children will "absorb" hostility between the parents even if it is not directed toward them. When young couples are upset, it is hard for them to remember these connections. As we explain further in Chapter 7, it is sometimes appropriate for you to interrupt negative exchanges and redirect the couple's attention to the long-term goal of creating a positive environment for their child.

The link between the quality of co-parenting relationships and parenting is particularly strong for young fathers. Mothers tend to draw parenting support from several sources, but fathers are much more dependent on their partners for co-parenting support. When the relationship is good, a young father is likely to benefit from his partner's guidance and encouragement and remain engaged with his child. When the relationship is poor, a young father has more difficulty staying engaged, particularly when he must go through the mother to have access to his child. Even if the young mother is willing to grant access (as is usually the case), young men are notoriously unskilled at managing interpersonal strain and tend to become progressively more disengaged from parenting. Helping a young expectant father learn to constructively respond to interpersonal conflicts will help him remain engaged with his child.

PHASES OF CO-PARENTING COUNSELING

The Young Parenthood Program is implemented in six phases, which are described in-depth in upcoming chapters. Counselors can track a couple's progress within each phase in their counseling notes. Couples may move through these phases at differing speeds; determining how much time to spend on each depends upon the couple's and counselor's abilities to meet phase goals.

The phases are designed to be implemented sequentially, but there may be situations in which they are best implemented out of order. For example, during

Table 2.1 PHASES OF THE CO-PARENTING COUNSELING INTERVENTION

Phase 1	**Introduction, Assessment, and Engagement** (1–2 sessions). The counselor introduces the goals and philosophy of the program; describes confidentiality; obtains consents; and begins to address relevant social and cultural issues.
Phase 2	**Goal Setting** (1–2 sessions). The counselor assists the couple in identifying (a) personal strengths and areas for growth, (b) relationship strengths and areas for growth, and (c) relationship goals. Issues related to culture, race, poverty, immigration, or discrimination that may be relevant to goals are addressed. At the end of this phase the counselor and couple create an individualized plan for the YPP.
Phase 3	**Interpersonal Skill Building** (4–6 sessions). The counselor and couple work on relationship development. The specific interpersonal and communication skills targeted will depend on the particular needs and priorities identified by the co-parenting couple. These skills are outlined in Table 6.2.
Phase 4	**Role Transitions** (2 sessions). Counselor and couple focus on the changes in life roles and relationships as a result of becoming parents. Exploration of these transitions includes examining shifts in relations with the couple's own family and friends. The counselor works with the couple on how to ask for support from others. The process may include inviting members of the family to participate in a counseling session.
Phase 5	**Summing up/Looking Forward** (1–2 sessions). The counselor helps the couple consolidate the development of key skills and generate a plan for reducing stress and optimizing strengths during the transition to parenthood.
Phase 6	**Follow-up Co-parenting Support** (2–3 sessions). The counselor conducts this "booster session" after childbirth to support the couple's adjustment to parenthood and address their most salient relationship needs. These two sessions offer the opportunity to reinforce previously learned skills and positive intentions about parenthood.

the goal-setting phase (Phase 2), a couple may discuss problems with one partner's mother who is always getting into "their business." The counselor should validate this issue, and then decide whether to proceed with interpersonal skill building (Phase 3) or move to the role transition phase (Phase 4) and re-visit Phase 3 later. In this particular case, it may make sense to first help the couple develop communication skills and later help them set appropriate boundaries with the grandmother, while remaining respectful and considering the possibility that she may be trying to offer support. A thorough knowledge of each phase and the associated goals and tasks will help you plan effectively, be flexible, and ensure that all program objectives are met. The phases of intervention are outlined in Table 2.1.

WHO WILL BENEFIT FROM THE YPP AND WHO SHOULD BE REFERRED ELSEWHERE?

For most young co-parenting couples, the prenatal phase offers an optimal time for delivering preventive services, such as the YPP. During this phase, young at-risk couples can be easily identified through prenatal clinics and schools with services for pregnant students. Young men are often resistant to the idea of counseling and some are averse to receiving any sort of social services. However, during the prenatal phase, an expectant father tends to be more open to participating in programs and receiving services, especially if he believes that doing so could benefit his family. The prenatal phase is somewhat of a "honeymoon" period for many couples. They are highly motivated to demonstrate their commitment as parents and co-parents even if they have doubts about each other and their relationship. We believe it makes sense to make use of their good intentions.

Clinicians and administrators may exclude couples from YPP who are clearly not suited for couples-based intervention. For example, youth who have serious cognitive deficits or developmental disabilities may not be able to make use of counseling that requires a fairly complex understanding of communication processes. Also, couples who are engaging in physical or sexual violence require a higher level of intervention, and it is appropriate to make a referral to another agency, perhaps recommending individual counseling for either or both partners. Finally, the age discrepancy between a mother and father should be considered before providing YPP counseling. In our experience, it is not unusual for one partner to be a legal minor and the other a legal adult. This can create legal issues for the couple and the counselor, depending on state-specific statutes regarding statutory rape; however, the fact that one partner is 16 and the other is 19 does not necessarily mean that the relationship is exploitative, coercive, or abusive. When one partner is a minor it is important to be particularly attentive to this possibility. In some circumstances the dynamic can change over time. When you are concerned that a minor is being victimized by an adult, it will be necessary to make a report to child protective services.

Determining if YPP is appropriate for a couple in this situation can be tricky. The decision should include the following factors: (a) Legal obligations related to child abuse reporting laws. Program counselors, supervisors, and administrators should be familiar with state laws regarding age of consent for sexual activity (typically 16) and when reporting is appropriate even for 16 year olds; and (b) Developmental discrepancies between the partners that suggest some level of exploitation and coercion. We have found that when one partner is a minor (under 18) and the other partner is more than five years older, the power imbalance is often significant and YPP can be an inappropriate intervention. Deciding if a couple would benefit from YPP should be done on a case-by-case basis following an in-depth interview with the couple during the Engagement and Assessment Phase (Chapter 5). Whenever YPP is not suitable, referrals to appropriate community agencies should be made by the counselor and/or care coordinator based upon the couple's needs.

WORKING EFFECTIVELY WITH ADOLESCENTS

Youth culture and language can be difficult for counselors to understand. Be curious, ask questions about the meaning of words and phrases used by your adolescent participants, but be aware that most young people are put off when adults try to adopt their language. This often comes across as phony and trying too hard. Most adolescents want adults to behave and talk like adults, which seems more genuine. That said, YPP counselors should be open to texting and e-mailing. Many youth and young adults are more apt to respond to these means of communicating, so ask YPP participants about their preferred methods of communication.

Young expectant parents vary greatly in how much they are able and willing to communicate with their counselors. Culture, developmental stage, self-confidence, personality, trust, and respect all impact how much young parents interact with their YPP practitioners. Some young parents will have no trouble expressing how they feel and sharing their thoughts, whereas others will struggle. When the latter happens, remain patient, focus on creating a safe, supportive environment, and work to build a positive relationship with your participants. You can offer your best guess about what they are feeling or thinking, but always ask their permission before doing so. For example:

COUNSELOR: You seem to be having a hard time figuring out how you are feeling or what to say, is that right?

YOUNG FATHER: Yeah.

COUNSELOR: Are you OK with me taking a guess? Then you can tell me if I got it right.

YOUNG FATHER: Sure.

COUNSELOR: I guess if I were in your shoes, I would feel angry and hurt but I would also feel like I didn't want to start a fight by saying that. Is that how you are feeling?

YOUNG FATHER: Maybe.

COUNSELOR (TO YOUNG MOTHER): Does that make sense to you? Is that what you might imagine he is feeling?

YOUNG MOTHER: I don't know.

YOUNG FATHER: I'm angry about what you said but I don't want to start an argument.

COUNSELOR: I think it's possible for you two to talk about this without getting into a big fight. Are you OK with me suggesting how to do that?

YOUNG FATHER: Yes.

COUNSELOR: Try to tell her why you are angry but do it in a way that does not blame her or put her down. After you do that, maybe you can soften things up a bit by reminding her of one important thing that you like about her. And if you have a hard time doing this, I can help.

This heavy-handed approach might be necessary to get some couples comfortable with using language to work on their relationship. When doing this, it is very important to be checking in to make sure that the couple is feeling supported and not manipulated. Young Parenthood Program counselors demonstrate respect to young participants by listening to them without passing judgment, asking about their ideas and perceptions, and encouraging them to use their strengths to find solutions that work best for them. Young Parenthood Program counselors can also role-model a high level of respect by being patient and by clearly demonstrating appreciation for the opinions, abilities, and interests of their participants.

WORKING EFFECTIVELY WITH THE FAMILIES OF YPP PARTICIPANTS

The YPP empowers young expectant parents to be positive and productive co-parents. At face value, few people would argue against supporting a positive co-parenting relationship. But consider the program from the perspective of the couple's parents who will be the grandparents of the child. In some cases, the grandparents may not approve of the couple's relationship and might prefer for the "other" parent to go away and leave their child and grandchild alone. Some grandparents may feel that YPP's focus on the young couple undermines their authority over their child. That said, most families of young expectant couples are ultimately supportive of YPP, although they are also understandably protective of their child's best interests. Almost always, they appreciate being included in the counseling process, if only as a gesture of respect for their position and perspective.

Counselors should consider extended families as potentially valuable sources of support. Although it is important to maintain your focus on the couple, it is also important to collaborate with their families as much as possible. Young mothers and fathers are often still dependent on the support and guidance of their own families, who are typically still invested in maintaining their responsibility for the well-being of their child. Anyone under the age of 18 is legally required to obtain parental consent in order to participate in YPP. Those over the age of 18 have the legal authority to make their own decision regarding YPP. Regardless of whether the YPP counselor *must* legally engage the family, it is a core value of YPP to involve and engage families in a useful manner based on each couple's needs.

Some families may be appropriately suspicious of you—you are a stranger offering to step in and help their child. In many contexts this may seem presumptuous or motivated by some hidden agenda. Some families may be uncomfortable with the close association between YPP and mental health, psychotherapy, and social services. Some cultures—including mainstream American culture—view people who *need* help as weak or flawed. Some families may feel that it is inappropriate to share personal concerns with strangers. These issues are best addressed by speaking directly with family members about their concerns and explaining YPP's rationale and purpose. Do not treat these conversations as a mere formality. Rather, use the opportunity to demonstrate respect for their role and authority and to solicit their perspective on how you can best support their child. For participants who are under 18, the need to obtain parental/guardian consent gives you a good excuse for connecting with the parents. If a participant is 18 or older, find out if talking with his or her parents would be useful. Older adolescents and young adults often appreciate the question because it conveys respect for their autonomy *and* their parents' position of authority.

Collaboration between counselors and the families of YPP participants can be critical to successfully engaging youth. The parents of young expectant parents experience a wide range of emotions and reactions to their adolescent's pregnancy, including sadness, anger, fear, guilt, excitement, happiness, and disappointment. They may have mixed feelings regarding the pregnancy and the relationship. Some parents will want to be actively involved in and informed about their child's participation in YPP; others will be less involved and will expect their son or daughter to take on more adult decision making and responsibilities in preparation for parenthood. When family members feel positively about the goals of the program, they are more likely to support regular participation (e.g., encourage, remind, provide transportation, open their homes up to be used for meetings). Remember to discuss the issue of confidentiality and assure families that any serious concerns regarding the safety of their child and grandchild will be conveyed to them promptly. Explain that the details of counseling session discussions will be confidential, but if they desire more information you can hold a joint session to address their questions and concerns. Adolescents and young adults will pay close attention to whether you keep your promise to respect their privacy; still, they may like seeing that you are willing to serve as a bridge between them and their parents.

CHAPTER REVIEW

The previous chapter served to set the stage by providing an historical context and a theoretical framework for program development. Now we switch our focus to describe in greater detail the roles of those implementing the key components of YPP, namely, the counselor and care coordinator.

THE ROLE OF THE COUNSELOR

3

INTRODUCTION

THE YOUNG PARENTHOOD PROGRAM IS BASED ON THE IDEA that relationships are central to almost every part of developmental process—from birth to death. Human beings grow and learn within the context of their relationships with parents, peers, and partners. In this clinical guide, we focus on the co-parenting relationship because we believe it is vital to the development of healthy children and the reconstruction of family life. This chapter is about *your* relationship with the young couple. In addition to our "naturally occurring" relationships, we all develop important relationships with a number of "professionals" in our lives, including teachers, physicians, and counselors. We believe that your professional relationship with the young men and women with whom you work is potentially vital to the quality of their co-parenting relationships, particularly for couples who are at high risk for disengagement or negative co-parenting. Your relationship with the young couples who participate in YPP is your primary tool for developing rapport, supporting growth and effecting change. As you read this guide (including this chapter, which provides a general introduction to the role of the counselor), remember that in order for the program to be meaningful and relevant to your participants, it needs to make sense to you and work for you. For this reason, we tried to design the program to be flexible enough to fit different counseling styles and professional orientations.

PRACTITIONER QUALIFICATIONS

A minimal requirement for YPP counselors is that they are in a graduate-level training program that will prepare them to conduct psychotherapy. Licensed psychologists, social workers, and marriage and family therapists are qualified to implement the YPP as long as they engage in the self-training process outlined in this guide to ensure that the program is implemented properly. A YPP counselor is expected to have basic couple's counseling/therapeutic skills including the capacity to (a) listen to both partners and empathically respond to individual and couple-level needs; (b) work with both partners to create a respectful atmosphere that encourages openness and sharing; (c) gently guide and redirect the process when one or both partners begin to engage in dysfunctional behaviors; and (d) focus on helping both partners learn and grow and experience forward movement in their relationship, even if that means deciding to break up as romantic partners.

In addition to having basic counseling skills, counselors need to receive some training on how to work with at-risk adolescents/young adults. This includes: (a) using simple language that can be understood by young people with limited vocabularies and concrete thought processes; (b) providing clear explanations of the counseling process (what the young person can expect will happen during the program) to ensure that everyone has a shared understanding of goals and activities; (c) demonstrating flexibility regarding the logistics of meeting, recognizing that young expectant couples are often overwhelmed by competing demands and may have limited control over their schedules; and (d) offering guidance and structure that are consistent with their level of development (15-year-olds are likely to have different relationship concerns than 25-year-olds). The interpersonal skill-building activities described in this guide are designed to help participants of various ages address their concerns, but you will have to figure out how to connect the dots between these activities and the particular goals of each co-parenting couple.

The Young Parenthood Program strongly emphasizes the therapeutic alliance between counselor and participants for two reasons. First, there is solid research evidence that a strong therapeutic alliance—characterized by a warm emotional bond—is the best predictor of positive therapy outcomes (Shirk, Carver, & Brown, 2011). Young people are more likely to be receptive to counseling if they feel respected and appreciated by their counselor; counselors are more likely to be effective when they are able to empathically connect with their participants' experiences and circumstances. When this emotional bond is missing, developing it will be an important goal for the counseling process (Karver et al., 2008). Second, YPP is about building relationship skills. Attending to the quality of the relationship between you and your participants is one of the best ways to model these skills. Young Parenthood Program counselors should be comfortable focusing on the relationship components of the therapeutic process, which may include self-reflection. The best way to accomplish this goal is to "be yourself" when interacting with participants. It is possible to maintain clear professional boundaries while allowing the young couple to get to know who you are and why you are interested in working with them. The more genuine you can be about your interest and investment in their relationship, the more invested they will become in the program.

As a counselor, you need to remain "couple-focused" and avoid the temptation to get drawn into individual concerns and problems. You may need to reframe a personal issue as a co-parenting issue that the couple could work on together. Consider, for example, a young father who expresses a great deal of anxiety about not getting a job. You may feel (appropriately) concerned and be inclined to coach him in how to solve the problem. In many cases, this would be a missed opportunity. Instead of responding directly to the father, you could encourage the couple to discuss the problem, providing your input only as needed. You may discover that the girlfriend has excellent suggestions about how and where he could find a job, but he is reluctant to take her advice. Guiding them through solving the problem themselves could result in the father seeing his partner as a resource and the mother feeling that her opinions are respected. It may be helpful for the couple to discuss ways that the father—if he cannot find work—could contribute to childcare so that he does not feel inept.

DEVELOP A STRONG, WARM CONNECTION WITH PROGRAM PARTICIPANTS

Couples are unlikely to continue attending their sessions or develop positive connections with you when they do not feel understood, respected, or valued. If you create an atmosphere of respect and appreciation, young parents will feel safe about sharing their feelings and more open to learning. Many young expectant parents have had difficult lives, have been in trouble with their parents, teachers, or police, and have felt put down for their mistakes. Often, their strengths are not regularly acknowledged. A simple expression of your appreciation for what a young parent has done well (e.g., "Great job with not interrupting. I know how hard that is!") or a specific strength (e.g., "You have never missed a prenatal appointment; that shows how hard you are working to be responsible for your baby.") demonstrates that you are paying attention to what is good and positive about him or her. Expressions of appreciation can subtly convey your understanding that life has been difficult and they are working hard to cope with it all. They are a simple way to give young parents hope that they will be able to meet challenges and that their efforts will pay off. It is important that your appreciation is genuine because unless you are an exceptionally good actor, most adolescents can see through any false compliments.

When you bolster a participant's sense of self-worth, he or she is more likely to come back for more because the experience is positive. Over time, the participant will begin to internalize your positive regard and will feel better equipped to do likewise for his or her partner and child. As an example, Samantha was a 17-year-old pregnant adolescent who, like many young mothers, had a very difficult childhood. She had been abandoned by her father, sexually abused by her mother's boyfriend, and subsequently ran away from home. She bounced from one living arrangement to the next and eventually became addicted to methamphetamines after hooking up with a dealer. She developed a very aggressive interpersonal style and was in constant conflict with people in her life. With her long blond hair, blue eyes, and cherub face, she looked like the all-American girl, but was unpleasant to be around because she was so angry and confrontational, often getting into physical fights. At some point, she recognized that her life was dangerously out of control and she needed to get clean and sober. She stopped using meth cold turkey and took steps toward reconciling with her mother.

Early in the YPP counseling process, her counselor asked Samantha and her boyfriend to identify their strengths. Samantha became tearful and said she was a complete screw up and had no strengths. She went on to say she didn't have a job, had dropped out of school, was pregnant, had no friends, and her boyfriend could hardly stand to be with her. Her counselor, who had worked in adolescent substance abuse clinics for many years, looked her in the eye and said, "OK, all that may be true, but you were able to stop using meth on your own, which is an incredible feat of strength. Honestly, I have worked with meth addicts for years and know that you did something that almost no one else can do. If you can do that, then I think there are a lot of other things you can do." Samantha smiled and looked genuinely pleased because the compliment was honest and accurate. It is the counselor's job to have at least one of those compliments on the tip of his or her tongue, ready for even the most difficult young parent.

PROVIDE CONCRETE HELP WITH BUILDING CO-PARENTING RELATIONSHIP SKILLS

The primary focus of YPP is to help young couples develop a broad range of relationship skills needed to establish a strong co-parenting alliance so they can effectively work together to provide a stable, supportive family for their child. Relationship skill building is the primary goal of YPP, and most of this guide focuses on helping you know how to accomplish this goal with young expectant couples. When YPP works well, couples will feel more confident about managing the interpersonal stress of parenting and learn to experience themselves more positively. Developing a strong therapeutic relationship opens the door for relationship skill building.

Generally, relationship skill building requires an active, solution-oriented approach to counseling described throughout this guide. Rather than focus on problems that have occurred in the past, counselors are encouraged to help couples focus on how they can make things better for themselves and each other now and in the future. Ironically, a solution-focused approach does not necessarily mean that couples should try to "solve problems" or come to concrete resolutions about disputes. Getting too focused on concrete solutions can get in the way of learning. Sometimes it is best to consider several solutions that might work. Your role as a counselor is providing couples with the interpersonal tools that will keep them engaged in trying out new strategies and broadening their interpersonal "repertoire." This involves teaching concrete relationship skills such as empathic listening, offering support, problem solving, reducing stress, and community effectively with extended family. Specific interpersonal activities are outlined in Chapter 7. Not all these new tools will help all couples, but you will be able to find two or three that will fit each couple.

CULTURAL AWARENESS AND CULTURAL HUMILITY

There are some important racial and ethnic differences in how young people think about and behave within their romantic and co-parenting relationships that may be based on cultural norms and beliefs, social and economic circumstances, or all of these (Burton, 1990; Harknett & McLanahan, 2004; Milbrath et al., 2009). In this guide, we do not attempt to describe or delineate such differences for two reasons. First, doing so would require writing a chapter on each of many racial or ethnic group you might encounter in your practice. Although this is beyond the scope of this book, we encourage you seek to understand how the cultural particularities of the couples you might work with in YPP could affect the counseling process. Second, we do not want to reify stereotypes by suggesting or recommending that you use a certain approach with this or that particular group. We believe that making cultural adaptations is sometimes necessary, but a "cookbook" approach to addressing cultural differences in relationship functioning is not useful because there are too many individual differences within any particular cultural group.

When working with YPP couples, you should be aware of each partner's cultural background and make efforts to address cultural values and norms that might pertain to co-parenting and the counseling process. Cultural values can play important roles in defining relationship goals, identifying strengths, finding acceptable solutions or even receiving help from outsiders. You are encouraged to explore the research and clinical literature that will help you understand the cultural and social contexts of the young men and women you encounter in your practice. As suggested, there is a delicate balance between cultural understanding and ethnic bias; there is a difference between appreciating distinct cultural perspectives and assuming differences based on race or ethnicity.

Throughout this guide, we encourage counselors to adopt a position of "cultural humility" (Anderson Juarez et al., 2006; Tervalon & Murray-Garcia, 1998), which is the practice of reflecting upon one's own cultural values and beliefs, while reaching out to better understand the cultural values and beliefs of others. Your capacity to reflect upon your biases and consider how your interpersonal style and social position affects others will increase your effectiveness as a YPP counselor. For example, a counselor who grew up in an upper-middle-class white family might track how his experience of privilege affects his capacity to fully appreciate the experience of an economically disadvantaged, African-American pregnant adolescent. This reflection might keep him from making assumptions and encourage him to elicit more information from his participant about her experience.

Cultural differences between parents can impact co-parenting. When two partners have been raised with different beliefs about parenting, they may have difficulties understanding or appreciating each other's parenting values or styles. It is also possible that two partners who belong to the *same* ethnic or racial group have "cultural" conflicts related to differences in national origin, rate of acculturation, religion, politics, socioeconomic status, and so on (Szapocznick & Kurtines, 1993). As a YPP counselor, you can assist a couple in understanding and appreciating each other's cultural beliefs and values, helping them to blend different worlds, set expectations, and create a family culture that will work for their child (who may need to navigate several cultural contexts). However, to be useful in this way you must first demonstrate your appreciation and respect for both participants' beliefs and values.

Cultural humility involves treating everyone as a local expert in their own culture. Ask questions and seek information about the participant's experiences and understanding of race or ethnicity (Altarriba & Bauer, 1998). This can be challenging and even awkward when you are working with participants whose backgrounds are significantly different from your own (Comas-Diaz & Jacobsen, 1991). But it is an important step toward understanding your participants' strengths and developing strong therapeutic alliances.

HELP COUPLES MAKE GOOD USE OF OUTSIDE RESOURCES FOR SUPPORT

As they develop new interpersonal skills and consolidate their co-parenting alliance, you may want to encourage couples to reach out to family members for support. Developing a strong social support network will be valuable as they navigate the transition to parenthood; others may assist in buying baby supplies, helping with childcare, and providing emotional support through stressful moments. Some young parents may feel pessimistic about their family's willingness or ability to provide support, based on recent conflicts. They often do not realize that if they were to approach their families from a different angle (with maturity and appreciation) they would likely receive a different response. As they try out new interpersonal skills with each other, YPP couples often begin to use what they have learned with their extended families. They are more direct and respectful when asking for help, they express appreciation for the support they receive, and they learn to avoid hostile exchanges and disengage from dysfunctional patterns of interaction. These changes are usually noticed and welcomed by extended family members, who begin to see the young couple as more mature and capable.

In addition to the support provided by family, young couples may be able to make use of support provided by teachers, nurses, doctors, clergy, and social service providers (Stoddard et al., 2011). Under some circumstances, probation officers and judges can also be supportive when they are approached with a genuine request for help. Young men and women may not be fully aware of how much support is available to them in their immediate environment. After the engagement, goal-setting, and skill building phases of YPP are complete, your role will include helping YPP participants consider these other sources of support, muster the strength to risk reaching out for it, and find the words to ask for it. For example, many young parents have done poorly in school or dropped out, but would like to return either to complete their high school education or get their GED. Most have bad memories of school in general but remember one or two teachers or school administrators who they liked. The idea of talking with one of these people about how to return to school might evoke a great deal of anxiety, but it might be a good place to start. Seeking this sort of support is also something that partners could help push each other to do.

GENERAL COUNSELING STRATEGIES

Counselors often find it difficult to keep couples engaged in an intervention. This is particularly true with at-risk adolescents who are often reluctant to seek help or open themselves up to adults. Below are eleven general therapeutic strategies to help you keep couples engaged in YPP and more likely to reach the program's goals.

(1) **Highlight and reinforce positive, constructive behaviors**. Highlight examples of how the couple is demonstrating the skills they are learning. When you observe a partner using positive, healthy relationship skills, point this out, label the behavior by referring to the skill, and relate it to parenting (if possible). Praise the couple and/or individual for their good relationship skills. Acknowledging when partners make efforts to be more positive in their relationships, or work toward their program goals is vital to developing positive therapeutic relationships. Plus, modeling positive feedback helps couples learn to recognize and acknowledge the efforts made by their partners.

(2) **Interrupt nonconstructive behaviors**. As a YPP counselor, you likely will witness partners talking belligerently to each other. This might include name calling, swearing at each other, shouting, or threats about breaking up "getting back" at the other. How should you handle this? First, interrupt and ask both partners permission to act as sort of referee and coach to help them avoid these sorts of interactions. Usually couples readily agree even if tempers are flaring. Next, back it up a bit. Remind them that they have both agreed to participate in YPP because they want to work together to support their child and that they have acknowledged there are better ways to communicate. Third, ask each parent to re-state their message in a way that is less hostile and easier for the other person to hear. It may take significant work on your part to move from someone saying "Fuck you" to "I am feeling really hurt by what you said." But if you have a solid therapeutic alliance, you can get most of the way there in a relatively short period of time.

(3) **Positively reframe negative behavior**. Positive reframing can help you shift the couple from hostility to warmth. This involves uncovering the positive emotion beneath a negative, maladaptive behavior to help both partners soften a bit and find their common ground. For example, Shelly was a 17-year-old young woman with a long history of depression who was tearfully questioning her ability to be a mom. She was upset because her boyfriend, Chris, was impatient with her constant crying. Chris responded by saying, "Look, you know I'm ain't the warm, cuddly type and I'm sure as hell not going to pamper you and treat you like a baby.... Hell, we got a baby coming!" In response, Shelly turned away and began to pout. The counselor turned

to the Shelly and said, "You know I have this idea that there is something about Chris's tough love style that you find sort of appealing and reassuring." Puzzled but curious, she asked the counselor what he meant. The counselor reframed what Chris had said. "I think there is a big part of you that wants to be with someone who treats you like an adult. I also think Chris is trying to say that he sees you as strong, capable person. I just think it would be easier for you to hear if he could say it more positively."

After you make a positive reframe like this, it is helpful to ask each partner to experiment with a more positive statement about how they feel or what they want. It is all right to provide a lot of coaching. It can be somewhat entertaining for the couple if you state what you think they are trying to say, using their language and then ask if it is in the ballpark, going back and forth until you get the language right. Then ask them to say it to their partner and ask the partner to respond. This is an active, solution-focused approach to breaking out of negative cycles.

(4) **Help couples slow down their interaction and move in a more positive direction.** A less heavy-handed approach to supporting positive interactions is to interrupt the couple as they are getting upset with each other and ask them to stop, listen, and think carefully before responding. Adolescents often get themselves into trouble simply because they act and react before processing information. When forced to think before they speak or slow down, they are able to respond quite well. By slowing down the communication process, negative interpersonal behaviors are less likely to occur and escalate. This approach works best once you know that a couple has an essentially warm connection with each other and has basic communication skills. You can say something like, "I think it would help you guys to slow this interaction way down, which will allow you time to think before you talk. Are you two OK with me acting as referee for a little while to help you slow things down and think carefully about how to make your point in a respectful way that moves things forward rather than backward?" This helps to structure the conversation yet leaves the couple a great deal of latitude. In Chapter 7, we describe a number of approaches to helping couples become and stay more positively engaged.

(5) **Help couples be more clear and direct about their feelings.** Young couples can often be sarcastic or use nonverbal language to convey their anger and disapproval of each other. For some couples, this is not much of a problem because neither partner takes the behavior too seriously. However, some couples get into big fights about small hostile gestures or inflections. The person being accused of being negative or hostile often denies that he or she is doing anything wrong ("I was just kidding around"). This puts you—as the counselor—in the uncomfortable position of being a witness and taking sides. One way to handle this is to sidestep the issue of indirect hostile communication and simply ask both partners to start over and state their feelings clearly and constructively. However, sometimes it is useful to educate the couple about mixed messages (messages that simultaneously express hostility and warmth, or agreement and disagreement). Explain that the problem with these mixed messages is that person sending the message is probably not communicating exactly what they mean and the person receiving the message is confused and likely to respond to the negative part of the message. Without being

accusatory, you can help couples become more aware of their nonverbal messages and "clean up" their communications by becoming more direct.

(6) **Stay focused on a limited set of manageable issues and goals.** At times, couples will jump from issue to issue in a matter of five or ten minutes and need help settling on one. You, too, may get caught up in trying to address too many issues in a single session. As a YPP counselor, it is important to avoid overwhelming couples with too many issues. To prevent this from happening, use the information you gathered during the assessment phase and during your sessions to identify (in consultation with the couple) two or three core relationship issues. Then, help them set priorities based on those core issues. If you try to do too much, couples are likely to experience the sessions as unpleasant and unproductive. The Young Parenthood Program is quite brief, which means you are required to make strategic decisions (e.g., When should I focus on an individual versus the relationship? How much should I focus on the past versus the present or future? How much should I focus on parent education issues?) This guidebook is intended to support you as you think through these decisions and make choices about what to focus on, while maintaining program fidelity and efficiency. Upcoming chapters offer specific strategies for working with participants efficiently and effectively.

(7) *Attend to cultural gaps in understanding.* When you invite a couple to participate in the YPP, you are asking them to enter a world that probably feels quite foreign and perhaps intimidating. Young men and women are often not comfortable with the idea of therapy or talking openly about their relationships. Essentially, you are asking them—perfect strangers—to buy into your belief system about what will help them with their transition to parenthood. Although we (the program developers) believe in the value of this program, we also recognize that the there is something implicitly presumptuous about our convictions. There are three fundamental ways that you should try to deal with this potential gap in belief systems:

- First and foremost, recognize that one size does not fit all. The YPP is designed to be flexible enough to adjust to the particular needs and concerns of young parents in different cultural and social contexts. Beyond the basic assumption that positive (e.g., supportive, constructive) co-parenting is good for children, YPP allows for differences in beliefs about romantic relationships, family structure, the value of marriage, and the role of parents in child development. Throughout this guide, counselors are instructed to tailor the program to the individual circumstances of each couple and meet the couples "where they are" developmentally and—to the extent possible—culturally.

- Second, strive to understand each participant's cultural beliefs and practices and modify the program's goals and tasks to be in sync with what makes sense for them (without sacrificing fidelity to the basic program principles). For example, some cultural groups have prescribed gender-based parenting roles that you might find inequitable. Remember that the goal of the YPP is not to alter cultural beliefs or practices, but to help couples develop communication skills that will help them negotiate well as a co-parenting couple.

  As indicated earlier, use "cultural humility" when you talk with young parents about their background, their families, and their hopes and expectations. Do not make assumptions about their beliefs, values, and behavioral norms, and be open to learning about cultural differences through open dialogue and exploration. Inform yourself by reading the literature on the ethnic or racial groups that you encounter in your practice. Enlist the help of cultural insiders who might have a useful perspective on the unique challenges facing African-American, Mexican-American, Navaho, and Hmong co-parents that might never have occurred to you. Most importantly, remain continuously reflective about how your beliefs, values, and experiences influence your ability to connect and understand your participants. A "culturally humble" counselor knows that bias is often expressed in implicit subtle ways and prejudice is often unconscious. Consider how your own biases or prejudices may be creating a gap in understanding.

- Third, demonstrate a willingness to admit your mistakes and missteps. Anticipate that there will be misunderstanding between you and your participants. These can be simple, such as when participants and counselors use vocabulary or slang that the other does not understand. They can also be profound, such as when a participant feels judged or put down by you, perhaps because you are trying to help him change his behavior, which could imply he is doing something wrong. The research literature on ethnic and racial matching suggests that although participants often prefer to receive counseling service from someone who is ethnically/racially similar, matching does not predict outcome. What matters much more is the quality of the therapeutic alliance and the counselor's capacity for repairing disruptions in the alliance related to culture, race, or ethnicity (Owen et al., 2012). You are not expected to walk on eggshells around cultural issues or pretend to be someone other than who you are, but do not be defensive about your limitations. Participants tend to appreciate counselors who are comfortable with themselves, open about who they are, and respectful of others.

(8) **Stay balanced.** It is important to build a solid therapeutic alliance with both partners and act on behalf of the co-parenting relationship. Make it clear to YPP couples that your job is to support both of them and that you will try to keep things balanced between them. Be watchful of yourself to ensure that you spend equal time focused on each individual. Often, you will feel more at ease with one of the partners. Do not give in to the tendency to engage more fully with one person. Instead, use this as a cue to yourself that the other partner may be feeling left out, isolated, or unable to find his or her "voice" in the counseling sessions or in the relationship. The best way to accomplish this task is to engage the more active partner in drawing out the less active partner, rather than trying to do this yourself.

For example, consider the case of Carla and Jose who had met through their gang affiliations. They hardly knew each other when Carla became pregnant. Carla was a tough kid—having grown up in a family that was deeply gang involved—but also was extremely shy. She essentially refused to tell Jose anything about herself because she did not trust him. She was so profoundly mute during their sessions that the counselor wondered if he could continue with couples' sessions without meeting with Carla individually. However, he was able to discern that Carla had a sense of humor and that he could get away with teasing her a bit about her refusal to speak. After two painfully one-sided sessions, the counselor engaged Jose in a game that involved trying to guess what Carla was thinking, based on subtle changes in her facial expression. Carla was amused and seemed to enjoy the attention she was receiving from Jose, for he was making a good effort at charming her. In this way, the counselor was able to avoid a lopsided therapeutic relationship and by the end, Carla and Jose were both fully engaged in the program.

There will be times when you think it is in the couple's best interests for you to weigh in with an opinion that might come across as taking sides. Although it is rarely appropriate to lecture or blame, it is irresponsible to remain neutral in some situations; for example, if one partner is engaging in seriously dysfunctional behavior, particularly if safety is a concern. If you find yourself "taking sides," it is important to explain the rationale for doing so and to avoid arguing. Be respectful of different perspectives and approaches—even if you regard them as fundamentally dysfunctional. Your goal (and role) is to advocate for health and safety, not to be "right."

High conflict couples often push counselors' personal buttons. It may help to use the consultation or supervisory process to sort through any personal reasons for siding with one partner. Understanding these personal issues usually helps counselors control their emotional responses and maintain their balance.

(9) **Maintain a present and future orientation.** As indicated earlier, counselors are encouraged to focus on the present and future issues rather than past difficulties. However, the past can be important when one or both partners describe expectations about relationships based upon either past experiences or current maladaptive patterns. A pregnant teen may distrust her partner either because he has been unreliable or her father was unreliable. Based on her previous experience, she may expect her partner to disappoint her. In this situation, the counselor could either dig into the past and/or suggest strategies to break negative patterns so as not relive the past. Sometimes it is necessary to do both, but it is often useful to start by providing the couple with a way out of the entrenched pattern *before* trying to understand where the pattern comes from. In the example that follows, Sheila is upset with Eddie for not calling her to let her know that he would be late for their appointment. Now she does not want to hear his explanation. Whenever Eddie makes these sorts of mistakes, Sheila jumps to the conclusion that he will ultimately fail as a partner and father and throws her disappointment in his face.

Sheila: It doesn't matter because I know you are not going to stick around anyway.

Counselor (*to Sheila*): Are you OK if I interrupt here?

Sheila: Fine.

Counselor: I have heard you say that before and I have a hunch that your low expectations of Eddie are related to your past experience. (*Note: It could be her past experience with Eddie or other men in her life.*)

Sheila: Yup.

Counselor: So if Eddie was to not get offended or defensive (*looking at Eddie*) and tell you that he's not going anywhere and that he will help you raise this child, would you be able listen and really take in what he's saying?

Sheila: He might mean it now but he might change his mind.

Counselor: Do you think you could tell Eddie how worried you are about having to raise this child without him? And do you think you could say it without it sounding like he's already been tried and convicted (*smiling*)?

Sheila (*smiling*): I suppose I could try to do that. I guess I am not always fair to him.

This sort of intervention is intended to help shift the conversation about the past to a conversation about the present and future. Sheila is likely trying to protect herself against disappointment by pushing Eddie away, but she is sending Eddie the wrong message, and he is beginning to internalize her low expectations of him. In this situation, the counselor focuses on helping Eddie reassure Sheila and helping Sheila become more direct (and less blaming) when expressing her anxieties. If the counselor believes that Eddie is not able to provide reassurance (that he will stick around), a different strategy will be needed, but it should still be "present and future" focused.

(10) **Be patient and remember that development is a slow process.** Growth and change often occur in a nonlinear fashion. Couples may take two steps forward, then one step back. The process of change is often discontinuous and couples may demonstrate new competencies but then fall into old interaction patterns. As a YPP counselor, try not to expect immediate results. Slow progress can be frustrating, but keep in mind that it is sometimes difficult to know when change is happening. The following highlights some guideposts for noting change:

- The level of hostile escalation is less extreme, of shorter duration, and more easily de-escalated or blocked.
- The couple recognizes a problematic interaction and attempts to interrupt the sequence, leading to a less negative emotional outcome.
- Reparation or solution-seeking behavior occurs more quickly after problematic interactions.
- The couple resolves a problem without resorting to dysfunctional behavior.

(11) **Know the limits of the YPP.** If you feel that the relationship between the couple is truly destructive and you do not believe that you can have a positive impact, you may need to discontinue co-parent counseling and make appropriate referrals.

ADDITIONAL CONSIDERATIONS

Engaging young expectant couples in co-parenting counseling is not easy. At times you may feel that you are "chasing" couples who are not invested or are too busy. This can be frustrating. The process of engagement is addressed throughout this guide, with an emphasis on how to think about young parents through

PRACTICAL TIPS

BUILDING THE THERAPEUTIC ALLIANCE

Be supportive of both partners.

- Establish a positive connection with *both* partners. Express warmth and positive regard toward the couple in a balanced fashion.
- Do not allow a session to become focused on one partner over the other.
- Acknowledge the strengths of both individuals and the couple.

Focus on their relationship.

- Emphasize that the program's goal is to help couples work together to make sure their child will be brought up in a healthy family.
- Make the distinction between their "romantic relationship" and the "co-parenting relationship."
- Emphasize that this is not a one-size-fits-all program and you will tailor the program to fit them and their relationship.

Be respectful, appreciative, and genuine.

- Convey respect for the couple's and each individual's cultural beliefs and values.
- Let the couple know how much you value their participation.

Make the sessions interesting.

- Keep the sessions action-oriented and interactive.
- Do not talk too much and when you do, use clear, simple, and direct language.
- The intervention process does not need to be fun, but it should be engaging and interesting.
- If the couple seems bored, detached, or confused, consider whether: (a) you are not allowing them to be interactive (you are talking too much) or (b) you are making things too complicated and they do not understand the goals or tasks.

Highlight connections between the couple's relationship and parenting.

- When the couple engages in a positive interaction, find a way to link their behavior (warmth, nurturance, attunement) to effective parenting.
- If the couple consistently engages in negative behavior, educate them regarding the negative impact of hostile behavior on the child's emotional and cognitive development.
- Regularly commend the couple for their investment in becoming good parents and co-parents; this reinforces their engagement in the program.

Give yourself (and them) enough time at the end to wrap things up so that couples do not leave the session feeling angry or distraught.

a developmental lens. Keep in mind that adolescents and young adults often lack the skills necessary to seek out help when it is needed. The process of just talking with you about their relationship can be an important developmental (growth) experience in and of itself. As you look for ways to engage the couple, keep these considerations in mind:

(1) Pregnant/parenting adolescents are in the midst of a difficult transition between adolescence and adulthood. The couple's participation in YPP may be one way for them to learn how to establish some stability and consistency in their lives. You can provide a model for being flexible when possible and providing structure when necessary, which couples will need to do with their children and each other.

(2) Typically YPP participants are dealing with a variety of challenges and stressors, and may feel that things are piling up on them. Many are trying to juggle school, jobs, relationships, pre-natal appointments, and preparing for the baby's birth. Even the most responsible and motivated YPP couples will have some difficulty making time for YPP. When couples fail to show up for appointments or cancel at the last minute, do not assume it is because they are not interested or resistant. It is important to inquire about whatever got in the way (so you can help problem solve), but avoid coming across as judgmental or reprimanding.

(3) Persistent, supportive, and sensitive counselors can model and demonstrate the basic importance of consistency, follow-through, and acceptance in relationships. As a YPP counselor, you can reinforce the idea that these are important traits for a co-parenting partner.

4 THE ROLE OF THE CARE COORDINATOR

WHAT IS CARE COORDINATION?

YOUNG PARENTHOOD PROGRAM COUNSELORS ARE PRIMARILY RESPONSIBLE for helping couples develop interpersonal and co-parenting relationship skills. However, the couple may need help with other life stressors, including finding a job, completing school, finding a place to live, dealing with immigration issues, or having enough to eat. These real-life problems often become the source of interpersonal conflict, but cannot be fully addressed by simply focusing on relationship issues and interpersonal skill building. Couples will quite naturally turn to their counselor for help, which creates a dilemma; if counselors put their time into these issues, it will be at the expense of helping the couple with co-parenting and interpersonal skill development. Yet the counselor cannot ignore important life stressors that are affecting the couple's well-being and their ability to function as parents and co-parents.

To address this common dilemma, we recommend YPP counselors work closely with care coordinators, whose role is to help couples learn to effectively cope with life stressors. Within the context of YPP, care coordination is defined as the process of helping young parents gain access to their community's medical, social, educational, psychological, and vocational services that will help them function better as parents and co-parents. Care coordination is a collaborative process in which the care coordinator works with the couple to evaluate their needs, develop an action plan, take action, and monitor progress toward goals.

In this chapter, we describe a model of care coordination that is based on a team approach to social and psychological services, involving both a YPP counselor and a care coordinator. Your agency may use such an approach in which psychologists or social workers provide counseling and community health workers or prenatal care coordinators provide "case management" services. Some organizations contract with independent case management agencies to provide these sorts of services. However, we recognize that in some settings, counselors may be expected to fill both roles and function as both a therapist and a care coordinator. Although this is possible, it is very difficult because the two roles are very different and equally time consuming. As indicated, when you get drawn into addressing a couple's care coordination needs, your efforts to address their interpersonal skills are likely to become diluted.

We have written this chapter assuming that the counselor and the care coordinator are two separate people working together. We provide a detailed description of the care coordination process so that you—the counselor—have a clear understanding of the care coordinator's role in the YPP model. We encourage you to share this chapter with whomever will be providing these sorts of services to the young people you are counseling. We believe he or she will appreciate the approach and the opportunity to work with young co-parenting couples.

If you need to function as both counselor and care coordinator, the information provided in this chapter will help you understand how to differentiate between the two roles. Being conscious and deliberate about whether you are wearing your counselor "hat" or your care coordinator "hat" will help ensure that you are getting both jobs done more effectively and will reduce the likelihood that either role will be diminished. If you are able to work with another person who will function as the care coordinator, make sure that he or she has a clear understanding of the YPP model and your distinct roles. One way or the other, integrating these two services increases the likelihood that both expectant parents will get what they need to make a successful transition to parenthood.

Although the counseling aspect of YPP is couple-focused, the care coordinator will often work with individual partners on individual issues. The care coordination component is more flexible because care coordination needs are sometimes specific to each young parent. For example, one partner may be more interested in getting a job, whereas the other is focused on getting enrolled in a school that provides daycare. At times, the care coordinator may be asked to provide help to the couple's extended family members because some issues, such as housing and food security, are related to the extended family's needs and circumstances. The care coordinator will decide to work with individual participants or couples on a case-by-case or situation-by-situation basis.

Note that we use the term "care coordinator" as opposed to "case manager" because we do not think of young couples as "cases" (too clinical) and we do think this role should stress guidance and teaching rather than managing. Plus, the term "case manager" is sometimes negatively associated with social service agencies that seem bureaucratic or intrusive. A care coordinator emphasizes warm guidance and facilitating a participant's sense of self-efficacy through active instruction. For example, instead of telling a young mother to apply for public housing, the care coordinator accompanies her to the public housing office and teaches her how to fill out an application and constructively engage with the housing administrator. Every problem or need can be turned into a valuable learning experience.

CHARACTERISTICS OF A SUCCESSFUL CARE COORDINATOR

There are five characteristics of a successful YPP care coordinator.

(1) Young Parenthood Program care coordinators are engaged. Care coordinators are encouraged to be very active in the engagement and follow-up process because many adolescents and young adults are not mature enough to address their care coordination needs on their own. Some simply do not know how to advocate for themselves or constructively engage with employers, teachers, daycare providers, medical professionals, and so on.

(2) Young Parenthood Program care coordinators teach independence. Care coordinators teach participants how to independently address their own needs. A care coordinator must know how to teach self-advocacy to his or her participants through modeling, instruction, and then supporting them as they take steps to advocate for themselves. The process is a little like teaching someone to ride a bike; at first you need to run along beside him or her and hold onto the seat until the person develops the capacity for balance.

(3) It is important to remember that many of the young parents who participate in YPP are highly stressed adolescents who require generous portions of warmth and patience. This approach requires that the care coordinator be an excellent communicator and teacher. In this respect, YPP care coordinators function as short-term mentors.

(4) In addition, an effective YPP care coordinator needs to be familiar with the developmental, social, and healthcare needs of participants. They also need to know about community resources and social services available to young participants (e.g., housing, family planning, education, job training programs). In many communities the healthcare and social service systems are complex and difficult to navigate; it requires experience and skill to effectively guide others through the process of finding and enrolling in appropriate services and programs.

(5) Finally, an effective care coordinator should have some knowledge of how to work with young couples who are in crisis and/or how to get help if the crisis requires a higher level of intervention. Typical crises involve intimate partner violence, the occurrence of child abuse or neglect, eviction, deportation, or other legal problems. Crises are time-consuming for the care coordinator and potentially traumatizing for the young participant, but with appropriate support, they can also provide opportunities for growth and learning.

PRINCIPLES OF YPP CARE COORDINATION

(1) Care coordinators should respect their participant's autonomy and services should be oriented toward helping the participant be in charge of his or her life (as is age appropriate).

(2) Young couples should be actively involved in determining the goals and guiding the implementation of their care coordination plan to ensure that the plan is participant driven. Care coordinators should use motivational interviewing techniques to get "buy in" and avoid imposing goals on their participants. Describing the details of the motivational interviewing approach is beyond the scope of this chapter, but we list excellent resources in the references (Naar-King & Suarez, 2011).

(3) When appropriate, YPP care coordinators should encourage (and teach) couples to constructively engage their natural support systems (family, school, religious organizations) and access local healthcare and social service agencies when necessary. Before making referrals, it is important to know the context. Do not encourage an adolescent to seek support from a potentially abusive parent or blindly refer a young couple to a healthcare provider who may have a poor record of service.

(4) Care coordination is partly about *helping* participants gain access to services, but mostly about *teaching* participants about how to access services. In this respect the process is like planting seeds for later growth. It is often the case that care coordinators will help young participant find services and then there is no follow through. This may be because the services were not a good match, were no longer necessary, or the participant was not ready to make use of the service. Care coordinators should be nonjudgmental in this situation, allowing young expectant parents to move at their own pace.

(5) Care coordination services should focus on safety first. A care coordinator's primary goal is to ensure that the young couple is not in immediate danger of harm or injury as a result of family violence, substance abuse, homelessness, and so on.

(6) Care coordinators should work closely with counselors. When the collaborative relationship between a counselor and a care coordinator is strong and effective, the couple will feel as though they are part of a team. Frequent

discussions between the counselor and care coordinator and joint access to clinical notes will help them coordinate the couple's services. Couples often bring up relationship issues during their care coordination sessions and care coordination issues during their co-parenting counseling sessions. Sharing this information in a systematic way (i.e., shared access to clinical notes) is important to the effective integration of services.

THE SIX STAGES OF CARE COORDINATION

Stage 1: Engagement

Getting a participant interested in care coordination services is an important first step and it may require some concerted effort. Young expectant parents may not recognize that they could benefit from care coordination until they sit down and talk to a care coordinator. The best way for the care coordinator to engage a reluctant participant is to be clear and concrete about how care coordination works and to emphasize the end result—that the care coordinator is there to help participants achieve their goals (i.e., getting a job, enrolling in school, finding a place to live.)

It is often helpful for care coordinators to meet with the families of participants and introduce themselves and the goals of care coordination. For this reason, a care coordinator should be included in the first meeting between the families and the YPP counselor. Family members can be powerful allies during the process of developing a positive working alliance with participants and can encourage their son or daughter to remain engaged in the program. The following are some helpful messages that care coordinators may convey to the parents of YPP participants (the grandparents of the baby):

- My job is to work with young parents to find out what their needs are and find solutions and resources to help them meet those needs and the needs of their baby.
- Your ideas and thoughts are important and I would like to know as much as I can from you so that I understand your expectations and hopes for your son/ daughter and your grandchild.
- In order for this to be most effective, I would like for the things I talk about with your son/daughter to be confidential because privacy is very important to most adolescents. That said, I will let you know if I have any concerns about your son or daughter's safety or the baby's safety.
- (If the participant is under 18.) Ultimately, you have authority here, and I want to make sure that I do not overstep my boundaries.
- I will try to find services and programs for your son or daughter that will help him or her meet his or her goals. My role is to facilitate and open doors, but ultimately it is up to you and your son/daughter to decide if the services are useful.
- If you or your son/daughter feels I am pushing something too hard, or not hard enough, let me know.

When working with participants who are more than 18 years old, care coordinators should still be mindful that a participant's parents may have some strong feelings and opinions about issues related to jobs, school, and living arrangements. It is perfectly acceptable for the care coordinator to consult with the parents of YPP participants who are 18 years old or older as long as he or she obtains a release of information to allow those conversations to occur. Going through the formal process of asking for that release is important because it demonstrates to the participant that you take their confidentiality very seriously. In most cases, they will welcome your connection with their parents. When family members feel they have been included and fully informed about the goals of the program (counseling and care coordination) they will be more likely to assist and support. After the first meeting, the care coordinator should work with each member of the couple to determine the ways care coordination could be helpful to him or her.

Both the care coordinator and counselor should make it clear that the goal of the program is to accomplish as much as possible prior to childbirth and in the weeks or months immediately afterward. Because participants often become attached to YPP providers, it is always important to say how long services will be available to prevent them from being surprised (and feeling abandoned) when time runs out.

Stage 2: Care Coordination Assessment and Planning

In individual assessment and planning meetings, the care coordinator explores each participant's primary needs (e.g., housing, food, healthcare) and goals (e.g., complete high school, find a better job) and identifies resources to meet those needs and goals. Many adolescents and young adults may not be able to immediately recognize or verbalize their needs and goals. Simply asking, "What do you need?" will often lead to blank stares or to a discussion of nonessential needs like videogames, hair products, and so on. The care coordinator should explain to participants that he or she will ask about a broad range of typical issues and concerns in order to help them clarify their most important needs and goals.

Using Table 4.1 (or something similar), the care coordinator helps participants think through what they need for themselves and their child in order to prepare for parenthood. The table is a tool designed to help participants rate their needs and assess the stress they feel about each need on a 10-point scale. It is important to emphasize that many young expectant parents will be considering these questions for the first time and may have a hard time quantifying their stress or the relative significance of needs. Stress can be a powerful motivator, and the care coordinator can use a participant's sense of urgency to identify specific and manageable goals. Note that when the counselor is also providing care coordination services, the assessment process can be integrated into the initial intake process. When the counselor and coordinator are working as a team, the care coordinator should conduct this assessment independently.

Once the primary goals are clarified, the care coordinator can begin to identify resources for meeting them. The script and table below is intended to help facilitate that process.

> Now I'd like to take some time to look at your responses and talk about the top two to four goals where you might want some help. Please let me know what you think will be helpful and what will **not** be helpful... if you have any idea about that. After we get a good idea of your top priorities, I will work **with** you to make appointments or do whatever needs to be done to help you meet your goals.

Table 4.1 CARE COORDINATION NEEDS ASSESSMENT

How Strong Is Your Need in Each of The Following Areas? (0 = no need, 10 = high need)	How Stressed Out Do You Feel About This? (only for those needs >0) (0 = low stress, 10 = high stress)	What Is Your Main Goal for Meeting This Need?
1. Poverty issues (food security; utilities; rent) 0 1 2 3 4 5 6 7 8 9 10	1. Poverty issues (food security; utilities; rent) 0 1 2 3 4 5 6 7 8 9 10	
2. Baby supplies 0 1 2 3 4 5 6 7 8 9 10	2. Baby supplies 0 1 2 3 4 5 6 7 8 9 10	
3. Stable living situation 0 1 2 3 4 5 6 7 8 9 10	3. Stable living situation 0 1 2 3 4 5 6 7 8 9 10	
4. Safe place for baby to live and sleep 0 1 2 3 4 5 6 7 8 9 10	4. Safe place for baby to live and sleep 0 1 2 3 4 5 6 7 8 9 10	
5. Transportation 0 1 2 3 4 5 6 7 8 9 10	5. Transportation 0 1 2 3 4 5 6 7 8 9 10	
6. Mental health concerns 0 1 2 3 4 5 6 7 8 9 10	6. Mental health concerns 0 1 2 3 4 5 6 7 8 9 10	
7. Substance abuse/drinking 0 1 2 3 4 5 6 7 8 9 10	7. Substance abuse/drinking 0 1 2 3 4 5 6 7 8 9 10	
8. Reproductive health/family planning 0 1 2 3 4 5 6 7 8 9 10	8. Reproductive health/family planning 0 1 2 3 4 5 6 7 8 9 10	
9. Parenting knowledge (e.g., infant care) 0 1 2 3 4 5 6 7 8 9 10	9. Parenting knowledge (e.g., infant care) 0 1 2 3 4 5 6 7 8 9 10	
10. Health concerns 0 1 2 3 4 5 6 7 8 9 10	10. Health concerns 0 1 2 3 4 5 6 7 8 9 10	
11. Education/school issues 0 1 2 3 4 5 6 7 8 9 10	11. Education/school issues 0 1 2 3 4 5 6 7 8 9 10	
12. Employment/job 0 1 2 3 4 5 6 7 8 9 10	12. Employment/job 0 1 2 3 4 5 6 7 8 9 10	
13. Other (list) 0 1 2 3 4 5 6 7 8 9 10	13. Other (list) 0 1 2 3 4 5 6 7 8 9 10	

Based on the results of this process, the care coordinator should identify two to four top goals (Table 4.2). Some goals may be couple focused (i.e., find an apartment together), whereas some may be individually focused (i.e., find a job).

Stage 3: Facilitating Access to Resources and Services

Young expectant parents often do not know how to access community resources and are not skilled in asking for help. If accessing services becomes too frustrating, they may give up and fail to meet their goals. For many YPP participants, it is useful to "grease the wheels" before handing over a referral. Once a need has been identified and discussed, but before making recommendations, the care coordinator should investigate potential resources in the community. Often, the care coordinator will make the initial contact with a service provider to confirm a participant's eligibility and identify the best person at the agency to talk with about signing up for services. Finding resources available in the young participant's neighborhood is best because they are more likely to use services that are convenient and in a familiar setting. When this is not possible, a care coordinator should be prepared to help the participant solve any transportation issues.

Some young expectant parents will be able to take a referral and make an appointment on their own, but many will need some help navigating the system, talking on the phone, providing necessary information, and so on. For this reason, providing *active* coordination—with timely follow-up—is an important programmatic aspect of YPP. An active care coordinator will promptly follow up on a referral's status (i.e., did the participant follow through with a given referral? Are there challenges with the service? Does the participant have additional concerns or questions?). When a referral falls through, an active care coordinator quickly reassesses the situation to determine what went wrong and revise the plan of action. In all cases, the active care coordinator gauges the level of guidance and oversight needed, based on the participant's skills and capacities.

Not uncommonly, a participant will identify a goal, and then fail to take the necessary next action steps. In such a case, the care coordinator should discuss options with the participant, including the option of temporarily doing nothing. Some adolescents and young adults are ambivalent, confused, preoccupied, or lack confidence, all of which can get in the way of achieving their goals. Rather than nag or push, the care coordinator can help a participant take ownership of goals when he or she is ready to do so. Here, motivational interviewing techniques can be effective. For example:

- **Validate the participant's ambivalence:** "I'm thinking (or hearing) that you are not quite ready to get a job yet. Is that right?"
- **Acknowledge that the participant is in charge of making decisions about his or her life:** "It's up to you to decide when you are ready to look for a job."
- **Help the participant consider the pros and cons of getting a job:** "What would be good about getting a job? What is the downside of getting a job?"
- **Kindle whatever motivation exists:** "On a scale of one to ten, how close do you think you are to taking action on this goal? (If the participant says "two," ask why he or she did not pick one, so as to underscore the positive.)"
- **Leave the door open for further thinking and discussion:** "Are you OK with me checking in with you again about this at our next meeting?"

Table 4.2 GOAL IDENTIFICATION

Goal	What and Who Can Be Helpful in Meeting the Goal?	What Are the First Three Steps to Achieving This Goal?
1.		1. 2. 3.
2.		1. 2. 3.
3.		1. 2. 3.
4.		1. 2. 3.

Table 4.3 GOALS AND PROGRESS

Goal	Level of Need (score 0–10; 0 = low, 10 = high)	Current Stress (score 0–10; 0 = low, 10 = high)	New Resources	Progress Toward Goal
1.				
2.				
3.				
4.				
5.				

When that moment arrives and the participant is motivated to take action (even just a *little* motivated), the care coordinator should be ready to help by guiding the young expectant parent through the concrete steps (i.e., resume writing, finding transportation, making phone calls) and by providing plenty of positive reinforcement for whatever progress is made.

Stage 4: Documenting Care Coordination Progress and Activities

Once the care coordinator develops a plan, he or she should create a system for helping the participant reach his or her goals (Table 4.3). It is important to track progress over time so that the care coordinator and the participant can discuss whether progress is being made. Optimally, the participant's resources will increase, stress levels will decrease, and goals will be partially or fully met.

Stage 5: Maintain Regular Contact

Routine contact between the care coordinator and expectant parents builds good working relationships and can play a decisive role in helping couples meet their goals. For example, regular contact increases the likelihood that the couple will ask for assistance when new challenges present themselves. If the lines of communication are open and the couple knows their care coordinator is invested and available, they will get better at identifying and taking care of their own needs before they become unwieldy. Most young couples need weekly contact to help ensure that their goals are being met. Regular contact is often needed to troubleshoot, but it is also an opportunity to give positive feedback when a participant takes a step forward toward meeting a goal. With high-risk expectant parents (such as those with mental health concerns or violence in the home), it is best that weekly contacts be face-to-face rather than on the phone. Young participants may minimize their problems over the phone. Face-to-face contact is usually much more informative and productive.

Stage 6: Reassessment and Follow-up

At some set period of time (we recommend 12 weeks after the initial meeting), the care coordinator should review the plan and decide whether to continue or discontinue active care coordination services. The following considerations should be made before discontinuing active care coordination services:

- Are there any urgent needs that must be addressed?
- Does the couple have a viable support system in place?
- Does the couple understand how to access resources in the community?
- Has the couple made progress toward identified goals?

If further care coordination services are not needed, the care coordinator can meet with the couple to review their progress, commend them for their work, and encourage them to contact the care coordinator again if necessary. If additional active care coordination services are needed, goals can be revised as appropriate. However, it is important to remember that care coordination should not become an interminable process; at some point it is necessary to let go of the bicycle and let the couple ride away on their own pedal power.

THE CARE COORDINATOR AS EDUCATOR

The care coordinator may believe that a certain issue warrants attention, even though the participant did not identify it as a need. A good way to provide input and guidance at such times is to provide a mini information session or series of sessions. For example, many young expectant parents may need some information about how to find (and keep) a job. Some may benefit from a little education about family planning options to avoid a "sudden" second child. Some couples may need help in knowing how to care for their infant. These information sessions can be accomplished in a variety of ways, but here are some rules of thumb: (a) Ask the individual (or the couple) if they are open to having you spend a few minutes talking with them about the issue you have identified. (b) Keep the conversation as interactive as possible. (c) Do not try to provide too much information (not more than 15 minutes at a time) and stay focused on one topic. (d) Consider providing information about a specific topic over multiple meetings throughout the intervention. This can be more effective than a single, dedicated conversation.

Example 1: Employment

For many youth, finding employment can be a challenging experience filled with disappointment, frustration, and various obstacles and roadblocks. Factors such as the participant's age, lack of previous experience, educational status, transportation, and maturity level can make it difficult to secure a job. The care coordinator's role is to help the participant think through options and prepare for an appropriate job search. It may be especially important for the care coordinator to work closely with the YPP participant to identify specific measures that will improve his or her chances of getting a job. In this domain, the care coordinator can serve as a job coach by providing practical guidance and advice. For example, some participants may benefit from basic guidelines regarding what to wear to a job interview, how to introduce themselves to a potential employer, how to fill out an application, how to write a resume, how to address questions about criminal history or immigration status, or how to create a voicemail message that sounds professional. Some young men and women may avoid looking for a job because they already feel defeated and expect rejection. The care coordinator can be empathic but also point out that the job will not come looking for them. The care coordinator should be ready to coach a participant through experiences of rejection or discrimination, and encourage him or her to persist despite these challenges.

Example 2: Family Planning

Most YPP couples will not include family planning as a goal because they are already pregnant and unconcerned about future pregnancies. However, many young expectant parents get pregnant again shortly after giving birth. It is important to ask the young mother or father if they have thought about when or if they may want to have another child and if they are willing to spend a few minutes discussing family planning.

It is not YPP's goal to prescribe which methods a couple should use to prevent a pregnancy. In discussing family planning, it is the care coordinator's role to provide accurate and thorough information about pregnancy prevention and to help the couple consider which method would be right for them. Although the co-parenting counselor may work with a couple to communicate about family planning issues, the care coordinator can make sure the couple has access to the birth control they want (and need) to avoid an unplanned second pregnancy. The care coordinator should have a basic, working knowledge of a variety of family planning and birth control options, and community resources that the couple can access so he or she can give accurate guidance.

Example 3: Communication with Healthcare Providers About Infant and Child Care

Medical settings can often be rushed, hectic places, where healthcare providers have many patients to see in short periods of time. Young expectant mothers and fathers may have questions about childcare, infant health, safe sleep, immunizations, feeding, and so on that they do not know when or how to ask. The care coordinator can help the expectant parents develop the skills to ask for information from their provider and seek information from other resources. A brief session on how to ask questions, make sense of the information received, and request services may be particularly useful. Consider, for example, participants who have questions about immunizations. Although the care coordinator may not have the answers, he or she can help by searching for information from reliable sources (the American Academy of Pediatrics or the Centers for Disease Control and Prevention) so the participants know what to ask their pediatrician. Similarly, a young expectant parent may have questions about bed-sharing and safe sleep and need help sorting through online information. Usually, it is best to coach the participant on how to ask clear questions of a medical provider.

CARE COORDINATION VIGNETTES

The following examples demonstrate some of a care coordinator's tasks and roles. They specifically illustrate the various approaches to helping adolescents access and receive community services, from simply providing advice to doing things directly on their behalf. In all cases, the care coordinators tailor their approach to each participant, always working toward helping him or her learn to be a self-advocate capable of finding his or her own resources and meeting his or her own needs.

Destiny

Destiny is 16 years old and six months along in her pregnancy. She told her counselor that she has been finding it very difficult to attend school regularly because she has felt very sick throughout the pregnancy. When she does attend school, she has a difficult time staying focused. She is worried that there might be something wrong with her or the baby. Her grades have dropped and she is getting worried that she will not have enough credits to graduate on time. The care coordinator assures Destiny that feeling so tired and unfocused is not unusual during pregnancy, and encourages her to discuss these concerns with her doctor just to rule out any other possible issues.

Destiny tells the care coordinator she has not seen her doctor in two months; she missed her last prenatal appointment and does not have another appointment scheduled. Her mother took her to her first appointment but cannot take off work to take her again. Her mother expects Destiny to take the bus to the doctor. Tearfully, she tells the care coordinator she does not know the bus route and does not want to go alone. The baby's father has to work all the time, she says, and cannot get the time off to go with her.

On the spot, the care coordinator calls the clinic to facilitate scheduling a prenatal appointment. After the initial contact, she hands the phone to Destiny, who makes an appointment. After determining that no one in Destiny's support network can accompany her, the care coordinator offers to ride the bus with Destiny and attend the upcoming appointment to help her become more comfortable with the process of getting herself to her prenatal appointments and communicating with her doctor. Destiny agrees.

At her prenatal appointment the following week, the doctor reassures Destiny that her worries and symptoms are normal, but that she will write a note to the school so that she gets accommodations for her pregnancy as needed (e.g., packets of work dropped off at her house by a tutor). The doctor tells Destiny that she knows this is something the school offers to pregnant adolescents, but says it is also good for her to attend school and be with her peers if she is feeling up to it.

The doctor also offers to see her again the following week to check in, and that the clinic provides free bus tokens for patients. Destiny looks visibly relieved and says she will stay in school. With the care coordinator's encouragement, she asks questions about the baby's development and about her weight gain, which is embarrassing her. She leaves the office in better spirits. When they finally get back to Destiny's apartment, it is dark and she is exhausted but feels empowered by the experience. She tells the care coordinator she thinks she can manage the bus alone and get herself to school.

Ricardo

Ricardo is a 17-year-old expectant father who speaks Spanish only. He and his girlfriend are expecting a child in four months. Ricardo tells the care coordinator that his biggest worry is that he has multiple unpaid parking tickets. He keeps receiving notices and thinks his car registration has been suspended. He would like to find out how to get the tickets paid off so he can drive legally before the baby is born but knows he cannot pay all of them right away.

The care coordinator looks over Ricardo's tickets and finds a phone number and an office location. She suggests they call the number together, right then, and find out how much money he owes and whether they can put him on a payment plan. Because Ricardo is concerned about being able to speak to someone in Spanish, the care coordinator places the call. When they get through, the care coordinator asks to speak with someone who speaks Spanish so that Ricardo can understand the conversation. Ricardo observes the care coordinator asking questions about the amount owed and payment options, including how he may make smaller payments over time, and what each option mean in terms of Ricardo getting his registration reinstated. They are told that he can set up a payment plan but that he needs to come in to the office and meet with a clerk. One of the clerks speaks Spanish and an appointment is set.

With a better understanding of his options, Ricardo talks with the care coordinator about how much money he has, what money he expects to earn from the upcoming jobs, and how much he needs to set aside for baby supplies. Together they determine a plan for how he will pay these tickets off over time. The care coordinator checks in with Ricardo the next week to see how the meeting with the clerk went. Over the course of this process, Ricardo tells the care coordinator he would really like to learn to speak English. The care coordinator identifies an

English as a Second Language (ESL) program at a community center not far from Ricardo's house. She helps him enroll in the class.

Devon

Devon is an 18-year-old expectant father whose partner is due in two months. They have an on-again, off-again relationship. Devon tells his care coordinator that his main concern is being able to provide for the baby financially, but he has not applied for a job. He has never held a job and does not know how to get one. Devon feels overwhelmed by the pressure to finish high school and get a full-time job. He often considers dropping out of school to work full-time. The care coordinator knows that one of Devon's goals is to earn his associate's degree in business. She talks with him about the importance of completing his high school education so he can get a better job in the long run. The care coordinator offers to help Devon determine if there are options that would allow him to continue school while working as much as possible.

Together, they gather information about various part-time jobs that would fit with his school schedule and they fill out a couple of online applications. During this process, the care coordinator learns that Devon is on probation for getting into a fight at school. He does not know if he should admit this when he is applying and interviewing for jobs. They discuss the importance of being upfront with employers; some will still consider hiring him and others will not, but they will find out anyway if they do a background check. They do a couple of role-play exercises in which the care coordinator pretends to be a manager at a fast-food restaurant and a warehouse, one friendly and one not so friendly.

The care coordinator also finds a vocational training program that helps with job placement. Devon asks what would happen if he gets a job, but they want him to work during school hours. The care coordinator tells him about an alternative high school program that offers a flexible schedule, so he may have greater availability to work throughout the week. Devon seems very interested in this option, but the care coordinator suggests that he take it one step at a time and apply for some jobs first. Nonetheless, she offers to arrange for him and his mother to meet with a counselor at the alternative school to gather more information. Devon seems energized and applies for several jobs.

These simple scenarios illustrate a few situations in which young expectant fathers and mothers need some help managing their lives. In many respects, the care coordinator is functioning like a parent figure or mentor, walking and talking them through the typical challenges involved in growing up and becoming more independent. Most young men and women want to function independently, but often lack the fundamental skills needed to navigate the world and are too embarrassed to ask for help. The care coordinator's approach should be tailored to enhance young people's ability to accomplish tasks for themselves.

WHEN PARTICIPANTS DECLINE SERVICES OR REFERRALS

Some participants may be uncomfortable receiving help in specific areas of functioning, particularly mental health–related services. Referrals should not be made for services that the participant clearly does not want. For instance, a care coordinator may believe that a participant needs therapy for past experiences of sexual abuse. Unless the participant also identifies this as necessary or desired, he or she is unlikely to follow through with a referral and may get irritated with the care coordinator for being too pushy.

That said, it may be beneficial for the care coordinator to plant the idea of getting some services at some point in the future. When a participant initially resists services, it is always helpful to frame the suggested support in a way that is congruent with the participant's belief system and within his or her comfort zone. For example, some adolescents feel more comfortable seeking mental health counseling if they know it will improve their parenting or if it is affiliated with their religion. Some might be more comfortable attending a support group than talking with a counselor. If counselors and care coordinators understand and respect a participant's discomfort with receiving help, that discomfort is more likely to diminish over time.

CHAPTER REVIEW

The previous two chapters detailed the roles of counselor and care coordinator, which we describe as two distinct positions. Although we believe that having a separate care coordinator to assist couples in addressing their psychosocial needs is important, we also realize that this is not always practical. Therefore, we encourage counselors to network with social service providers in their respective agencies/clinics/schools or outside agencies as appropriate to assist in providing support in common areas of need (e.g, housing, employment, school) to program participants. With clinical roles and responsibilities defined, we now turn our attention to the individual phases of the Young Parenthood Program, starting with Phase 1—engagement and intake.

PHASE 1: ENGAGEMENT AND ASSESSMENT

5

INTRODUCTION

PHASE 1 BEGINS WHEN YOU, THE COUNSELOR, meet with the young expectant mother and father together to discuss their participation in YPP. Optimally, this two-hour engagement and assessment meeting should occur during the mother's second trimester; the couple has passed through the initial shock of the pregnancy but has time to make progress on co-parenting skills before their baby arrives. During this meeting, you will explain the goals and structure of the program, begin to develop a therapeutic alliance, and complete an assessment of the couple following the process outlined in this chapter. This first meeting is unusually long because the assessment process is fairly extensive. Explain to the couple that subsequent sessions will last no more than one hour each.

WHEN AND WHERE TO MEET

Young couples have little control over their school and work schedules and may not have reliable transportation, which means that scheduling sessions can be difficult. As much as possible, be flexible and recognize that many couples can meet only during evenings or on weekends. Some young couples may need assistance in determining when they can meet because they are not practiced at making (and keeping) appointments. They may not directly ask for your help when they are having difficulty scheduling appointments; rather, they may hesitate when scheduling appointments, frequently miss appointments, or arrive too late to meet with you and leave frustrated. Although these behaviors might signal problems in the therapeutic relationship, they might simply be the result of difficulties with scheduling or transportation. Be patient yet persistent about resolving such problems. Many adolescents do not know how to manage their schedules and need adult guidance to learn how to request time off from work or resolve transportation issues. Ask the couple if they would like a little help with problem solving around their schedule or transportation.

Many programs for young mothers are home visitation programs based on a public health model in which nurses check in on new mothers to ensure that they are able to attend to their newborns' basic needs. The YPP is not designed to be a home visitation program, but it may be practical and efficient to provide in-home counseling for some couples. Some young expectant parents are completely overwhelmed by the demands of their lives and frequently miss scheduled appointments. That said, providing YPP in a participant's home can be challenging for the YPP counselor and requires a little extra instruction.

First, remember you are a guest in your participant's home. Be sure to thank the family for inviting you in and providing you with needed space. You may want to explain the importance of the young couple's confidentiality, which means that you would prefer to meet in a room in which you can close the door. Second, as a member of the mental health profession, you may be looked upon with suspicion;

do not take this personally. Case workers are often regarded as distrustful because they have a reputation for "getting into other people's business." Third, be prepared to respond to home life activities (TVs, phone calls, children running in and out) that otherwise can be distracting and diminish the focus of the sessions. If you want to alter the home environment (e.g., by turning off the TV, having the children leave the room), make a polite request. For example: "Would you be OK with turning off the TV for a few minutes? What you have to say is really important to me, and unfortunately I get distracted by hearing the TV." Finally, pay attention to your own safety. If you are feeling unsafe in the neighborhood or the home, find another location for your sessions.

PRACTICAL TIPS

MEETING PARTICIPANTS IN THEIR HOMES

- Begin the visit by thanking the participant and family for receiving you in their home. If it seems appropriate, make positive comments about the home's appearance.
- Introduce yourself and explain your purpose and role. For example, "As we talked about, I'm here for us to set the goals for our future meetings."
- Ask questions such as, "May I sit down?" or "Where would you like us to talk?" to indicate that you know you are a guest in their home.
- Acknowledge possible feelings of judgment or invasion. Explain that you are there to support them, not judge them. You can say, "Some people find it strange that I want to visit them at home. But I've found it's usually less of an inconvenience. I hope I won't be in your way and that you'll let me know if there's a problem."
- Accept offers graciously. It can feel uncomfortable to accept an offer of food or drink, but especially on the first visit, it can be helpful to do so. Let the participants or their families know that you do not expect such "royal" treatment each time you visit.

At the beginning of an in-home meeting, set the stage by discussing and agreeing upon a plan for how long the meeting will last, where you should meet next, and who should participate. At the end of the session, make sure that you thank the family for inviting you and helping you find a quiet, private place to work with their son/daughter.

Some young people will neither make it to your office nor want you in their home. If you are flexible about where to meet, you will increase the likelihood of providing YPP counseling to the broadest range of couples. (We have commonly met couples in prenatal clinics and public libraries). It is best to be creative when scheduling appointments. Transportation presents the biggest obstacle for some couples. Some have never used the public transportation system and feel intimidated by the prospect. Some are uncomfortable traveling to or through unfamiliar neighborhoods. Again, be flexible, discuss options, and coach the young parents through their obstacles.

THE YOUNG PARENTHOOD PROGRAM

Table 5.1 PHASE 1: GOALS AND TASKS

Goals	Tasks
1. Begin to develop a therapeutic alliance with the couple (and their families as appropriate).	1. Obtain consent to participate in the YPP (for participants under 18). 2. Schedule an initial meeting to explain the purpose of the program. 3. Explain YPP goals and objectives. 4. Explain confidentiality. 5. Explain the structure of the YPP. 6. Help the couple tell their story.
2. Gather information from the couple through structured. interviews and questionnaires.	1. Conduct individual YPP interviews using the YPP Individual Interview Script (Table 5.2). 2. Administer self-report questionnaires.
3. Develop an initial YPP counseling plan and case formulation.	1. Review information you have gathered. 2. Develop a YPP counseling plan based on gathered information using the YPP Case Formulation Template (Table 5.3).

GOAL 1: DEVELOP A THERAPEUTIC ALLIANCE

In this section we outline all the details of getting started with counseling, beginning with obtaining consent for treatment. We regard every interaction as an opportunity to develop a positive therapeutic alliance… or not. Attention to the interpersonal details of the consenting process, such as obtaining parental permission, can be a "make it or break it" moment because not only are you explaining the purpose of the program, but you are also addressing some very fundamental concerns, such as confidentility and parent authority. In the sections that follow, we describe the elements of setting up the counseling relationship.

Task 1: Get Consent for Participation in the YPP

You are required to obtain parental/guardian consent for YPP participants under the age of 18. Obtaining signed consent from a minor's parents is often complicated and a common obstacle to treatment. Ideally the minor's parent accompanies him or her to the first session but this rarely happens. Instead, you may need to make several phone calls before connecting with the parent, explaining the program and figuring out a way to get a signed form in your hands.

Talking with the parents (of the expectant mother and/or father) provides you with the opportunity to begin developing a positive working relationship with the extended families. Regular contact with some parents can help obtain their support. Although parental permission is not a legal necessity for participants 18 and over, it may be useful to engage with the parents, solicit their input, and demonstrate your respect for their role and position. Before doing so, first ask the expectant mother or father for permission and have them complete a formal "release of information" form. For some YPP couples, your relationship with their extended families will not be important. But for others, it will play a critical role in their success with the program. Their parents, for example, might be a very important source of support and encouragement. Plus, in some cultural groups, not including the young couple's parents might be seen as disrespectful and undermining of the parents' authority.

Engaging the participants' parents demonstrates respect for the family hierarchy and acknowledges the significant role that parents play in the life of youth.

Task 2: Schedule the Initial Meeting to Explain the Purpose of the Program

At the start of the first session, meet with the expectant mother and father together, either in your office or a location more convenient for the father. Meeting both parents together at this time is important for two reasons. First, it helps establish parity in your relationship with each individual (which will increase your credibility when emotions run high). You want both partners to feel like you are equally there for both of them (and their baby). Second, it is the best strategy for ensuring that both partners will stay engaged throughout the program. If you do not get the young father in the door for the first session, it is likely to only get more difficult as time passes. If you are working with a care coordinator (case manager) it is best for him or her to be present for this introductory session. This allows the couple to meet and learn about your complementary roles. Your primary concerns at this time are to explain YPP's purpose and address the issues of consent and confidentiality before the counseling process.

Task 3: Discuss the YPP Goals and Objectives

Discuss the overarching program philosophy. Use your own language to provide the information below, but be sure to touch on each of these points:

- The goal of this program is to help you develop the sort of relationship with each other that will be good for your child. How you treat each other is very important to your baby's development. The healthier your relationship is, the better off and healthier your child will be.
- New parents who "take care of their relationship" are likely to become better parents because they will have more emotional energy left over for their child. Parenting can be a bit of a roller coaster ride; there are ups and downs. You may have family problems, money problems, or legal problems that are upsetting to one or both of you. If you can work together to deal with these problems, parenting will be a better experience for both of you.
- The program focuses on mothers and fathers because both of you are important to your child's development. Most children get different things from their mother and their father and it is important that your child benefits from what each of you has to offer.
- The sessions will help you clarify what sort of parent you want to be and how you can help each other become that sort of parent.
- If you have conflicts, the program will help you handle them in a safe, respectful, and productive way. This is an extremely important parenting skill. You will need to do this with each other, and before too long, you will need to do it with your child.
- What happens in your relationship with each other is entirely up to you. You will not be encouraged to marry or stay together as a couple. You will also not be encouraged to break up. Instead, I will guide you toward developing the relationship skills you need to raise a healthy and successful child no matter what happens in your romantic life. Everything you will be working on together will be useful if you stay together for the next 50 years or if you break up tomorrow.
- There is no set idea about what a good relationship looks like or how you two ought to get along. There are a lot of types of co-parenting relationships

that work. The goal is to make your relationship work as best it can in a way that fits with both of your personalities and provides a good environment for your child.

- We will not focus much on specific parenting behaviors, but if you have questions about parenting (practical or even philosophical), they can be addressed. We can also provide referrals to parenting classes.
- You will get the most from the program if you talk openly about yourself and your relationship.

Task 4: Explain Confidentiality

Young Parenthood Program participants are more likely to be open and fully engaged if they trust that the counselor will treat the content of their interactions as confidential. Confidentiality—its definition and limitations—may be unfamiliar or misunderstood by YPP participants, so explain it carefully. Assure the couple that you will not talk with others about what they share with you unless you become seriously concerned about someone's safety. For example, you *cannot* maintain confidentiality when a participant confides about child abuse, neglect, or endangerment or exhibits suicidal behaviors or other self-harming behaviors. Adolescents commonly complain that therapists promise confidentiality but talk with their parents anyway. However, a frank and open discussion of the limits of confidentiality can build trust in the therapeutic relationship.

Task 5: Explain the Structure of the YPP

After discussing the YPP goals, outline the program's structure so the couple knows what to expect. Using your own words, cover the following points:

- The first sessions will focus on making personal goals, relationship goals, and identifying your strengths and weakness as individuals and as a couple. This will help us plan what to work on during our next few meetings.
- Our focus will depend on your needs, your wishes, and your personalities. We might focus on listening skills, problem-solving skills, or learning how to accept and support each other. All these skills will help you create a warmer, more secure home for your child.
- If you have problems or issues with your own families, or if they play a big part in how you will work together, we can include that in the program. If it makes sense, we can invite them to join in some sessions.
- After your baby is born, we will want to meet with you a couple more times to see how you are adjusting to parenthood and being co-parents.

ENGAGING EXPECTANT FATHERS

An expectant father may be willing to come to the initial meeting because his partner insisted or persuaded him. His continued participation will be contingent on whether he feels the program is useful for him and whether he connects with you. It is important to recognize that co-parenting counseling is probably not his top priority. Many expectant fathers are stressed about making enough money to support the baby. Some are preoccupied with school, friends, and other things.

You should work to help each young man identify his primary concerns and his questions about becoming a father. Do not try too hard to sell the program or convince the father he "needs" co-parenting counseling. Listen and respond in a nonjudgmental way while identifying (and pointing out) his areas of strength. Many of these young men have not received much positive feedback; a little support and appreciation—even for just showing up—can go a long way (Kiselica, 2011).

TIMING OF SESSIONS

Spend a few minutes talking about the pace of your meetings. Ideally, a couple should have at least 8 to 10 sessions before the birth of the baby. The pace, therefore, depends on how much time you have until the baby is born. If there is plenty of time (e.g., the baby is not due for five months), it may be useful to meet once a week for four or five weeks to engage the couple and establish a working alliance. Then, you might meet less frequently to allow the couple to practice the new skills. If the baby is due sooner, you might push to meet twice a week to maximize the number of sessions before the baby's birth. If the YPP program phases are not completed before the baby's birth, the program can continue following his or her arrival. However, this is likely to be a challenge, as the couple's time and energy will be focused on their newborn.

Task 6: Help the Couple Tell Their Story

Many adolescent couples will have no idea about how to begin the counseling process, what they should expect from it, or even what they hope to gain. A typical method for establishing a therapeutic relationship is to ask an open-ended question such as, "How might I be helpful?" followed by silence. With young expectant couples, this is generally not a useful way to begin. After setting the stage with the couple about what they can expect through their participation in YPP, let them know you are interested in learning more about them both as individuals and as a co-parenting couple. Ask them to share their story by opening with something like, "Tell me your story, I'm interested in how you guys met and got together in the first place." Generally, this is a good icebreaker. You might use the following questions as prompts:

- What happened between the time you first met (and got together) and now? How did your relationship develop over time?
- What do you like about your relationship?
- What has been difficult in this relationship?

- What feelings do you have regarding the pregnancy?
- What are your feelings about becoming a parent?

Couples will vary in how much they disclose and which one does most of the talking. Try to draw both of them into the conversation, but do not push a participant who seems reluctant. Some couples will quickly bring up problems. In this case, make sure that conflict level does not overwhelm either partner.

It can be challenging when conflicts emerge right away and you should always be prepared for that possibility. Couples will often feel safer if there are some established ground rules for dealing with conflicts. Effective couple's counselors are able to create a safe environment by making it clear that they will prevent conflicts from getting out of hand. Establish ground rules early in the therapeutic relationship; if a couple engages in serious conflict before the ground rules are in place, interrupt them. You might suggest the following ground rules:

GROUND RULES FOR MANAGING CONFLICTS

- The basic ground rule is to be respectful; partners should not interrupt each other, yell at each other, swear at each other, or call each other names.
- Both partners should agree to let the counselor use the "time-out" hand signal (or something similar) to stop them from being disrespectful.
- When the counselor interrupts a conflict, he or she will help both partners to take a moment (maybe just a deep breath), return to the issue, and express themselves more respectfully.

GOAL 2: GATHER INFORMATION THROUGH STRUCTURED INTERVIEWS AND QUESTIONNAIRES

As described, the first session begins with you meeting both partners together. If they are interested in co-parent counseling and agree to participate, then it often makes sense to immediately begin the assessment and intake process. During this initial phase you will meet each partner individually to conduct an in-depth interview about their relationship and administer a number of brief questionnaires. This process will help you assess how both partners were functioning before their participation in YPP across several key indicators of interpersonal health. The information will be used to develop a case formulation (explained below) and to tailor the program to fit the couple's specific needs. Questionnaires can be re-administered at program completion to assess changes in functioning and help determine if YPP is helping you to support the development of your clients.

In some clinic settings, the intake process is conducted by someone other than the counselor. If possible, personally conduct the assessment; it can help you to build rapport with each partner in a balanced way. For efficiency, ask one partner to complete the self-report in one room while you meet privately with the other in another room. When the first private interview is completed (approximately 30 minutes) switch and meet with the second partner.

Task 1: Conduct Individual YPP Interviews

The private interview is an opportunity for you to get to know each partner individually. It is designed to explore the partner's relationship with the co-parent, feelings about the pregnancy and future parenting, family relationships, and support network. Conducting these interviews privately allows each partner to express thoughts and feelings they otherwise might not. They may have different agendas regarding what they hope to get from the program. For example, one partner may want to focus on strengthening the other's level of commitment, whereas the other may want his or her partner to be less controlling and demanding. Individual interviews provide a different window into the relationship. They also allow you to ask personal questions about family relations.

The questions to be asked during the individual interview are listed in Table 5.2. Consider asking follow-up questions and probe as necessary to understand a participant's responses and what he or she is trying to relate. It is very important to ask questions in an open-ended way and to avoid suggesting responses when a participant seems confused by the question. It is better to explain or rephrase the question and acknowledge that some questions are difficult to answer. Let the person know that you may ask some questions he or she has never thought about before, and you will allow some time to think if needed.

Table 5.2 YPP INTERVIEW

I am going to ask you a number of questions to better understand you, your relationship with (co-parenting partner), and your family. This information will help me determine how the Young Parenthood Program may be helpful to you as you prepare to become a parent and co-parent. Some of these questions might have been discussed when we met together with (co-parenting partner), but I am also asking you these things individually so that you have an opportunity to share anything that you didn't feel comfortable sharing when (co-parenting partner) was with us. What you share with me individually will be kept confidential between us. I won't bring up anything you tell me now with (co-parenting partner) unless you want me to. I will ask these same questions of (co-parenting partner) when I meet with (him/her) in a little while. Answer these questions as much as you feel comfortable. Let me know if you have any questions or concerns along the way.

The Couple's Relationship

1. Please provide three words you would use to describe your relationship with (partner's name); please provide examples or explain what you mean by...?

2. What are your feelings about (co-parenting partner)?

3. How has the relationship changed since finding out about the pregnancy?

4. What would you change about (co-parenting partner) if you could?

5. What can you do to make the relationship better?

6. What can (co-parenting partner) do to make the relationship better?

7. Please provide three words you would use to describe your partner; provide examples.

8. Please provide three words you would use to describe yourself; provide examples.

(continued)

Table 5.2 CONTINUED

Conflicts in the Relationship

1. What do you and (co-parenting partner) disagree about? Can you give me an example?

2. How do you and (co-parenting partner) usually work things out when you have a disagreement?

3. Are there any issues you think the two of you need to resolve?

4. What is the most serious fight or argument you have ever had with (co-parenting partner)?

5. Have you ever gotten into a physical fight with (co-parenting partner)?

6. Where do you want this relationship to go in the future?

Parenthood

1. Have either of you been with other partners since you started going together? (Probe about whether the partner knows, and if it remains an issue.)

2. What are your feelings about becoming a parent?

3. What do you imagine it will be like to be a parent?

4. What kind of parent do you want to become?

Relationship with Parents and Extended Family

1. Please provide three words you would use to describe your mother; provide examples.

2. Please describe your relationship with your mother.

3. What has been her response to learning about the pregnancy?

4. Please provide three words you would use to describe your father; provide examples.

5. Describe your relationship with your father.

6. What has been his response to learning about the pregnancy?

7. Please describe your parents' relationship with each other.

8. How would you like to do things differently with (partner)?

9. Please tell me about other people in your family that you'd like me to know about (siblings, grandparents)?

10. Please describe your relationship with your partner's family.

Living Arrangements and Support Network

1. Who do you live with now?

2. Who will be most helpful to you when the baby is born?

3. In what ways will they support you (e.g., financially, physically, emotionally)?

The Young Parenthood Program

1. How can this program can be most helpful to you and your partner?

2. Can you tell me about any problems that would be useful for me to know about (health, family, legal, school)?

3. Do you have any questions of me at this time?

4. Is there anything else you want to me to know about you or your relationship?

Thank you for taking the time to talk with me and for all that you shared. As you know, I will be asking the same questions of (co-parenting partner). Part of my job as your counselor is to try to understand where each of you is coming from and be balanced when I work with the two of you together. What you've shared gives me a good understanding of how things are for you, personally and in your relationship with (co-parenting partner).

Table 5.2 also includes a sample introduction to the interview. Notice the counselor's acknowledgment of the confidentiality of the individual interview. A sample closing statement is also provided. The intent of the closing statement is to clarify that the counselor's empathic listening/responding (affirmative statements, affirmative body language) is not confirmation that the counselor takes everything the individual says as fact, but rather that the counselor heard the individual's perspective.

Task 2: Administer Self-Report Questionnaires

The goal of the assessment process is to get to know the couple as best you can in a short period of time. It is hard to gather all the information you might want. Self-report questionnaires are efficient tools for gathering information because the questions are brief and the responses are to the point, not allowing for elaboration. Some young people are more comfortable sharing sensitive information on a questionnaire than in a face-to-face interview. Self-report questionnaires are particularly good for gathering information about drug and alcohol abuse, intimate partner violence, mental health, and stress. Table 5.3 contains a list of measures that we have used with some success. There are many measures available on the Internet and we encourage YPP counselors to find ones that work best for them and their participants.

There are many other questionnaires and screening tools that could be added to the assessment process. The questionnaires listed above cover areas that we believe are essential, but it is also worth considering measures that focus more explicitly on depression, trauma, or antisocial behavior that could interfere with co-parenting. More detailed information is almost always useful. However, the risk of asking too many questions is twofold. First, many of these questionnaires focus on the negative aspects of the young parent's life. This is the nature of screening instruments; however, too many in one sitting can be overwhelming. Second, we have found that when the assessment process is very long and arduous, the young couple is less likely to want to continue with co-parenting counseling because they believe it will require too much time. Before adding other questionnaires, consider these factors.

Table 5.3 RECOMMENDED MEASURES FOR THE PRE-PROGRAM ASSESSMENT

Drug and Alcohol Abuse. The *CRAFFT* is a recommended screening tool for identifying drug and alcohol abuse concerns (Knight et al., 2003). It is designed for use with youth under the age of 21 and recommended by the American Academy of Pediatrics' Committee on Substance Abuse. It is short (six items) and reliable and can help you determine if a longer conversation about drug and alcohol use is warranted. The CRAFFT and instructions for its use can be accessed through the following website: http://www.ceasar-boston.org/clinicians/crafft.php.

Intimate Partner Violence/Relationship Conflict. The *Conflict in Adolescent Dating Relationships Inventory* (CADRI; Wolfe, Scott, Reitzel-Jaffe, Wekerle, Grasley, & Straatman, 2001) is a recommended questionnaire for assessing both positive and negative behavior between intimate partners. The measure focuses primarily on the negative behaviors but includes some questions regarding positive approaches to addressing disagreements. The introductory section about dating history may not be necessary during a YPP assessment, so consider dropping that part. Ask each participant to focus on his or her relationship with the co-parenting partner specifically, even if the co-parents are not together as a romantic couple or they are dating other people. This measure, along with information regarding its development and validation, was published in *Psychological Assessment*, Volume 13, Issue 2 (2001).

General Mental Health. The *Youth Outcomes Questionnaire: Self Report* (YOQ-SR; Ridge et al., 2009) is recommended as a quick and easy way to assess social, emotional and behavioral symptoms. For YPP participants who are 18 or over, there is an adult version called the Outcomes Questionnaire (OQ). These instruments are brief measures of mental health that can be used repeatedly with participants and are sensitive to changes in functioning over time. The YOQ and OQ are not in the public domain but are inexpensive and can be purchased at http://www.oqmeasures.com. If cost is a factor, there are several symptom checklists/screening devises that are in the public domain, such as the Strengths and Difficulties Questionnaire (Goodman, 2001; http://www.sdqinfo.com)

Perceived Stress. The *Perceived Stress Scale* (either 4 or 10 items) is a recommended tool for assessing the degree to which situations are appraised as stressful (Cohen, Kamarck, & Mermelstein, 1983). This brief measure can be easily used to track perceived stress over time. The PSS-4 and PSS-10 can be found at the following website: http://www.psy.cmu. edu/~scohen/scales.html.

Resilience. The *Child and Youth Resilience Measure-Short Version (CYRM-12;* Liebenberg et al., 2013) measures resilience in youth at three levels of experience (individual, family, and community context). The CYRM manual defines resilience as being comprised of three capacities: (a) The capacity of individuals to navigate their way to resources that sustain well-being; (b) the capacity of individuals' physical and social ecologies to provide those resources; and (c) the capacity of individuals, their families and communities to negotiate culturally meaningful ways for resources to be shared. The 12-item version of the CYRM is based on the longer 28-item, original measure (Unger & Liebenberg, 2011). Both versions have been found to have adequate content and construct validity, test-retest reliability, and internal consistency. The CYRM-12 can be obtained from the primary author (Dr. Linda Liebenberg, Co-Director of the Resilience Research Centre, at Dalhousie University, Halifax, NS Canada; linda.liebenberg@dal.ca).

Trauma Symptoms. The *Screen for Posttraumatic Stress Symptoms* (SPTSS; Carleson, 2001; Caspi et al., 2007) is a 17-item brief screening measure designed to identify people with high levels of posttraumatic stress symptoms. Items closely match the DSM-IV criteria for PTSD and are written in simple language making the instrument suitable for use with a wide variety of populations. One of the advantages of the SPTSS is that trauma symptoms are not asked in reference to a specific event, which allows it to be used with individuals who may have experienced multiple stressful events. The SPTSS has been found to have adequate psychometric properties (Caspi et al., 2007).

GOAL 3: DEVELOP AN INITIAL COUNSELING PLAN AND CASE FORMULATION

Creating a case formulation and a plan will help you clarify your thinking and approach to a couple. This step is integral to the YPP counseling process. You will have collected a great deal of information about the couple, including information about emotional health, drug and alcohol abuse, relationship conflict, and stress. Before Phase 2, you should review your notes and impressions from all interviews. Next, review the scores derived from the self-report questionnaires. Take all this information into consideration and write up an initial case formulation and a co-parenting counseling/care coordination plan. In the formulation, include your impressions of each partner's strengths and weaknesses and your impression of the couple's strengths and weaknesses. Your plan should contain your preliminary thoughts about how to address strengths and weaknesses. If possible, discuss your plan with your clinical team before your next session with the couple.

Task 1: Review the Information You Have Gathered

Review your notes. The first YPP session and private interviews should have provided you with ample information. In your review, pay attention to the following issues:

- The expression of warmth and hostile feelings toward each other
- The level of openness and interpersonal comfort/connection
- Power and control dynamics
- Issues of trust/distrust
- Each partner's capacity for verbal self-expression
- How the couple copes with difficulties and stress
- The couple's feelings about pregnancy and parenthood
- Commitment/investment in the relationship
- Discrepancies between how partner behaved when together and when alone with you

Next, review the questionnaires, which can help you identify red flags. Although each questionnaire listed has instructions for scoring (so that you can create total scores and subscale scores) it is often clinically useful to examine the item level responses. For example, it would be important for you to know if the couple is getting into fist fights (reflected in a single item on the CADRI); this information would significantly raise the level of concern about fundamental safety. When reviewing the information gathered through the self-report questionnaires, pay particular attention to the following risk factors that could interfere with co-parenting and parenting: (a) hostile, aggressive interpersonal behavior; (b) significant drug or alcohol use; (c) symptoms of depression, anxiety, or trauma; and (d) high levels of stress. Any red flags that you identify may warrant some follow-up. For example, a young expectant parent might report suicidal behavior and/or ongoing abuse and you will need to respond immediately. It is important to remember that when serious risks such as these emerge during the assessment process, it is likely that the participant is both wanting and expecting you to notice and respond.

In subsequent couple's session, moderate levels of hostility and aggression can be effectively addressed, as can individual-level issues, including trauma, depression, and anxiety. That said, be careful not to raise an issue that emerged on the self-report questionnaire without first getting permission to do so. Young Parenthood Program counseling is not intended to treat individual mental health concerns; information about individual functioning is gathered and used when working with couples because each partner's mental health affects the relationship. When serious mental health issues arise during the assessment, consider making a referral for additional assessment and treatment. For example, a young father's substance abuse problem is likely to become a primary focus of the co-parenting sessions. A frank discussion of this issue may motivate him to seek treatment, hopefully improving his ability to function as a co-parent and parent. Table 5.4 provides a template for a YPP co-parenting counseling plan.

Task 2: Develop a Counseling Plan Based on the Information You Have Gathered

DESCRIBE THE COUPLE'S DEMOGRAPHICS

This section of your plan should include the basics (such as age, living situation, grade in school, employment status and ethnicity), but also information

Table 5.4 TEMPLATE FOR A CO-PARENTING COUNSELING PLAN

1. Demographic background of each partner

   a. Her age, education level, school and/or work situation, ethnicity/culture/religion, due date, location of prenatal care, involvement with any other services

   b. His age, education level, school and/or work situation, ethnicity/culture/religion, involvement with any other services

2. Family history

   a. Her family of origin and family history (parents' relationship with each other, quality of her relationship with parents, extended family resources)

   b. His family of origin and family history (parents' relationship with each other, quality of his relationship with parents, extended family resources)

3. Couple's story (relationship history and interpersonal dynamics)

   a. How they met and the duration of their relationship

   b. Relationship quality; warmth, power dynamics (control, autonomy)

   c. Communication skills

   d. Primary relationship strengths

   e. Feelings about pregnancy and impact of pregnancy on relationship

   f. Readiness for parenting

4. Risk factors and co-parenting concerns

5. Targets for preventative and intervention (actual goals will be formulated with the couple)

that may be relevant to care coordination goals (including how they are doing in school, whether the family is struggling to pay rent). Many young expectant parents live on the brink of a crisis or are struggling with school and/or work; include any potentially pressing concerns that would warrant the care coordinator's attention.

DESCRIBE THE COUPLE'S FAMILIES

First, describe the family structure of both the young mother and father. For some couples, the structure may be complex and nontraditional. Assess the quality of close family relationships as best you can; this may be difficult because adolescents and young adults often have very mixed feelings about their families and these feelings change from day to day. Sometimes it is difficult for adolescents to provide useful information about their families because they do not like talking about them or they have a hard time explaining the complex relationships. As best you can, given the limited information you have, assess the strength of each person's bond with each parent. Knowing what an expectant father admires most about his mother, for example, can be useful as you work toward drawing out his strengths. Who are their primary positive and negative role models? Who is likely to be primary sources of support and/or conflict? Many young parents say they want to do things differently than their parents; the reasons why they want their child's life to be different from their own can help you clarify program goals and be a motivator for change.

Second, assess the level of family chaos and identify pockets of stability. This can help the young parents decide where their child should live and who they can turn to for support. Some young men and women have a difficult time evaluating risk and protective factors within their families. For example, one young mother lived with her father—an alcoholic who had served prison time for molesting children. Initially, she planned to have him babysit her infant while she was at school. She was so excited about having recently reconnected with her father that it did not occur to her that this plan might not be in the baby's best interest. A discussion about how this young mother wanted her baby's family life to be different from her chaotic upbringing helped her consider other options. As you describe family risk factors in your counseling plan, consider how the young couple might create a positive environment for their child within the context of their existing relationships.

Third, identify the couple's resources for emotional, social, financial, and parenting support. It is important that you evaluate both current and untapped potential resources within the extended family. Adolescents often underestimate the level of support that is available to them. Additionally, with some readjustment of family roles, sources of conflict sometimes can be converted into sources of support. One of the most interesting aspects of working with young expectant couples is that they are in rapid transition and their family relationships can be positively "realigned."

DESCRIBE THE COUPLE'S RELATIONSHIP HISTORY AND INTERPERSONAL DYNAMICS

The relationships of YPP couples tend to be complex and you should do your best to describe all you have observed during your joint and individual meetings. Note your concerns about the couple's relationship, particularly as they relate to how YPP might help them strengthen it. Focus your report on what aspects of their relationship are strong and what aspects could be strengthened.

Describe the stability of the couple's connection. Some young couples may seem intensely engaged with each other, but the bond may be explosive or fragile. Others may seem unsure about their long-term prospects as a couple, but are nonetheless able to express compassion for and understanding of each other. Important factors to include in your evaluation are: (a) level of warmth and fondness expressed, or the basic temperature of the relationship; (b) capacity for empathy and acceptance of the other; (c) level of intimacy between partners, defined in terms of how well they know each other and how much personal information they share; (d) levels of hostility, anger, and distrust, especially if there has been infidelity; (e) controlling and distancing behavior between partners. It is particularly important to note the occurrence of aggressive, abusive, and violent behaviors and to follow up with a risk assessment if you have concerns about harm to either partner or the baby. The issue of intimate partner violence is addressed in more detail in Chapter 11.

RISK FACTORS

Some young parents have individual risk factors or problems, such as substance abuse, depression, a history of behavior problems or a history of criminal activity (Fagot et al., 1998). Describe each partner's level of individual risk and how they might negatively interfere with co-parenting and parenting. These individual risk factors may be appropriate to address through care coordination services (with a referral for additional counseling) and/or during co-parenting counseling if they are straining the relationship. Also consider how the co-parenting relationship could positively impact a pre-existing individual risk. Impending parenthood can motivate some young men to become more responsible, for example, particularly if they feel their partner values their contribution as a parent.

Describe negative life experiences (abuse, trauma, feelings of abandonment and neglect) that may relate to the co-parenting relationship. Direct questions about child abuse and trauma are not part of the YPP assessment protocol, but these issues often come up during the evaluation process. Past trauma and abuse experiences are almost always relevant to the co-parenting relationship and parenting. For example, adolescents who have a history of being abused often have residual feelings of anger, distrust, and betrayal that can spill over onto their current relationships. However, finding a safe way to discuss these feelings can create moments of compassion and connection between co-parents. Consider how past difficulties can be addressed in the co-parenting counseling process in ways that will help the couple move forward.

In addition to the typical risks that accompany young parenthood, some young expectant parents may have cognitive limitations because they are developmentally delayed or have a severe mental illness—such as psychosis—that affects their social functioning. Although we do not ask direct questions about these issues, it is important to keep these questions in mind because YPP may not be appropriate for young parents with low or impaired interpersonal-cognitive skills. If you are concerned that a parent is not able to make use of YPP, you may refer for a different sort of intervention. However, also consider if a simplified approach to interpersonal skill building would be useful.

INDIVIDUAL AND RELATIONSHIP GOALS OF THE COUPLE

End your YPP plan/case formulation by including potential individual and relationship goals and tasks. A more collaborative approach to identifying goals is part of Phase 2, described in the next chapter. It is likely that the relationship goals you identify (improved listening skills, improved empathy and acceptance) will be different from what the couple identifies as their relationship goals in Phase 2. It is best to follow the couple's lead when setting goals, but remain aware of the goals you selected that you might insert into the counseling process as co-parenting issues emerge.

Be realistic about what you can accomplish in a brief intervention. Do not try to "remake" the relationship or change either partner's personality. For example, if one partner is quite controlling and the other is very independent, YPP is not going to dramatically change this dynamic. However, it may be possible to "warm things up" so that the controlling partner becomes more nurturing and less managerial and the independent partner becomes more disclosing about themselves and less distancing or disengaged. As you write your formulation, consider how small shifts in the dynamic might help the couple become more balanced and stable.

Clearly state all primary strengths and weaknesses as they relate to co-parenting. Your summary should include some discussion of how to involve the extended families in this process, with an emphasis on how to help the couple make the best use of resources available to them. Your plan should also include care coordination goals. Some couples may have relatively few care coordination needs, particularly if they have a lot of family support, whereas others may need a great deal of very basic help. Finally, you should write the report in a way that it helps you know how to provide the couple with concrete and positive feedback when they need it. It will serve as your map and keep you from getting "lost in the trees" (the current conflicts) and losing sight of "the forest" (the long-term best interests of the child). Your impressions of the couple's strengths and weaknesses will likely change over time, and revisiting your plan should help you track their progress (or otherwise).

SAMPLE CASE FORMULATION AND YPP PLAN

(1) **Demographics.** Marlana is a quiet, 17-year-old who is five months pregnant, and lives alone with her parents. She has two older siblings who live in the area. Marlana is a high school senior and doing well in school but has a long history of depression and seemed quite depressed during the initial meeting. She makes poor eye contact, seems somewhat irritable, has a hard time expressing herself and is quite self-critical. Marlana's partner, Andy, is an outgoing 19-year-old, who is living with his mother and brother, working at a Pizza Hut. His head is shaved, he has earrings in both ears, and has the words "FUCK YOU" tattooed on his arm. Andy is on probation for drug possession and is required to get a drug test every week. He recently skipped his drug test because he could not afford to pay for it. He said it is likely that because of this, his judge will put him in jail for a few days. Both are white, but seem to come from different socioeconomic backgrounds. Marlana is middle class and seems a bit sheltered; Andy grew up poor and clearly has seen some difficult times, having spent significant time in youth corrections for various nonviolent criminal activities.

(2) **Family context.** Marlana reported that she has a close relationship with her father, but that he really hates Andy and wants her to break up with him. At one point, he threatened Andy with a gun when he snuck into Marlana's bedroom through the window. Marlana feels supported by her father, who has said he will help her take care of the baby, but she feels torn about this because her father is so adamantly against her relationship with Andy. She has a bad relationship with her mother, who she describes as mean to her, putting her down for everything she does wrong. Her mother does not like Andy either but was willing to sign the consent form allowing her to participate in the co-parenting counseling sessions, explaining that Andy should take responsibility for this baby. Marlana has two older siblings but does not have much of a relationship with either, although one or the other may be an untapped source of support.

Andy's mother has been diagnosed with schizophrenia and his father has been out of his life for many years. Andy seems to feel responsible for taking care of his mother, but is clearly fed up with that role. He speaks disparagingly about her crazy behavior and does not know how to help her, but clearly does not want to make things worse. His brother and he are friends and drinking/drug buddies. Andy said they had to raise themselves and they are pretty tight.

(3) **The couple's story and relationship dynamics.** In their introductory meeting with the counselor, Andy and Marlana bickered and argued about a number of issues, including whether Andy had been mean to Marlana that morning, whether Marlana talked too much, what Andy did with his money, and so on.

Andy has a gruff and aggressive style, dominating the conversation. He does not seem threatening or abusive and there is no indication that they have been in physical fights. He demonstrates some capacity for self-reflection and seems slightly amused by his own exaggerated behavior and Marlana's response. Despite her quiet demeanor, Marlana does not seem frightened or intimated by Andy. In fact, she seems a bit energized by his behavior and also somewhat amused. The arguing seems to be part of the way they connect with each other. When asked about how they got together, Andy said that he met Marlana on a bus, that he "hit on her" and she gave him her number. They started talking on the phone and then dating. Marlana did not elaborate on this, except to correct Andy on the small details.

During their individual interviews, they both said they were committed to the relationship but also said they had a lot of problems and argued all the time. Although they each blamed the other for the arguments, they also acknowledged they were both stubborn and irritable. They both seemed to lack much empathy for the other. This does not seem related to a lack of care. It seems partly a result of immaturity in the sense that both lacked the fundamental skills needed to listen and take in what the other was saying. This also seems partly because they are temperamentally very different. Andy is extroverted and probably conduct disordered; Marlana is introverted and possibly depressed. Their experiences of themselves are so different that it will require a great deal of effort to understand the other's point of view. As such, they seem to constantly misunderstand what the other person is saying. Marlana reports they have broken up several times and she does not really expect that the relationship will last. Nonetheless, both say they want to give the YPP a try and seem open to outside input. There are no signs of infidelity or jealousy. Neither seems particularly intent on controlling the other person. Despite an underlying fondness for each other, there is little intimacy or capacity for expressing warmth, care, or concern.

(4) **Risk factors.** There are a number of notable risk factors. Andy has a history of getting into trouble with the law and seems to have developed a "bad boy" identity. He also has a history of drug use and drinking. Based on what he reports about the pattern of use, he does not appear to be drug or alcohol dependent. Nonetheless, his chronic irresponsible behavior could interfere with his functioning as a father. For example, going to jail for missing his meeting with the probation officer could result in losing his job. It also does not bode well for building a more positive relationship with Marlana's family. Marlana appears to be at risk for significant depression. She is fundamentally pessimistic and clearly feels negatively about herself and her relationships (says disparaging things). Interpersonally, she seems younger than 17 because she lacks much insight about herself or others, and seems quite confused and defeated by her life.

(5) **Individual and relationship goals of the couple.** Despite these risks, Andy and Marlana demonstrate motivation for growth and learning. Individual goals for Andy may include abstinence from all drugs and alcohol, which seem to clearly interfere with his judgment. Being in trouble with the law seems like his chosen lifestyle and he may need some help thinking about his long-term prospects if he continues on this trajectory. He seems capable of finding an

approach that will lead to more stability and security for his child. Marlana might benefit from further assessment of her depression. Related to this, it will be important to help her build on the positive components of her life. She does well in school and it may be best for her to continue her education after high school, if this is a source of strength.

With respect to relationship goals, Andy and Marlana would benefit from learning fundamental listening skills and learning to provide emotional support for each other. As a couple, they do not seem particularly focused on or aware of their role as co-parents or parents, so it may be helpful to be explicit about how their relationship is relevant to parenting. Finally, it will be important to explore sources of support from extended family members. It is unclear if there is any room for Andy to develop a more positive relationship with Marlana's father or for Marlana to develop a more positive relationship with her mother. As it stands, if the baby lives with Marlana at her parents' home, it will be difficult for Andy to be able to provide much help because he is not allowed to be there. These issues could be explored in Phase 4 and it may be useful to engage Marlana's parents in a session intended to build bridges.

Document YPP Activities and the Couple's Progress

Once the case formulation and YPP plan is complete, you will be ready to move into Phase 2 and begin working with the couple to determine their goals. As you move through the phases, each couple's challenges and successes should be monitored using a standard Data, Assessment, and Plan (DAP) or Subjective, Objective, Assessment and Plan (SOAP) note-writing format. These notes help you track a couple's functioning from session to session. Notes should be concise but provide enough information to adequately describe what happened, what you think it means, and what you plan to do to facilitate progress. Documenting this information is required by most agencies and clinics. It can also help you reflect upon a couple's strengths/challenges and stay focused on meeting identified goals and track your activities. An example of a counselor note is provided in the following, using the DAP format.

> **D:** Met on 11/6/12 for 50 minutes and continued to work on reducing hostility. FOB and MOB were better able to remain connected and warm even when discussing conflicts. MOB talked about how she has been moody and irritable during the week, exhausted by the pregnancy. FOB agreed and reported they had several intense conflicts in the last couple days. FOB said that he had been trying to be nicer to MOB, but she was still trying to control him by making him to do things with her family without asking him first. When discussing this issue, both did a better job (than previously) listening and responding appropriately to each other. At times, one or the other became blaming, but responded positively to my redirection. To reinforce warmth in their relationships, I commented on how important it was for both of them to get positive feedback/support from the other. FOB readily acknowledged that this was important for him and MOB said that she would try to be more positive and encouraging. FOB admitted to smoking pot before they came to the session. In addition to focusing on listening skills and mutual support, I actively interrupted negative exchanges and tried to model the process of providing positive feedback.

A: Both FOB and MOB appear to care about each other and remain invested in their relationship but have not developed the basic skills for supporting each other. They get into intense conflicts and then make up, but they have not developed much capacity for ongoing compassion or kindness. Progress has been slow but both seemed to make some positive gains in the session today. FOB's continued substance use is a concern because he is currently on probation for other criminal activities and will be sent to jail if he is caught with a "dirty drug screen."

P: Continue to work on listening skills and learning to provide support to each other. Continue to acknowledge and reinforce FOB/MOB positive traits with the idea that they may both need affirmation. Address FOB's substance use issues related to fatherhood responsibilities, including staying out of jail.

Clinical notes help you maintain running narrative of the counseling process and keep a clear focus and direction, specific to each couple. To complement this narrative approach, we developed a simple system for tracking fidelity to the program, which we define in terms of: (a) number of sessions attended; (b) the extent to which you completed the phase specific goals described in this guide; and (c) whether the couple experienced the sessions as helpful. As a YPP counselor, you are encouraged to be flexible in the application of the YPP model to the particular needs of individual couples, but you are also expected to adhere to the fundamental structure and engage in core YPP activities. The purpose of the YPP fidelity worksheet (which can be found in the Appendix) is to assist you in monitoring your adherence to the model. YPP participants complete the top part of the worksheet, which asks them to report on "helpfulness" session by session. You complete out the bottom half of the sheet, which documents activities and "dose" (number of sessions), phase by phase. Although this tracking process may seem awkward to administer at first, it provides a simple and quick way to check in with couples regarding their feelings about the program. Hopefully, you and the couples you work with will feel comfortable being open when completing the worksheet. You should explain that their honest input can provide you with important feedback and help you make changes in your approach to maximize potential program benefits. We re-visit the issue of fidelity in Chapter 12, which focuses on assessment and program evaluation.

CHAPTER REVIEW

The following tasks should be accomplished by the end of Phase 1:

- The participants understand the goals of the YPP.
- The counselor has reviewed confidentiality.
- The counselor has developed a written initial case formulation, with particular attention to the couple's strengths.
- The counselor has selected a note-taking strategy and understands the importance of documenting fidelity to the YPP model.

With these foundational elements in place, you are now ready to engage in Phase 2 program activities, which focus on setting individual and co-parenting relationship goals with the couple.

6

PHASE 2: SETTING PROGRAM GOALS

INTRODUCTION

AT THIS POINT, YOU AND THE CO-PARENTING COUPLE have completed the introductory session and the assessment process. Now it is time to work with the couple on setting goals for their YPP sessions. Phase 2 consists of one or two sessions that allow for each partner to discuss his or her individual strengths and weaknesses (or areas for growth) and for the couple to set goals for their co-parenting relationship. Work with each partner to custom-fit the intervention to their needs and clarify relationship goals, as this usually increases their investment in YPP.

As a note of caution, keep in mind that at this point it is tempting for counselors to focus on the couple's weaknesses because it give you something to work on right away. Phase 2 is a good time to point out any strengths you have already observed in the couple and then probe for a little more detail. Specifically, ask what they like about the relationship and what keeps them together. Answering this question can be difficult or risky. Some partners might have a hard time saying what they like about each other. Others might say that the pregnancy keeps them together, an answer that may upset their partner. It is worth the risk and important to get those issues on the table, but be prepared to (a) help identify positive aspects of their relationship, and (b) engage in some positive "reframing" (damage control) when lukewarm statements leave one partner feeling rejected. When both partners are committed to the relationship, which is usually the case, discussing relationship strengths will help the couple feel appreciated, understood, and hopeful about working on problems and setting realistic goals (Table 6.1).

Table 6.1 PHASE 2: GOALS, TASKS, AND RESOURCES

Goals	Tasks
1. Identify strengths, weaknesses, and goals 2. Set program priorities that focus on the co-parenting relationship	• Link relationship strengths and weaknesses to personal strengths and vulnerabilities. • Link relationship strengths and weaknesses to co-parenting issues. • Identify and discuss relationship goals. • Identify personal goals. • Discuss conflict and convergence between personal goals and relationship goals. • Make a joint decision about which interpersonal relationship skills will be addressed and when (i.e., reflective listening, problem-solving, expressing needs and feelings).

Additional Resources

Personal Goals: Strengths and Weaknesses Worksheet
Relationship Goals: Strengths and Weaknesses Worksheet
Areas of Change Checklist: Solvable Problems

GOAL 1: IDENTIFY STRENGTHS, WEAKNESSES, AND GOALS

Sometimes relationship goals can interfere with important individual goals and vice versa. For example, a young father may feel torn between getting a job to provide financial support for his child and staying in school and on the football team because he has dreams of getting a college scholarship. Interpersonally, many young parents are either (a) unwilling to make small personal compromises in their relationships or (b) unable to speak up for their needs in a positive, assertive way. A common challenge that many co-parenting couples face is how to coordinate personal and relationship goals. This is particularly challenging when the personal goals of one partner are in conflict with the personal goals of the other. This frequently occurs later in their relationship if they are depending on each other to care for the child while they pursue their personal goals (school, sports, other relationships). The YPP is intended to help each partner clarify personal goals and identify how they relate to their partner's goals and their respective roles as parents and co-parents. Apparent conflicts between personal and relationship goals can be turned into opportunities for understanding and a deeper appreciation for how the relationship can support personal growth.

You may need to provide a lot of support to both partners as they discuss their personal strengths and vulnerabilities and consider how these are likely to influence co-parenting. This sort of discussion is not easy for many young expectant parents, as they may have a hard time clearly expressing themselves or even thinking about strengths, weaknesses, or life goals. Work with the couple to complete the "Strengths and Goals Worksheets" from the Toolbox at the end of this book. This can be a great conversation starter and will better understand the couple's interpersonal dynamics. Working interactively with the couple can lead to some good discussions. After each person identifies and articulates their own goals, strength, and weaknesses, ask for their partner's input. For example, when a young mother cannot think of any personal strengths, her partner may be able to help, volunteering that she is patient. This small exchange tells you a great deal about the mother, her partner, and their relationship.

If the couple is too guarded to work on this together and shuts down when you ask them to discuss their strengths and weaknesses, ask each partner to complete the exercise on their own. Younger adolescents may be more comfortable with this because it feels more like a school assignment, which they are used to doing on command. Once this is complete, help them discuss what they wrote by finding connections between personal goals and relationships goals. Either way, all program participants should complete the Phase 2: Strengths and Goals Worksheet. The essential outcomes of this task are outlined in the following.

- Each partner identifies at least one relationship strength and one weakness.
- Each partner identifies at least one personal strength and one weakness.
- Each partner identifies at least one relationship goal.
- Each partner identifies at least one personal goal.
- Discuss how relationship strengths support personal goals.
- Discuss how personal strengths support relationship goals.

PERSONAL GOALS, STRENGTHS, AND WEAKNESSES WORKSHEET

This worksheet is to be filled out by the counselor in collaboration with the young parents.

Personal Goals—What *you* would like to achieve in the next few weeks, few months, or few years

Personal Strengths—Things that you feel proud of; areas in which you do well and see *yourself* as skilled or capable

Personal Weaknesses—Things about yourself that you would like to change; ways in which you would like to grow

Young Mother	Young Father
Personal Goals	*Personal Goals*
1.	1.
2.	2.
3.	3.
Personal Strengths	*Personal Strengths*
1.	1.
2.	2.
3.	3.
Personal Weaknesses	*Personal Weaknesses*
1.	1.
2.	2.
3.	3.

RELATIONSHIP GOALS, STRENGTHS, AND WEAKNESSES WORKSHEET

This worksheet is to be filled out by the counselor in collaboration with the young parents.

Relationship Goals—Goals for your relationship in the next few weeks, months, and years

Relationship Strengths—Things about your relationship that make you feel good, that give you hope

Relationship Weaknesses—Things about your relationship that you would like to change; ways in which this relationship could become better for both of you

Young Mother	Young Father
Relationship Goals	*Relationship Goals*
1.	1.
2.	2.
3.	3.
Relationship Strengths	*Relationship Strengths*
1.	1.
2.	2.
3.	3.
Relationship Weaknesses	*Relationship Weaknesses*
1.	1.
2.	2.
3.	3.

GOAL 2: SET PROGRAM PRIORITIES

The next step in the YPP process involves prioritizing the couple's relationship goals. By ranking goals, the couple is less likely to become overwhelmed. Start with easy goals and work up to more difficult goals. For example, it is easier to get a couple to be quiet and listen to each other (using the reflective listening exercise) than it is to get them to problem solve and compromise. Your guidance can help ensure some immediate sense of success or accomplishment. This will help them feel good about themselves and the program and embolden them to work on more difficult goals.

It is important for you to accomplish two things with respect to setting program priorities. First, give the couple a brief description of what they will do next: interpersonal skill-building exercises. Briefly describe one or two exercises that you think are directly relevant to their goals. For example, if the couple identifies "arguing less" as a priority, explain just a little bit about the reflective listening exercise they could work on in their next session. Having a menu of the skill building exercises to show them (Table 6.2) may help the couple understand what you

Table 6.2 MENU OF RELATIONSHIP SKILL-BUILDING EXERCISES

1. Expressing Needs/ Feelings	Helps couples learn to open up and express themselves in positive, respectful ways. Good for conflict resolution and for couples who want to open up and share more of their thoughts and feelings with each other.
2. Reflective Listening Skills	Couples learn to be quiet and listen, to speak more directly and clearly, to pay attention and "take in" their partner's thoughts and feelings.
3. Support Skills	Helps both partners learn how to ask for and accept their partner's support. Partners also learn how to provide support to each other in helpful ways.
4. Problem-Solving Skills	Couples learn to brainstorm solutions to ongoing conflicts. Focus is on finding compromises that work for both partners and ensuring both agree to keep up their end of the deal.
5. Stress Management Skills	Couples learn how to calm down when stressed out and help their partner calm down when he or she is really stressed.
6. Acceptance Skills	Helps partners learn to accept and/or appreciate each other's personal flaws. Focus is on knowing the difference between what one can control and when one should "just let it go." This includes learning to adapt to things that will not change.
7. Conflict De-escalation	Helps couples to recognize when conflict is escalating, how they may cool down before the conflict rises too high, and how they can later talk about the conflict in a way that feels safe and calm. This is important for preventing violence between couples.
8. Family Planning Skills	Helps couples discuss family planning issues such as if and when they might want to have another child, how they will avoid pregnancy in the meantime, preferred contraception, and where to acquire it.
9. Minimizing Negativity	Helps high-conflict couples determine how they will continue to co-parent and communicate productively but keep their distance in order to avoid unhealthy conflict that could upset or harm their child.

are talking about. Second, work with the couple to identify two or three goals that are their highest priorities. Try to come out of Phase 2 with a rough plan of what you might do for the next two or three sessions, letting the couple know that this plan is flexible, depending on what other issues or concerns come up.

ADDRESS FEARS

Couples may express some of their fears about becoming parents in the first few counseling sessions. Take these fears and concerns seriously, but also let the couple know that most new parents have fears. Compliment the couple for being upfront about their fears, and let them know that the healthiest way to deal with anxieties, doubts, and worries is to be honest and gather more information. Here are a few common concerns of young parents.

- Childbirth will be painful.
- The baby could have health problems.
- They might lose friends because of parenting responsibilities.
- Parenthood will make them feel trapped.
- They may not have enough money to take care of the baby.
- They might break up.

These fears can be a good stepping-stone for setting relationship-based co-parenting goals, particularly around expressing feelings and asking for support. If the expectant mother is afraid of childbirth, you can help her set a goal around asking for help from her partner. This might lead to coaching the father on how he can reassure her in simple ways (staying by her side and talking her through the labor and delivery). Although this may not relieve her of the fear (which is reality based), it may help her to feel stronger and more capable of managing the pain (which will diminish the fear).

It is more complicated to address a young woman's fear that her boyfriend will break up and abandon her. If the boyfriend is telling her that he does not want to break up, but she does not believe him, help the couple set the goal of building security between them (e.g., by expressing positive emotion, providing emotional support, listening and reflecting), with a particular focus on absorbing their partner's support. If the boyfriend is not able to commit to the relationship, help him express his commitment to parenting together. This might help reassure the young woman that the boyfriend will stick with her to raise their child no matter what happens to them as a couple. Although this reassurance will not relieve all her anxieties, it may help her build resilience.

SUMMARIZE

Talk with the couple about how their relationship and personal goals are directly or indirectly related to co-parenting, parenting, and their child's well-being. Young expectant couples often need some help making these connections because parenting is still hypothetical for them, especially for fathers. For example, if a personal goal is to stay in school, you can support that goal by just reflecting back that if they complete high school and even go to college or a vocational school, they will be in a much better position to get a good job and support their child. If they say their goal is to argue less, which is a common goal, you can commend them for that goal and provide a little education about how intense arguing or aggression can disrupt a infant's brain development because stress hormones are released when infants and children sense intense hostility. On the other hand, when children see their parents getting along—even when they disagree—they feel more secure and are more likely to copy their parents' positive communication skills.

CHAPTER REVIEW

The following tasks should be accomplished by the end of Phase 2:

- Each member of the couple identified their personal goals based upon exploration of personal strengths and weaknesses.
- The couple identified their co-parenting relationship goals based upon relationship strengths and weaknesses.
- The counselor has linked the couple's strengths and weaknesses to issues related to co-parenting.
- The counselor and the couple have decided which interpersonal relationship skills they want to work on first.

With mutually agreed-upon program goals in place, the couple is now ready to launch into the heart and soul of the counseling process—Phase 3, Interpersonal Skill Building.

PHASE 3: INTERPERSONAL SKILL BUILDING

7

INTRODUCTION

PHASE 3 OF THE YPP IS DESIGNED TO ENGAGE COUPLES in a series of exercises that will help them learn skills needed to develop and maintain a positive co-parenting relationship. These skills include the ability to regulate emotional reactions, express positive feelings, listen carefully, become more interpersonally flexible, and remain focused on the child's well-being. In many respects this phase is the core of the YPP. It typically consists of three to six sessions. As a YPP counselor, you should work with each couple to select three to four of the nine exercises. It is recommended that every couple receive the "Communications about Family Planning" module as one of the selected exercises. The others should be selected based on each couple's specific needs and wishes.

Phase 3 borrows heavily from a number of intervention programs for married and co-parenting couples, tailoring exercises and concepts to better fit the circumstances of young, unmarried expectant couples (Gottman, 1999; Jacobson & Christensen, 1996; Stanley et al., 1999). Using the menu of skill modules (see Table 6.2) in the previous chapter, you should begin with exercises that are likely to be relatively easy for a couple. Do not try to do too much or you will risk overwhelming the couple. Depth of skill development is more important than breadth. Be thoughtful in your selection of which skill to teach based on your assessment

Table 7.1 PHASE 3: GOALS, TASKS, AND ADDITIONAL RESOURCES

Goals	Tasks
1. The couple and counselor identify specific areas of communication or co-parenting relations that would benefit from interpersonal skill development	Teach the couple to communicate more effectively using skill-building exercises that address three or four of the nine core skill areas:
2. The couple learns core interpersonal/communication skills	1. Expressing needs and feelings
	2. Reflective listening
3. The quality of the couple's relationship improves	3. Support skills
	4. Problem solving
4. The level of relationship stress decreases	5. Stress reduction
5. There is a decrease of risk factors (such as aggression and hostility) for intimate partner violence and child abuse	6. Acceptance
	7. Conflict de-escalation
	8. Communicating about family planning
	9. Minimizing negativity

Additional Resources

Areas of Strength Checklist
Areas of Disagreement Checklist
"What I like about you/What I like about us" Worksheet
Areas of Change Checklist
Acceptance Worksheet

of each couple's particular needs. Throughout Phase 3, many couples will focus on their romantic relationship because the idea of parenting or co-parenting is still quite hypothetical because their baby is not yet born. Their romantic relationship often feels like the most important, pressing issue. It is fine to focus on their romantic relationship during this phase as long as you—as their counselor—help the couple identify the link between a healthy romantic relationship and the skills needed for positive co-parenting and parenting.

The rest of the chapter is focused on exploring the principles behind each of the skill areas listed in Table 7.1 and discussing how these skills can be further developed in YPP sessions.

SKILL 1: EXPRESSING NEEDS AND FEELINGS

Introduction

Young people differ in their abilities to express their needs and feelings. Some have not developed the language skills to express themselves clearly or may lack the cognitive skills to even know how they feel or what they need. This may be because of immaturity or lack of exposure to other people talking about their needs and feelings. Consequently, some young parents feel uncomfortable when asked to talk about what they want, how they feel, or what they are thinking. A counselor's typical questions like, "How did you feel about that?" may be confusing or feel like a test or an interrogation. Some young men and women are so focused on the external world that they do not know what to make of these internally focused questions. It can be helpful to explain that you know it may take them awhile to figure out how they feel or what they need or want in a relationship.

Context can influence an adolescent's ability to express himself or herself freely and openly. In one context (at home or with their friends) they know what to say and can clearly communicate their feelings, but in another context (with their partner or in your office) they feel tongue-tied or confused. For most people, our ability to communicate depends on our mood. When we are upset—the very time when clear communication is most important—we are most prone to communicate poorly and say things we later regret. Our ability to communicate effectively when challenged, stressed, or angry develops slowly over time, with a great deal of trial and error. The YPP aims to speed up this developmental process and your role is to help make the learning process explicit and manageable.

Some YPP couples do not know each other very well; they just met before they got pregnant or they have known each other for a while but have not yet learned how to talk about what is going on in their hearts and minds. At this point in the YPP process, you should have a pretty good idea of how comfortable a couple is with talking to each other. For couples who are very uncomfortable talking about feelings or expressing needs, this exercise will be a good place to begin. It is intended to help couples develop the basic skills they will need to get the most out of the YPP program as a whole. Couples who are comfortable with expressing their feelings and needs can skip this exercise entirely.

The purpose of learning to express feelings and needs is to help co-parenting partners communicate more directly and—in some cases—get to know each other better. The basic premise is that co-parenting couples will benefit from sharing their feelings with each other. Participants sometimes challenge their counselors as to whether there is really much value in talking about feelings. Indeed, many people are skeptical that talking can help them deal with problems or concerns; they may believe that when there is a problem, you should either do something useful or stop doing something that is causing the problem. As a YPP counselor, it helps to explain the value of talking and learning to communicate more effectively. There are two primary reasons we think talking about feelings and needs is important.

Talking can prevent negative actions. When young people lack words, they often just act, by responding to their emotional experiences immediately with behavior. When in conflict, the behavioral response is often aggressive. When young people learn to express how they feel with words, it tends to slow down their impulses and allows them time to reflect and come up with a more civil response. At times, after expressing the words—"I am really angry"—a person no longer feels any angry action is necessary, especially if the other person responds in a constructive way. This skill can carry over to parenting: Helping children talk about their feelings will give them better self-control over their behavior. Children who see their parents talking about their feelings and thoughts will grow up to be more verbal and expressive.

Talking strengthens bonds. Sharing thoughts and feelings can help to create a sense of connection and empathy that adds to a couple's physical connection. Young mothers commonly complain that their partners do not talk enough, leaving them guessing about their feelings. Of course it works in the reverse, some young mothers are less expressive than their partners, but women tend to be more verbal and more comfortable talking about feelings. The YPP is particularly effective in helping young fathers develop the skills to open up and share their thoughts with their partners, setting the stage for a higher level of intimacy.

There is a very important caveat that goes along with the endorsement of talk therapy. There is no doubt that people are wired very differently, and although some of us want to talk out problems as soon as they emerge, some of us need time to digest, settle, reflect, or cool down before its possible to have a constructive conversation. Some of us need more closeness than distance and others need more distance than closeness. Although we believe learning effective communication is essential to positive co-parenting, we also respect that some young parents will need to balance all this talking with some quiet time and space to be alone.

Getting Started

The mere idea of talking about feelings can make some people anxious and want to clam up. Explain to the couple that you may be asking them to do things that are outside their comfort zone, but also assure them that are not required to discuss their deepest feelings or reveal too much about themselves. What they say (or do not say) is completely under their control and you will always respect their boundaries. Expressing feelings can be about sharing simple things, such as what they liked about a movie or how they feel about coming to YPP sessions or what sorts of things they would like to buy for the baby. One of the goals of this exercise is to simply get more comfortable with talking with each other because this skill is an important part of successful co-parenting.

Some YPP participants may get nervous about expressing their feelings because they do not want to get into a fight with their partner. They may equate expressing feelings with arguing. It may be useful to explain that this exercise is not about starting arguments. The exercise will probably involve learning to express upset feelings in ways that are helpful and constructive. But expressing upset feelings does not mean letting loose and saying whatever comes to mind. The idea is to open up and be honest while respecting the other person's feelings. You should reassure the couple that it is possible to talk about angry or hurt feelings without getting into a big argument. This requires choosing words carefully and learning self-control.

This exercise can also include expressing positive feelings, such as what the partners like about each other or what they like about their relationship. This too can be difficult for some young men and women because they worry that the feelings will not be reciprocated. Expressing positive feelings can open oneself up to a level of intimacy or closeness that feels to raw and vulnerable, particularly for young people who have experienced a great deal of loss or disappointment. Yet, learning to express these sorts of feelings—and have them acknowledged and reciprocated—is something for which many young men and women secretly wish.

There are two versions of this exercise. The first is for couples who have a hard time expressing any feelings; the second is for those who have difficulty expressing negative feelings (anger, hurt) in a respectful way. The first step is to select a topic for discussion. The couple may easily come with something or you may have an idea of a good topic for discussion based on your previous session when the couple identified their relationship goals. If the couple is having a difficult time identifying something to discuss, you may use one of the several conversation starter worksheets in the Toolbox (such as the "Areas of Disagreement" worksheet). A list of worksheets for use throughout YPP can be found in Table 7.3 at the end of this chapter. Some counselors have used therapeutic games such as LifeStories (by Talicor) to help with couples who need a great deal of support developing basic communication skills.

FOR COUPLES WHO HAVE A HARD TIME EXPRESSING
ANY FEELINGS OR NEEDS
Ask the couple to pick a topic and then give them some instruction on how to get started. One approach to working with couples who are having a difficult time knowing how to begin is to use the "What Do You Know About Each Other?" worksheet, which asks each person to list things about their partner that they *think* they know (favorite color, earliest memory, their favorite pet) or that they *want* to know. You can instruct each partner to complete the worksheet and then use it as a way to get them talking about topics that are nonthreatening. Do your best to let them carry the conversation forward. As necessary, interject with open-ended, follow-up questions to model how they can help each other further explain their thoughts and feelings.

- Show interest in your partner's feelings and ideas. For example, ask, "What do you think about this?" Or "How do you feel about that?"
- Give your partner enough time and space to sort out his or her feelings. Be patient if your partner says, "I do not know how I feel about that." People often do not know how they feel or what they think until they have time to figure it out.

- Show appreciation that your partner expressed himself or herself. Even if you do not agree with what your partner said, take a moment to just "take in" the information. This can be difficult if you get upset by what your partner says. Do not argue against it, do not put your partner down or do anything that punishes your partner for expressing needs and feelings. Just breathe and let it sit for a moment. If possible, it may be useful to say "Thank you for letting me know how you feel about that!"
- Ask for more information about your partner's feelings or ideas. You can simply say something like, "Hmm. Can you tell me more about that?" or "Can you give me an example?"
- Share an experience from your own life that seems similar or related to what your partner shared with you.

Guide the young couple through the process of eliciting thoughts and feelings from each other in a manner that seems comfortable for them. This is likely to seem awkward and staged at first, but most couples open up with time.

FOR COUPLES WHO COULD BENEFIT FROM LEARNING TO EXPRESS THEIR FEELINGS AND NEEDS MORE CONSTRUCTIVELY

Some couples need help learning how to talk about feelings without blaming the other person and getting into arguments. Some young men and women have grown up in families in which the expression of feelings led to conflicts, which taught them to either keep their feelings to themselves or let their negative feelings fly without restraint. These young men and women need help learning to express their feelings, including negative feelings, in a more constructive way. It is sometimes helpful to provide communication tricks or tips borrowed from the marital and family therapy literature. The goal of expressing oneself is usually to be heard. These tips are generally intended to help both partners achieve that goal.

Tip 1: Use "I" Statements

When a couple is talking about a conflict, they often fall into blaming each other with "You did this…"–type statements. When this happens, intervene and offer this piece of advice, using your own words:

> A good trick for helping you make your angry or hurt feelings sound less blaming and easier for your partner to hear and take in is to focus on how you are *feeling* rather than what your partner *did wrong*. This involves changing "You" statements to "I" statements.

You may want to provide the couple with some concrete examples, outlined in the following:

Blaming/Hostile Statement	Suggested ways to open up a dialogue
You do not care about me....	I feel bad when I do not hear from you…
That's stupid....	I have a different opinion about that....
You were flirting with her/him…	I sometimes get jealous…
You blew all our money....	I am worried that we are not going to have enough money to get the stuff we need for the baby....

The value of using "I" statements is that if the partner is not put on the defensive he or she is more likely to respond more constructively. This can be a difficult exercise for some couples because sometimes one partner wants the other to feel guilty and apologize. Sometimes this may even be quite appropriate. However, in many cases, the best way to get people to take responsibility for themselves or their behavior is to refrain from blame or control. If both partners can be assertive and disclosing by saying, "this is how I feel" or "this is what is going on with me" or even "this is what I want" without controlling or putting down the other person, he or she is more likely to respond positively.

Tip 2: Avoid Using the Words "Never" and "Always"

Another communication trick is to avoid the use of words like never and always because these words also tend to put people in the defensive position. For example: "You always come home late" or "You never call me" can be turned into "Last night when you came home late, I got really worried" or "When you do not call or respond to my texts, I start to panic."

The idea is not to globalize the problem, because when this happens, the person who is being blamed has an easy out—"I do not always come home late"—and misses the point. Also, when someone is told that he or she always does something wrong or never does something right, it can feel like character assassination. When someone feels slammed, he or she is unlikely to listen.

Tip 3: Stay Focused on Future Solutions Instead of Past Problems

One reason young people wish to avoid discussing conflicts or disagreement is that they anticipate they will be forever blamed for past mistakes. If one partner senses that he or she is about to "get it again," you may encounter some resistance to this exercise. Fortunately, it is possible to express feelings and needs without getting into any recounting of what happened in the past. You can genuinely reassure couples that this exercise is not about rehashing old complaints. It is designed to help couples move forward. If you sense some resistance to discussion of an old conflict, you might try saying something like:

> Here is another communication trick. Do not focus on what went wrong in the past. Rather, make a suggestion about how you two might handle things differently in the future. This gives your partner a way out of feeling blamed. It keeps the conversation positive and constructive.

Tip 4: Establish Ground Rules

The greatest risk in asking young couples to discuss conflict is that the discussion gets out of hand and feelings get hurt. This is never helpful and it is important for you have strategies that prevent destructive exchanges from occurring in your sessions. Couples who have a tendency to get very hostile and volatile will appreciate having you set some basic ground rules that will help contain their anger and/or their partner's anger. Being a good referee helps both partners feel more emotionally (and perhaps physically) safe. Ground rules for managing conflict also make the sessions more productive and give you confidence that couples will not leave their sessions feeling worse than when they arrived.

You might introduce the idea of ground rules by saying something like: "Some couples think it helps to have some guidelines for expressing their feelings so that they do not end up in a conflict. Do you think setting some rules or guidelines would help you?" The following are sample ground rules that some couples may find useful, but it is often a good idea to ask them to come up with their own set of ground rules for keeping it fair and respectful.

(1) Be respectful of the other person's feelings and opinions; do not use insulting language.

(2) When you are upset, count to 10 or take a deep breath before you talk or respond.

(3) Do not ambush. Give your partner the *option* of having a discussion now or later, "I am upset and I want to tell you how I am feeling. Are you OK with that?"

(4) Promise to stay connected even when you are upset. "I am upset with you and I want to talk about it, but I promise to be respectful and to listen to your side."

(5) End the conversation with a positive statement.

(6) Stop talking when the counselor says "time out" and allow for him or her to intervene.

SKILL 2: REFLECTIVE LISTENING

Introduction

Reflective listening is particularly useful for couples who (a) interrupt each other, (b) do not hear what their partner is saying because they make assumptions about their partner is going to say, or (c) are so determined to get their own opinions heard that they have stopped listening. Several models of couples' therapy emphasize the importance of reflective listening, which helps partners slow down and listen to each other more carefully (Stanley et al., 1999). We have found that YPP couples value this exercise because it is easy to do and usually produces immediate results.

It is very common for couples to misunderstand each other and/or feel misunderstood. One partner may not say what he or she means to say. The other partner may hear only what he or she expects to hear. They may be cutting each other off and talking over each other. Ambiguous statements are commonly misinterpreted in the worst possible way. For example, the statement, "You think I do not care about the baby? Well, I wouldn't be sitting here if I didn't care about the baby!" could be interpreted as "I wouldn't be with you if I didn't screw up and get you pregnant." Alternatively it could be interpreted as "This is hard for me too but I want to work this through because it is really important." When stressed, we tend to say things in a more negative way and we tend to hear things in a more negative way, so miscommunications are common. Reflective listening allows for clearer communications to occur. Developing good listening skills will not necessarily solve a couple's problems, but it will help them understand each other more fully. Generally speaking, a full understanding will lead to more positive feelings than a partial understanding.

The Basic Steps in Reflective Listening

Reflective listening can be introduced at any time during Phase 3. It is most effective when a couple is having an exchange during which they are not listening to each other. Consider introducing it when you anticipate such an exchange—at the beginning of a session when you know that the couple has a difficult issue to discuss. This will provide them with a sense of safety and structure. Most couples will present you with the opportunity to exercise this skill without you having to "prime the pump," but some couples may need a structured discussion activity to facilitate a dialogue about important relationship issues. The "Areas of Change Checklist" or the "Areas of Disagreement Checklist" (see Toolbox) is a good place to start. The exercise described in the following is designed to help couples speak more clearly and listen more accurately. Here are the basic steps:

(1) One partner (the listener) asks for the other partner's (the speaker's) feelings or point of view regarding a situation (usually a recent disagreement) and does not interrupt the speaker's response.

(2) When the speaker is done, the listener repeats back what he or she heard without adding commentary.

(3) The counselor asks the speaker whether what was heard was what they said or meant to say. The speaker clarifies any differences between the message sent and the message received.

(4) If the listener did not get it right the first time, he or she is given another chance to repeat back what was heard.

(5) When the speaker feels understood, the roles reverse. The process continues for a few minutes until both partners feel more understood.

(6) The counselor commends the couple for what they did well and asks if they could do this on their own when one or both feel misunderstood.

Guiding couples through the process of reflective listening can help them feel more understood and fully appreciated by their partner (Stanley et al., 2000; Tuerk et al., 2012). It also helps them learn to regulate their emotional response to each other because they are required (by you) to bite their tongue and listen. This is an important lesson in the development of close, enduring relationships (Bell & Calkins, 2000).

After taking turns as speaker and listener, couples may appreciate how easy it is to misunderstand, which may come as a relief to those who have felt misunderstood or have been accused of not listening. This exercise can help different types of couples in different ways. It helps people who tend to be impulsive or reactive to slow down, sit back, and absorb more information. For those couples who are constantly arguing and talking over each other, reflective listening offers a way to manage conflict. Some couples really appreciate this somewhat formulaic approach to interrupting their tendency to get into high-intensity conflicts. It provides them with the opportunity to step back and have a more civil discussion without giving up or giving in. For couples who have a hard time opening up with each other, reflective listening can help provide a safe way to share with each other. Often partners do not share with each other because they do not expect they will be heard or their feelings will be appreciated. Some do not share because they do not feel they are able to communicate effectively.

Your job is to help the listener hear more clearly, help the speaker deliver the message more clearly, or both. Focus on the distinction between what was said and what was heard, and work toward aligning the message sent and message received.

Throughout the YPP sessions, promote or reinforce reflective listening. For example, when one partner listens and reflects back to his or her partner, you should commend this behavior and help the other partner articulate his or her own positive response. Keep coaching couples who need some help in rephrasing what they say and clarifying what they hear. For example, when the speaker is blaming the other, help him or her rephrase the statement before asking the listener to reflect what was heard. This sort of reinforcement and promotion will help the couple develop new patterns of engagement.

SKILL 3: OFFERING AND RECEIVING SUPPORT

Introduction

Research indicates that parents who receive high levels of positive support from significant others (partners, parents, or friends) are better equipped to cope with the stress of parenting, more warmly engaged with their children, and less likely to become harshly punitive or abusive (Cutrona et al., 2005). This component of the program is designed to help couples learn the basics of asking for support and providing support. This skill is particularly important when one or both partners report high levels of stress. Stress can be contagious and reverberating; often when one partner is upset, the other also becomes upset. At times partners get upset because they want support but either do not know how to ask for it or do not like the type of support they receive from their partner. If parents can effectively support each other emotionally during rough times, their health outcomes and their children's functioning will be improved (Newman & Roberts, 2013).

What is support? There are many ways to define support, and because it means different things to different people, this can lead to misunderstandings. In YPP we draw from the vast research literature on social support (Cohen & Wills, 1985; Shumaker & Brownell, 2010) to define three types of support that are most pertinent to young co-parenting couples.

(1) **Emotional support** refers to expressing empathy or compassion, showing concern, providing comfort and affection, and giving encouragement. If all goes well, this type of support is conveyed with warmth and genuine concern and is experienced by the recipient as caring and affirming. Sometimes, just being present and aware (providing companionship) is experienced as emotional support.

(2) **Tangible support** refers to proving concrete help, such as financial assistance or physical assistance (e.g., babysitting or cleaning the house). This is sometimes called instrumental support, and typically involves doing something to assist or lighten the burden of another person.

(3) **Informational support** refers to giving advice or providing suggestions or offering useful information to someone. This type of support is most useful when a couple is engaged in problem solving, but can be perceived as intrusive or unwelcome when it is not elicited.

A number of common beliefs interfere with partners asking for support from or providing support to their partners. A partner may believe that "If I have to ask for support, it means he (or she) doesn't really care or doesn't want to help." Or, "If she is upset, I should just leave her alone till she cools down." In addition, some partners may not want support because they believe they should be able to handle things on their own. Others feel that when they try to give support, they get it wrong and only make things worse. Teaching couples the following basic steps will help them become more supportive and feel more supported. These steps will seem obvious to some, but new to those who are inexperienced with close, intimate, and supportive relationships.

(1) **The first step in offering useful support is to notice when someone is upset.** Interestingly, adolescents and young adults offer support to each other in ways that can sometimes be confusing for adults. Adolescents may display empathy by sending a crying text message face or saying something like "Man, that's fucked up!" These overtures can be loosely translated to mean, "I am sorry that happened" or "I see you are upset and want you to know that I am here to help or just listen." However, some young expectant parents respond to their partner's stress by getting angry or making jokes that do not help. Sometimes one partner may not notice that the other partner is upset. When such circumstances occur, it may be important to interrupt what is happening and help the couple frame and attend to the situation. Take the example of Dave and Jill that follows.

It seems to me that Jill is really upset, and you, Dave, are not sure how to respond. This sort of thing happens all the time between parents and I would like to use this as a chance to help the two of you figure out how to ask for and give support when it is needed. Knowing how to deal with these moments is important when it comes to helping each other with parenting. Dave, are you willing to give this a try? Jill, are you OK with using this moment as an opportunity to learn?

If the couple agrees (they usually do when asked) you can instruct Dave to tell Jill that he wants to hear why she is upset. This form of modeling is a message to Dave about how to best approach Jill and a message to Jill that Dave is trying to be helpful. In this case, Jill might think that Dave ought to know why she is upset and gets more upset because Dave is either "too thick to get it" or "is just pretending" that he does not know why she is upset. When this sort of exchange occurs, you should intervene and ask Jill to start with the more forgiving assumption that Dave might have some understanding of what is bothering her, but may need to hear it directly from her in order to be helpful and move forward.

(2) **The second step is for one partner to ask the other for help or support in a direct, nonblaming way.** Many people are very reluctant to ask for help or support. They want to be independent and deal with their problems on their own, and they do not think others want to help or they do not trust that others will be able to help. Emphasize that knowing how to ask for help directly is necessary if co-parenting is to be successful, and it is important to respect what each other defines as helpful. Requests for help should be simple and direct: "I just need you to hold my hand for a minute" or "I'm angry and I just want you to listen" or "I need help with my homework." It may take someone a while to figure out what, exactly, he or she wants from the partner. So this step may require some dialogue about what has felt supportive or helpful in the past.

(3) **The third step is for the other partner to respond in a way that is helpful and compassionate.** When Jill expresses why she is upset and asks for Dave's help, it is important that Dave listens empathically and responds positively. If Jill wants him to hold her hand and he is willing, they will have learned something from that moment. If Jill wants him to do something that he is unwilling to do, it becomes more complicated. In this situation, Dave could say he wants to be supportive and offer an alternative way of helping Jill. Some young men and women are unpracticed in how to offer support or empathy, so it is very hard for them to be genuinely compassionate. In your role as a YPP counselor it is fine to do some coaching if, for instance, Dave has no idea what to say that could be supportive or if he says something intended to be helpful but it comes out rudely. Point out that offering support does not come naturally to everyone and that it might take some work to learn how to be warm and supportive. Emphasize that it is important to try and then be sure to commend the effort.

(4) **The fourth step involves accepting the support offered and express appreciation.** Many people have a hard time accepting support. Some young people are so convinced that they are not going to get the support they want, that they refuse to take it when it is offered. The desire for support and the expectation of disappointment are overwhelming. This means that in addition to coaching partners on how to *give* each other support, you may need to coach them on how to *accept* support and allow themselves to feel supported. Complete this step by underscoring that all support—even if it is imperfect support—is valuable. If Jill is able to say thank you and acknowledge Dave's effort, it will help lay a foundation for managing similar moments in the future. If Dave's support was not particularly helpful, you can coach Jill on how to ask for a different type of support, again in a way that is appreciative of her partner's efforts. Despite the best intentions, the support or help that is given often falls short of what is wanted or expected, so it is important for couples to be able to gently clarify with each other what was most helpful about the support received and what would be even more helpful in the future. You can help couples have this discussion by stating that people need different types of support and it always takes a while to figure out this particular dance.

STEPS TO REMEMBER WHEN OFFERING OR RECEIVING SUPPORT

1. The first step in offering useful support is to *notice* when someone is upset.
2. The second step is for one partner to *ask* the other for help or support in a direct, nonblaming way.
3. The third step is for the other partner to *respond* in a way that is helpful and compassionate.
4. The fourth step involves *accepting* the support offered and express appreciation.

SKILL 4: PROBLEM SOLVING

Introduction

Problem-solving skill training is intended to give young couples a set of simple tools or procedures to help them work together so they do not feel overwhelmed or get into unnecessary conflicts. The strategies can help with big problems—one partner getting evicted or deported or losing a job—or small problems like who picks up the child from daycare. The first step in teaching problem-solving skills is to identify the problem. The problem is often a source of conflict, but it does not have to be; it can be something external to their relationship that they both have to figure out how to deal with, like where to live or how to get the car fixed.

Most couples will easily identify conflicts and problems to work on during their sessions. You, too, should not have much trouble identifying a conflict or problem for them to focus on for the sake of this exercise. If a problem cannot be identified, use the "Areas of Disagreement" or the "Conflict Start-up" exercise in the Toolbox. It may seem strange to dig up problems, but learning these skills will help partners function more adaptively. Pick a conflict that you think is resolvable. The following is an example of a common problem that might be presented by YPP couples:

> Selena is 17 years old and 6 months pregnant. Her parents disapprove of the baby's father, Theo, because he is not in school and is unemployed. Selena's parents are pressuring her to break off contact with Theo and raise the child on her own with their help. For example, whenever Selena spends time with Theo, they give her the silent treatment and refuse to pay for certain things she wants. Selena responds by becoming angry at her parents and at Theo; she and Theo have begun to snipe at each other and argue more frequently. Selena is feeling torn and Theo is distancing himself from her.

In this case, the process of problem solving could be approached from several different angles. As the counselor, you could help Selena and Theo identify what type of problem they have. Is this Theo's problem (e.g., he does not have a job) or a relationship problem (e.g., Selena and Theo are under great pressure and do not have the communication skills to talk through what they want as a couple and as co-parents)? Is the problem external to their relationship (e.g., do Selena or Theo need help talking to Selena's parents)? In some respects the problem is all these things. So where should you begin?

When a problem is complex, it may be useful to work on its different components. It seems obvious that Theo should be in school or looking for a job (or both), but he might need some help from Selena (and perhaps her parents) in making those things happen. The counselor could focus on understanding the following: (a) what is keeping Theo from being in school or getting a job; (b) how to deal with the pressure that Selena's parents are putting on the couple; and (c) how to cope with the strain and stress between Selena and Theo. Trying to do all this at once will overwhelm the couple and be less effective in the long run, so it will be important for the counselor to prioritize these issues.

The YPP focuses on helping couples develop problem-solving strategies that will allow them to separate what they can control from what is beyond their control. In this case, the couple cannot control Selena's parents, but they can control how they work together to manage external forces and pressures in their lives. We do not know why Theo is out of school and without a job, but that seems like a good place to start. The counselor might focus on Theo's job/school situation as the problem to be solved, to see if they can come together around helping Theo move forward. If they can come up with a good plan for solving that problem, it will be easier for them to come together on how to respond to the pressure Selena is getting from her parents. And if they can come up with a constructive plan for responding to Selena's parents, they are well on their way to resolving their interpersonal conflict.

Selena and Theo have a significant problem because it is complex and not easily resolvable. Couples cope with these challenges in adaptive and maladaptive ways. Maladaptive ways include: (a) drug and alcohol abuse; (b) hostility and blame; (c) manipulation and deceit; (d) controlling, demanding behavior; and (e) disengagement/withdrawal. Adaptive ways of coping include: (a) finding mutually acceptable solutions, which may involve compromise; (b) brainstorming different ways of dealing with problems and working together to choose a solution that works for both; (c) asking for outside input from a trusted adult; and (d) cooling down and re-approaching the problem when emotions have settled. When couples bring their problem to their YPP session, it provides you with the opportunity to help them replace maladaptive coping behaviors with adaptive ones. Your role as the counselor is to give the couple a method (outlined below) to think about their problem, consider solutions and select a shared plan.

Steps in Effective Problem Solving

(1) **Create space for problem solving.** One of the most important problem-solving skills is to create the interpersonal space for talking about problems in a respectful way. This is hard to do when tempers flare. The first step is for one partner to invite the other to talk about a problem as something to work on together, rather than something about which to fight. In the following are some examples of how one partner might invite the other to discuss a problem:

"I feel like I am getting blasted right now, it would really help me if we talked about this more calmly."

"Can we just take a step back and try to come at this again, maybe a little friendlier?"

"I see this is a problem we need to solve together. Do you think we can discuss this without it turning into a big fight?"

(2) **Create a shared understanding of the problem.** Make sure the couple agrees on the problem being discussed. The primary purpose of this is to make sure you and both partners have a shared understanding of the problem and what is at stake. For example, it would be easy for Selena and Theo to have different ideas about how to define their problem.

Couples often present with concrete problems (like what to name the baby), which might represent bigger issues regarding each parent's claim on the baby. Once the couple identifies a problem to work on, it may be useful to ask the couple to step back and give their individual perspectives on what the problem is about. Their response can help you decide whether to focus on the concrete (choosing baby names) or the abstract (paternity, family identity). Sometime it is helpful to work on the concrete issues, like naming the baby, while remaining cognizant of the larger underlying issues, such as family identity and paternity. It is often the case that if you can help a couple productively resolve the small, concrete issues, then the larger background issues get worked out too in the process. For example, naming the baby after someone on both sides of the family and including both surnames can be a powerful statement to the extended families about a shared sense of belonging.

(3) **Break big problems into smaller, manageable problems.** In the Selena/Theo scenario described above, multiple issues are wrapped up together. How are they are supporting each other? How do they establish better communication with Selena's parents? What are Theo's goals and plans for helping to support the child? What can be done to help him get back in school, find a job, or both? If the couple tries to address all these issues simultaneously, they will quickly become overwhelmed. It is usually best to start with what seems like the root problem (the problem that is causing the other problems). In this case, Theo's unemployment seems like the root problem. There may be disagreement about how to define the root problem. And it may turn out that Selena's parents are not going to accept Theo no matter what he does. But we will not know that until he at least tries to address what seems to be the root problem. If the couple cannot decide on which is the root problem, they should try to agree on which problem would be the easiest to solve.

(4) **Brainstorm solutions.** Couples often have conflicts because each partner gets locked into one way of thinking about a problem or one way of doing things. Brainstorming helps couple recognize that there are many ways to approach any given problem, some which may be better than others. Help the couple generate a laundry list of potential solutions. Write their ideas down for them. Reassure the couple that *all* ideas, even wild ones, are worth considering when brainstorming. If you have an idea that the couple has not thought of, it is fine to ask if you can add something to their list. You should not spend more than 10 minutes on brainstorming or you will have too many ideas to sort through.

(5) **Assess the pros and cons of possible solutions.** Hopefully the brainstorming session yielded some solutions that have good potential. The next step is to evaluate the ideas that were generated, which can—of course—lead to conflict if not handled respectfully. Frame this step by saying that this is an exercise in being tactful. It is okay to not like an idea, but you can say why it does not work for you without trashing the idea. It may be helpful to consider which solutions seem to benefit one partner much more than the other. Are there some ideas that are completely unacceptable? Explain that it may be efficient to just rule out those solutions that one or the other partner cannot live with, but also point out that it is not fair to say you can only live with the solutions that you proposed. Help the couple identify or create solutions that could be win-wins, benefiting both partners. Are there solutions that involve compromise so that both partners get some of what they want?

(6) **Come to an agreement about action**. If the couple is able to find a solution that seems agreeable to both partners, ask if they would like to create an action plan. If the couple is willing, outline a two- to four-step plan in which each partner has an identified role. Help the couple be clear about who does what, pointing out that this is good practice for co-parenting. Ask about a timeline for getting the plan done, and see if the couple wants you to check-in with them at the next session to hold them accountable.

If the couple cannot come to an agreement about a solution, do not try to force one on them. Sometimes the process of throwing out a number of ideas is enough to qualify as a success. Explain that some problems do not need to be solved right away. Sometimes it is best to have a good discussion and to spend some time pondering the range of possible solutions. Often, when a couple discusses a problem in a positive way, it gets resolved on its own. The important thing is for the couple to learn strategies for working on problems together.

(7) **Evaluate**. It is helpful to end the exercise with some self evaluation. How well did this approach to problem solving work for them? What did they learn? You can comment on what seemed to go well for the couple from your perspective. If the process was difficult or lackluster, it might be useful for you to comment on why you think it did not work and settle on next steps. Help the couple decide if they would like to try it again or move onto a different skill.

STEPS TO REMEMBER IN EFFECTIVE PROBLEM SOLVING

1. Create space for problem solving.
2. Create a shared understanding of the problem.
3. Break big problems into smaller, manageable problems.
4. Brainstorm solutions.
5. Assess the pros and cons of possible solutions.
6. Come to an agreement about action.
7. Evaluate.

SKILL 5: STRESS MANAGEMENT AND REDUCTION

Introduction

Young Parenthood Program couples face all the typical stress associated with adolescence as well as the stress that accompanies pregnancy and parenthood. Additionally, many young parents live with chronic stress because of conditions of poverty and disadvantage, and some are burdened by racism, discrimination, and a lack of opportunities (Bolland et al., 2007). Chronic stress is detrimental to the health of both the young mother and father, strains their relationship, and negatively impacts the development of their child even before birth (Austin & Leader, 2000; De Weerth et al., 2003; Huizink et al., 2002).

The most common symptoms of stress are irritability, fatigue, and lack of energy or motivation. Behavioral consequences associated with stress include overeating, eating unhealthy foods, getting into fights, and losing sleep. Stress is often expressed with psychosomatic symptoms, such as headaches, upset stomach, chest tightness, and dizziness. Pregnant women who experience high levels of unmanageable stress—stress that consistently overwhelms them—are at increased risk for early labor and delivery, and their babies are at risk for being under weight because of their indirect exposure to stress (Borders et al., 2007; Dole et al., 2003). When pregnant women are overly stressed, their sympathetic nervous system—which responds to stress—is overloaded. In an effort to compensate, the mother's body produces high rates of cortisol (the stress hormone) and may develop high blood pressure. This, in turn, will affect the developing infant, whose physical growth and development are linked to his or her mother's psychological state. High levels of stress also affect the parenting process. Mothers and fathers who are experiencing high levels of stress are less attuned to their infant's needs (because they are more preoccupied with their own) and more likely to react negatively to their infant's efforts to get attention. This can set up a cycle in which a stressed-out parent inadvertently stresses his or her baby, and the stressed-out (probably screaming) baby makes the parent even *more* stressed.

Helping young couples manage their stress will not remove the stressors in their lives, but it can increase their coping capacities and reduce the negative effects of stress on their health and wellness. Of course, some tangible stressors—such as poor housing—can be addressed directly through care coordination services. However, many of the stressors experienced by young parents are interpersonal and best managed through positive coping. When young parents are exposed to multiple stressors and have little control over the stress in their lives, relaxation exercises can help them regain mastery over their emotional responses and enhance their well-being.

Relaxation Techniques

Relaxation techniques—such as deep breathing and mindfulness—are most helpful for couples who are demonstrating emotional and physical symptoms of stress. These techniques can be used in sessions when one partner is very upset or there is tension between partners. Relaxation techniques provide a way to interrupt conflict or diminish hostility. When teaching couples relaxation techniques, you may also coach them on how to use the technique in their everyday lives.

There are a variety of relaxation techniques for stress management ranging from very simple to more complex exercises (see Baer, 2003; Kabat-Zinn, 2003). Which technique works best is a matter of personal preference. We briefly discuss two exercises in the following. The first is *deep breathing* because it is a crucial element of many other relaxation techniques. It is easy to learn and usually has immediate results. The second is an exercise in *mindfulness*, which is the practice of focusing one's attention on the simplest aspects of being alive as a way of re-setting one's emotional state and becoming more at peace by quieting one's thoughts. Before demonstrating or instructing your participants on how to use these relaxation techniques, you should practice them yourself.

DEEP BREATHING

Deep breathing helps an individual to control the physical symptoms and effects of stress. It expels carbon dioxide from the body, slows heart rate, lowers blood pressure, and promotes relaxation, calmness, and clear thinking. The convenient thing about deep breathing is that it only takes a minute, can be practiced anywhere, and can be done while standing, sitting, or lying down. Also, YPP couples can deep breathe together. When one partner is upset the other can suggest that they both take a moment to breathe deeply.

The act of taking notice, or observing one's emotional state, can be the first step in learning to calm down and regulate stress. You can help YPP couples recognize when they experience stress by identifying common symptoms such as increased heart rate and/or anxiety, rigid and tense body, clenched jaw, and dry mouth. When these symptoms occur, you can recommend that the couple take a break and practice deep breathing. Follow these steps:

(1) To start, place one hand over your chest and the other over your belly.
(2) Inhale slowly through your nose while silently counting to four. The hand over your belly should rise as your lungs fill up with air. The hand over your chest should barely move.
(3) Hold your breath while counting silently to four.
(4) Exhale slowly through your mouth.
(5) Repeat 10 times.
(6) It may help to choose a word or phrase to say silently while you breathe out. Choose words that help you calm down or remind you of a pleasant experience, such as "chill" or "lying on the beach" or "blueberry pie." Try to focus on that word or phrase and put your other thoughts away for the moment.
(7) Wrap up: Ask your partner how he or she feels.

Deep breathing is one of several brief stress reduction techniques that could easily be incorporated into the YPP. Others include progressive muscle relaxation and mindfulness meditation. These techniques can be taught quickly as a dyadic, couples-oriented activity and performed in the moment—such as in the car, at school, or in your office. After practicing a relaxation technique with a couple, debrief and discuss the experience. Ask each partner:

•   How did you feel before, during, and after the exercise?
•   Was this helpful?
•   Is it worth trying again?
•   How might you use the technique outside of YPP sessions?
•   How could you use this technique with each other to handle stressful situations?

The wrap-up conversation will help you decide whether to encourage the couple to continue practicing a given exercise or to try an alternative relaxation technique. When it works, couples may benefit from doing this at the beginning or the end of their sessions with you. Including relaxation techniques at the beginning of the sessions can help set the stage for a more productive exchange and repeating the exercise at the end can help couples internalize whatever learning has occurred.

MINDFULNESS

Mindfulness is defined as paying attention—without judgment—to what is happening in the present moment for the purpose of becoming more self-aware. Although the idea of mindfulness might sound passive, it is meant to be an active process that requires you to focus your attention on the present moment and away from past experiences or thoughts about the future. It also requires effort to let go of judgments as to what is right or wrong, good or bad. This means focusing on what you see, hear, smell, feel, and think; accepting those sights, smells, noises, and so on for what they are and then letting them go. This may sound too abstract, but the exercise that follows will help make these ideas more concrete.

Mindfulness is used to help people gain control over their mind and behavior by learning to step back and observe themselves (and others) without needing to do or say anything. This can help young people realize that there is an important distinction to be made between *thoughts* or *feelings* and *behavior*. We can think and feel without taking action. This helps us become more accepting. It also allows those pressured, anxious, or upsetting moments to pass, teaching us that just waiting can be a great way letting problems take care of themselves. Mindfulness helps to slow down racing thoughts and calm an overactive nervous system.

MINDFULNESS SCRIPT

This should be read slowly with pauses between points

- Pay attention to the natural rhythm of your breath and how the air comes in and out. Do not hold your breath or push air out more forcefully than normal...just breath naturally and be aware of your breath.

- Count your breaths as they come in and out. Stay focused on breathing. Count "one" as you inhale, and "one" as you exhale, then "two" inhale, "two" exhale, up to five and then return to "one. "Keep doing this for one to two minutes (e.g., one-one, two-two, three-three, four-four, five-five. One-one, two-two, three-three, four-four, five-five...). Even though you are trying to stay focused on your breathing, your mind is probably wandering. Maybe you are thinking about lunch or the baby or something that irritated you earlier. When these thoughts pop into your head, just take notice of them and return to counting your breath. Do not judge your thoughts or worry about them. Just let them be.

- Now say to yourself, "I wonder what my next thought is going to be?" and just wait for it to come. Imagine yourself writing down the thought on a piece of paper. Now roll up the piece of paper and tie it with a string. Attach the string to a balloon and then let it float into the air.

- As it floats far up into the sky and out of sight, wait for your next thought to emerge. Again, write down the thought, tie it with a string, and attach it to a balloon. Then let the balloon float slowly away as you keep your mind on it.

- Remain conscious of your breathing. (One, one. Two, two. Three, three.)

- If your mind goes blank and has no more thoughts, just imagine balloons emerging and then floating away.

THE YOUNG PARENTHOOD PROGRAM

There are many different mindfulness exercises. Breath counting (Fontana & Slack, 1997; Kabat-Zinn, 1990) is one of the most basic ways to help participants learn to focus on the present moment and calm the mind. Unlike the deep breathing exercise, breath counting does not involve controlling or changing one's breathing. It is just about paying attention to one's breath.

Ask the couple to find a comfortable place to sit together. Explain that you would like for one partner to guide the other through this exercise, reading from the script on the following page. If neither is comfortable with reading out loud (some may be too self-conscious about their reading ability), you should step in and read it to both of them. They will still get the idea that one person can help guide the other.

An immediate goal of this exercise is to help the couple relax and train their mind to let go of negative emotions and thoughts they might get stuck on. This is useful when one partner will not back down or let go of a pet peeve, a perceived insult, or a jealous moment. The larger goal of mindfulness is to help each partner (and the couple together) learn to be more patient and accepting of himself or herself, which relates to skill 6: acceptance.

SKILL 6: ACCEPTANCE

Introduction

At one point in the history of marital therapy, counselors mostly focused on helping couples change their behavior and fine-tune their relationship through behavioral reinforcements. Over time, many marital therapists shifted to a more emotion-focused approach, designed to help both partners learn to accept aspects of one another rather than try to change them (Christensen & Jacobson, 1999). The goal of acceptance in couples counseling is to increase intimacy, develop empathy, and remember the importance for liking someone for *who they are* instead of trying to make them into someone else. The following discussion between a YPP counselor and a couple illustrates this approach.

Rita is angry with her boyfriend Daryl because he is always late and does not call. He claims that he just cannot keep track of time. Daryl has chronically struggled with being where he is supposed to be and staying on top of his responsibilities. He struggles in school and his mother is constantly on his case about things he forgot to do. He recognizes that this is a problem but he is not doing anything to change it; he feels badly that everyone gets annoyed. To address this, the counselor asks Rita if she knew that Daryl was forgetful and a bit disorganized when they started dating. When she says "yes," the counselor follows up.

Counselor: Why didn't it bother you before?

Rita: Because we weren't having a baby together then!

Counselor: What is the worst thing about Daryl being late? What is the worst that can happen?

Rita: Well, he could miss the birth of his child! And it is just inconsiderate!

Counselor: OK, I can see why that is important. Why do you think Daryl is late all the time?

Rita: I don't know... it seems like he doesn't care.

Counselor: Can you ask him if he cares?

Rita (*to Daryl*): Why are you late all the time? Do you even care?

Daryl: I do care, but I'm just having a hard time keeping track of everything. I never know what I'm supposed to be doing. I know it's a problem, but I cannot seem to fix it.

Counselor (*to Rita*): Do you believe that?

Rita: I know that's the truth, but it still bugs me. How are you ever going to keep a job?

Counselor: So what is the cost of being irritated with Daryl about this all the time?

Rita: I guess we'll just be bickering until we can't stand each other no more.

Counselor: Do you think it is possible for you to let this go for the time being? To let Daryl figure this out on his own, so that it is not a big issue between the two of you? I'm not saying that you are wrong to be irritated, but trying to control Daryl might not be the best use of your energy right now.

Rita: I suppose.

Counselor: Really?

Rita: I know I'm not going to change him. He's gotta do it himself.

Counselor: Is it a deal breaker for you? Can you live with that?

Rita: I love him too much for it to be a deal breaker. But it sure is annoying.

Counselor: Daryl, what do you think about this?

Daryl: I feel bad about being late all time. I can try harder.

Counselor: Would it help to have Rita stop getting on your case?

Daryl: I don't know. I'm kinda used to it. It would be different, that's for sure.

Counselor: Yeah. If Rita loosens up, you might have to tighten up!

In this case, Rita's willingness to accept Daryl's behavior does not seem complete. Moreover, the dynamic between Daryl and Rita seems to be part of the problem—Daryl might even rely on Rita to remind him about things in the way that he relies on his mother and his teachers. In this case, Rita's ability to accept or live with Daryl's behavior might open more room for growth. This approach recognizes that: (a) all of us are flawed; (b) our partner's flaws can be acceptable or tolerable when considered in context; (c) it is folly to try to control or change another person's behavior; and (d) when people feel accepted, they are more likely to become more flexible and change their behavior. This perspective on the imperfection of relationships encourages couples to stop trying to force each other to become their perfect partner. This does not mean anything goes. Counselors who emphasize the value of acceptance help couples learn to differentiate between what is a deal breaker and what they can let go.

Learning acceptance can benefit all co-parenting couples, whether they remain romantically involved or not. In some respects, the process of accepting a partner's imperfections is simpler for couples who are not romantically involved because their expectations of each other are (or could be) more narrowly defined. As a YPP counselor, you can help each partner consider whether their partner's "problem behavior" will affect the fundamental health and development of their child (for example, smoking marijuana may or may not be acceptable, depending on how much and whether the child is exposed). If so, then expectations can be framed in terms of providing the child with a healthy, safe environment. For the partner who complains a lot and wants to control things that are beyond his or her control, letting go can help reduce their level of stress. If acceptance is achieved, the child will benefit from having two parents who get along and like each other.

Exercise 1: Accepting Your Own Undesirable Behaviors

One approach to helping couples develop acceptance is to ask them both to tell you something about themselves (not their partners) that they wish they could change. How would they feel if this behavior or trait could not be changed and they had to live with it? Would it mean they would not like themselves? Would they be able to adapt? Is there anything about this apparent flaw or weakness that is valuable or serves a purpose? The focus of this discussion is on learning to accept undesirable things about the self; to develop some self-compassion, which is an important step in developing acceptance skills. This exercise is intended to help young men and women take a step toward accepting their partners for who they are and letting go of who they want their partner to become, at least in some respects.

Exercise 2: Accepting Your Partner's Quirks

If the couple does relatively well with the first exercise, you can take it a step further with a second exercise. Ask them to identify things about their partner that kind of bother them but are not deal breakers. When they provide examples ("He's a slob!" "She never comes over when she says she's coming over!" "His friends are jerks." "She's too sarcastic with me."), ask if they know why their partner does these things. Why is he a slob? Why is she late? Why does he hang out with that group of friends? From the other person's point of view, what purpose could this behavior serve? Setting aside the fact that the behavior annoys you, is there a way to understand it? This exercise in reflection could lead to a more open, nonblaming discussion of these behaviors with the partner. Now you can ask what would it mean for the relationship if this trait or behavior never changed? Would that be so awful? Could you let it go? Most importantly, what is the cost trying to change your partner or get him or her to behave differently?

Hopefully, these discussions loosen up both partners so that they are able to have a more constructive discussion about their pet peeves. Teaching couples about acceptance is difficult, but it can have a powerful impact on those who tend to get locked into believing that "If only he or she would stop doing this or that, everything would be OK." Stepping aside from this rigid perspective can be a relief. If acceptance takes hold, some previously annoying behaviors and traits will matter less.

Exercise 3: Accepting Hurtful Behaviors

Some behaviors are much more difficult to accept than others. For example, after a co-parenting couple breaks up, it can be very difficult for one partner to accept that the other is with someone else. It is even more difficult to accept that the ex-partner could bring the baby to the new partner's house. It is not uncommon for one partner to say that any contact between the baby and the new partner is unacceptable. In this situation, the challenge is to help the co-parenting couple separate their hurt feelings from what is acceptable (or tolerable) co-parenting behavior. When partners are very angry with each other, especially after a break up has occurred, the capacity for empathy and acceptance is very low. When you engage in discussions related to letting go of the romantic relationship, it is often more useful to focus on feelings of loss and disappointment than feelings of anger and betrayal. If the hurt partner can mourn the loss of the relationship, it is will be easier for him or her to accept that it is time to let go and move forward.

It is important to note that some behavior may not be acceptable by any standard and it is important for one parent to draw a line and say, "This is unacceptable." For example, if one partner is exposing the child to drug use or criminal behavior, the other partner has reason to be concerned for the child's well-being. In some cases, like this one, you may need to educate one or both partners about child endangerment and how to draw the line between behavior that is annoying or hurtful (but ultimately acceptable) and behavior that is dangerous and unacceptable.

When having these sorts of discussions with a couple, it is important to be clear that a behavior may be deemed unacceptable, but this does not mean that the person engaged in the behavior is unacceptable. For example, if a mother believes her child is at risk because of the father's drug use, you many need to help her set parameters around the father's time with their child (never when under the influence) or restrict his involvement until he gets help with his serious substance abuse problem. The message conveyed is that the mother wants the father to be involved as a parent, but only when she can be assured the child is safe when in his care. These discussions are challenging, but it is possible to conduct them in a nonjudgmental manner.

The marital literature focuses on the value of acceptance for increasing intimacy between committed partners. As indicated, learning to accept and let go can be a very useful skill for couples who are no longer in a romantic relationship, but trying to co-parent. This particular skill may be one that you will want to return to later in the program (Phases 4, 5, or 6) if the couple breaks up and one or both partners are struggling to manage their anger or get over feeling hurt and disappointed.

SKILL 7: DE-ESCALATING CONFLICT

Co-parenting couples will inevitably have conflicts. The goal of YPP is not to solve or prevent conflicts, but to change the way that couples manage them. The following set of skills is particularly important for couples who have a history of aggressive behavior with each other. Unfortunately, pushing and shoving is fairly common among young couples. The skills that follow will help to reduce the risk that conflicts will lead to aggression.

(1) **Soften the approach.** John Gottman, who is a renowned marital researcher, emphasizes the importance of the soft start when working with high-conflict couples. The idea is that how a person starts a conflict can have an impact on how it ends. If it starts with hostility it is likely to end with hostility. Couples who are able to approach hot topic discussions in a positive, collaborative way are more likely to be effective co-parents. As indicated earlier, when working with high-conflict couples, you should ask their permission to interrupt hostile exchanges so that you do not come across as too controlling or judgmental when you step in quickly to redirect their behavior. When you observe one partner confront the other in a way that is potentially offensive, ask him or her to try a back up just a bit and try a softer, warmer approach.

(2) **Accept responsibility.** When couples get set on winning a conflict, they often become unwilling to take any responsibility for whatever problem is occurring. Conflicts become much softer when both partners are able to identify the role they have played in causing the problem or making things worse. Your role is to simply point out that relationship problems are very rarely just one person's fault. You can say something like "It takes two to tango" and then ask both partners to take responsibility for their own contribution. These sample statements might help a young person think about his or her responsibility in any conflict:

   · Yes, I have been stressed and irritable lately.
   · Yes, I have not been very nice lately.
   · Yes, I have taken you for granted.
   · Yes, I have been overly sensitive.
   · Yes, I have been too critical.
   · Yes, I dropped the ball.

   By accepting shared ownership of a problem, the couple is in a better position to de-escalate, reconnect and find a compromise.

(3) **Compromise/accept influence.** Partners should learn to look for points of agreement with their partner, even if such points are small or few. For example, if a young mother is angry because she does not like her partner's friends, ask him if he can find some way to address her concern—whatever it may be—without necessarily giving up his friendships. Could he curtail some activities? Could he spend less time with friends and more time with her? Learning to accept a partner's influence or meet in the middle when seeking a solution can help diminish the need to win fights. You can help the couple shift their perspective away from this need to win by helping them identify common goals and shared feelings.

(4) **Step down when conflict becomes too negative.** Partners should learn how to take a break when they become overwhelmed and are no longer communicating in a productive manner. Depending on the topic, sometimes the conflict is not worth pursuing, but other times it will be important for the couple to come back together when they are calmer and continue working on the problem. If the issue is something that will come up again and again, it may be helpful to use the problem-solving technique to help the couple work more collaboratively.

(5) **Repair.** In addition to accepting responsibility, it may also be important to apologize and end with a positive statement about each other or the relationship. This can help decrease defensiveness and re-establish a warm connection. Because they are young and often proud, many YPP coupes have a hard time with compromise and repair when their feelings have been hurt. This is particularly true when they are no longer in a romantic relationship. According to John Gottman, one of the most important components of an enduring relationship is the ability to say "I'm sorry" and ask for another chance to discuss a disagreement in a better way. The capacity to repair a frayed interpersonal connection requires humility and flexibility, which might be in short supply in the midst of a conflict. You can model repair behavior using role-play in which you adopt the position of both partners apologizing to each other and asking for a chance to try again. If commitments are made to try again, your role is to follow up and hold the couple accountable to their commitment.

SKILL 8: COMMUNICATING ABOUT FAMILY PLANNING

Introduction

If a couple gets pregnant again soon after the birth of their first child, it will likely lead to significant stress and diminish the quality of parenting attention they can provide to either child. If the co-parents are no longer together as a romantic couple, and the father gets another young woman pregnant, his ability to parent his first child will be negatively impacted. Unfortunately, rapid repeat pregnancies occur with some frequency, affecting approximately 20% of adolescent parents in the first 24 months post birth (Tocce et al., 2012). The reason for this is straightforward: A substantial percentage of young mothers and fathers use contraception inconsistently or not at all (O'Connor, 1997). Those who use long-term contraceptive methods, such as hormonal implants and injections, are less likely to have rapid repeat pregnancies, but most young people prefer other methods, which are less reliable unless they are used correctly and consistently.

Most couples will not bring up birth control or family planning. This can be an awkward topic to discuss, but should be broached in a matter-of-fact manner as it relates to co-parenting and parenting. The goal is to help the couple talk about family planning and birth control as a co-parenting issue. To minimize stress and strain, engage the couple in a structured dialogue about if and when they would want to get pregnant again. If they are not together as a couple, focus on whether they might have children with other partners. Be sure to include both partners in the discussion. Many fathers defer to their female partners, but you should work to help a father understand the importance of his involvement. The following guide is intended to help make this discussion easier.

(1) **Note the benefits of waiting.** Start with simple questions about whether they know if and when they want to have other children. *Have you thought about when you want another child?* This could lead to a discussion regarding the optimal spacing between children. You may discuss the value of waiting at least two years before getting pregnant again, underscoring that both the first and second child benefit from having at least two years between them. You should point out that their baby will benefit from having the couple's undivided attention for a period of time and the health of the second child is improved when mothers have adequate time to physically rebound from pregnancy. You might also link the benefits of delaying a second pregnancy to each young parent's life goals, particularly finishing school, finding a good job and saving money. Once the issue of family planning is on the table, it is easier to discuss contraception more directly and specifically.

(2) **Find out who makes decisions about contraception.** The goal is to introduce the idea that contraceptive use can be discussed, despite the awkwardness of doing so. *How do you feel about talking with each other about contraception? In the past, who has decided what contraception to use and when? Who will do so after the baby is born?*

(3) **Educate couple about different methods.** You may want to provide couples with a handout or website that describes the different forms of contraception and sexually transmitted disease (STD) prevention. You can take this opportunity to assess the couple's knowledge about protection against sexually transmitted diseases, and to educate them on which methods provide protection.

(4) **Address the issue of birth control with other partners.** If the couple is broken up, ask them to think about using protection with other partners. This conversation may be too challenging and emotional with both partners present. If so, you can collaborate with the care coordinator who can address the issue one-on-one with both partners.

(5) **Obtaining birth control.** Talking about using contraception is important but ineffective unless the young couple has access to affordable contraception. You should have a discussion with your participants that focuses on where they can obtain contraception, how they can pay for it and whether they are comfortable asking for it from their health provider. If either partner is uncomfortable or does not have access, use the problem-solving process to find a solution and develop a plan. Most states provide Family Planning Only Services that provide free or reduced-cost contraception to economically disadvantaged men and women through most clinics.

(6) **Include parents.** It may be useful to explore family/cultural values regarding sexuality, childbearing, and contraception and to encourage young parents to discuss birth control with their parents. Parents tend to be more supportive of birth control than most teens expect and the conversation can help reinforce the use of birth control.

When possible, YPP counselors should collaborate closely with care coordinators on family planning resources. Care coordinators may be able to help couples obtain the contraceptives they prefer. The following resources support discussions on birth control, STD, and family planning (Table 7.2)

If discussing sexuality makes you uncomfortable, ask yourself the following questions. (a) How can I increase my own comfort level when talking about sex and birth control with young couples? (b) What are my own values and assumptions about adolescent and young adult sexual behavior? (c) If young parents have different ideas and values about sex and birth control, how do I provide input in a way that is also respectful of their beliefs?

Table 7.2 BIRTH CONTROL RESOURCES ON THE WEB

Birth Control Methods: Frequently Asked Questions. U.S. Department of Health and Human Services, Office on Women's Health

http://womenshealth.gov/publications/our-publications/fact-sheet/birth-control-methods.pdf

STD Fact Sheets. Centers for Disease Control and Prevention
http://www.cdc.gov/std/healthcomm/fact_sheets.htm

Condom Fact Sheet in Brief. Centers for Disease Control and Prevention
http://www.cdc.gov/condomeffectiveness/brief.html

For example, if a young mother does not want to use birth control and intends to have another baby soon, you will be challenged to find a way to offer an alternate perspective on 'timing' without being judgemental. Answering these questions will help you become more at ease in these important discussions. And remember what you tell your participants—having these sorts of discussions gets easier with reflection and practice.

SKILL 9: MINIMIZING NEGATIVITY

Introduction

Throughout this guide, counselors are encouraged to adopt an optimistic, positive approach to co-parenting counseling, and couples are encouraged to express support, accept their partner's foibles, work toward positive solutions, listen and reflect, and so on. This sort of collaborative process assumes a basic level of respect between partners, or the capacity to develop respect. Unfortunately, some couples will not be able to make use of this approach because one or both partners are too hostile or angry to listen, accept, or engage in positive problem solving (Boyan & Temini, 2004). This can happen when one partner has a psychological disorder that interferes with emotion regulation or when one partner feels unforgivably hurt and/or betrayed.

Research indicates that when parents and co-parents cooperate, their children benefit; when they engage in high levels of ongoing conflict, their children suffer. All parents argue and get angry with each other, but chronic, intense conflict between parents is a serious problem (Grych, 2002). For some couples, the effort to resolve issues or support mutual understanding may be counterproductive, leading to increased conflict and stirring up hurt feelings. If co-parents cannot get along well enough to collaborate and manage their conflicts, then it is best for the counselor to help them disengage from each other and learn to communicate from a safe distance. Rather than try to change how they feel or behave, it may be best to lower their expectations of each other and their relationship. Help the couple find ways to minimize face-to-face contact and learn to focus on a small set of simple co-parenting's goals and tasks (e.g., pick up, drop-off, shared costs). If the counselor decides to encourage a couple to disengage, he or she should be clear about several points:

(1) Disengaging from the relationship (and the source of conflict) should not mean disengaging from parenting.
(2) Disengaging means avoiding contact with the other parent in order to eliminate conflict. In this respect, disengagement is the best solution to an unsolvable problem.
(3) Disengaged partners can still function adequately as co-parents if each learns to live and let live, assuming that neither is engaged in neglectful or abusive behavior.
(4) Disengaged partners still need to communicate with each other about important matters, like medical issues (if the child is sick, for example, what medication is needed, what has already been administered, and when should the next dose be given). Communications should be simple and factual. Text messaging can help minimize arguments because both partner can think before responding.

Under most circumstances, the goal of YPP is to keep couples engaged in negotiation and compromise. However, when either participant is unable to manage his or her feelings of hostility, it may be useful for the counselor to meet with each partner individually to allow them to: (a) express their hurt, angry feelings in a safe context; (b) discuss strategies for containing these feelings so they are not expressed inappropriately or destructively; and (c) work with the counselor to clarify co-parenting goals by separating essential from nonessential issues and concerns. In Chapter 11, we address the issue of meeting with individual partners in more detail.

Being Civil for the Child's Sake

When working with a couple who does not like, trust or respect each other, the goal is to eliminate harmful behaviors. Put more positively, the goal is to establish and maintain a basic level of civility for the sake of the child. Following are some modified co-parenting goals for couples who cannot manage a collaborative, cooperative co-parenting arrangement.

(1) Set minimum agreed upon goals for co-parenting with a clear focus on their child's health and well-being. Help partners agree that a fundamental co-parenting goal is to avoid intense conflicts that create instability and insecurity for the child. Some parents may need help remembering that how they treat their child's other parent will ultimately affect their child's emotional well-being.

(2) Clarify that YPP is *not* going to heal old wounds or address conflicts related to feelings of betrayal or injustice. Remind the couple that the goal of co-parenting communication is not to "fix" their relationship (or the other partner).

(3) Establish communication ground rules that include: (a) agreed-upon (safe) topics for discussion/negotiation (the logistics of childcare, shared costs, etc.); (b) mode of communication (face-to-face, phone, text); (c) style of communication (I-statements rather than you-statements; calm tone of voice).

(4) Consider writing a simple, mutually agreed upon co-parenting plan that couples can refer to when they disagree. Having a written co-parenting plan can help diminish the need to revisit old conflicts. The plan might address such topics as:

- Amount of time the nonresident father spends with the child each month
- Who pays for necessities such as food, diapers, child care, etc.
- What to do when conflict or disagreements occur
- Topics to avoid (other partners, past disappointments)
- What *not* to say about each other in public, including on Facebook, Twitter, or whatever social media is popular

(5) Emphasize that time is often a great healer of wounds. If both partners can maintain some level of civility despite their strong dislike for each other, they will feel less angry in a year or two.

The following is a list of practical tips to share with participants who are struggling with how to co-parent effectively while maintaining a safe distance. To avoid setting up unrealistic expectations, let the couple know that these tips are merely suggestions. Giving these tips is like planting seeds; it will take time for them to germinate and take root.

CHAPTER REVIEW

At the end of Phase 3, couples should feel more confident about their ability to communicate with each other, support their partners, and resolve conflicts that arise. This is a good time to review the skills that the couple has developed and let them know that as you move through the next phases of YPP, you will ask them to continue using these new skills, if only for the sake of practicing them.

After working with a couple on their communication skills, ask whether the approach helped them to express themselves more effectively. Did they feel that their partner was better able to listen and take in what they were saying? When you wrap up the sessions with a brief evaluation of what was accomplished, it can help the couple become more aware of their behavior and encourage them to practice using the new strategies on their own. As you move forward, track their progress with expressing thoughts and feelings. Point out what they do well and remind them that they can make use of these simple exercises when they stumble in their communications.

A brief synopsis of the interpersonal skills discussed in Phase 3 follows. Counselors should address at least three of the following interpersonal skills during this phase:

(1) **Expressing needs/feelings.** Helps couples learn to open up and express themselves in positive, respectful ways. Good for conflict resolution and for couples who want to open up and share more of their thoughts and feelings with each other.

(2) **Reflective listening skills.** Couples learn to be quiet and listen, to speak more directly and clearly, to pay attention and take in their partner's thoughts and feelings.

(3) **Support skills.** Helps both partners learn how to ask for and accept their partner's support. Partners also learn how to provide support to each other in helpful ways.

PRACTICAL TIPS

HOW TO REDUCE CONFLICT: SUGGESTIONS FOR DISENGAGED COUPLES

Set priorities and make requests, not demands or sarcastic remarks. Figure out what you want from your co-parent. Then ask for it clearly and simply. For example, ask, "Would it be OK if I took Julia for the weekend?" or "Would you be able to pick up some diapers?"

Do not interrupt, no matter how much you want to. Assume that disagreements will occur. When they do, let your partner speak his or her mind. Indicate that you understand (and even appreciate) his or her point of view. Remaining quiet and listening does not imply agreement, and you do not lose anything by doing so.

Sometimes it is a good idea to bite your tongue. Do not react to everything that upsets you. Hold onto the big picture—what is best for your baby in the long run. Ask yourself if the issue really matters to your child's basic health or if you are just upset because you feel disrespected or manipulated. Your ego can probably handle it, whereas a big fight or argument could harm your child. If the issue does not concern your child's health, it is probably best to let it go.

Separate your differences in parenting style from serious concerns about basic safety. Do not tell the other parent how to parent. When your partner tells you how to parent, let it go. If you have concerns that the child's other parent is endangering the child (driving while high or leaving the child unsupervised, for example), talk with others about how to express that concern directly and clearly or how to involve the child protective services.

Text rather than talk. In order to minimize the likelihood of arguments, communicate with each other by text messaging. Keep the messages simple and straightforward. Do not blame or ridicule or reprimand. Do not respond to provocation. Think before you text. Do not text when you are angry.

---

(4) **Problem-solving skills.** Couples learn to brainstorm solutions to ongoing conflicts. Focus is on finding compromises that work for both partners and ensuring that both agree to keep up their end of the deal.

(5) **Stress management skills.** Couples learn how to calm down when stressed out and to help their partner calm down when he or she is really stressed. Specific techniques include deep breathing and mindfulness exercises.

(6) **Acceptance skills.** Helps partners learn to accept and/or appreciate each other's personal flaws. Focus is on knowing the difference between what one can control and when one should just let it go. This includes learning to adapt to things that will not change.

(7) **Conflict de-escalation.** Helps couples to recognize when conflict is escalating, how they may cool down before the conflict rises too high, and how they can later talk about the conflict in a way that feels safe and calm. This is important for preventing violence between couples.

(8) **Family planning skills.** Helps couples discuss family planning issues such as if and when they might want to have another child, how they will avoid pregnancy in the meantime, preferred contraception, and where to acquire it.

(9) **Minimizing negativity.** Helps high-conflict couples determine how they will continue to co-parent and communicate productively but keep their distance in order to avoid unhealthy conflict that could upset or harm their child.

Table 7.3 BRIEF DESCRIPTIONS OF WORKSHEETS IN THE YPP TOOLBOX

Title:	What do you know about each other?
Description:	This worksheet can help facilitate conversation when couples are having a difficult time picking a topic to talk about or are having trouble talking in a constructive, non-hostile way. The goal is for the couple to learn more about one another while expressing their feelings in a thoughtful, respectful manner. The 11 statements included in the worksheet are written in a true/false format, designed to force each partner to indicate what they *think* they know about the other, intended to evoke sharing and positive dialogue.
Possible uses in YPP:	Phase 3 (Expressing Needs and Feelings exercise)

Title:	**Areas of Strength Checklist**
Description:	As the title indicates, this worksheet can help couples identify relationship strengths, while also allowing them to identify areas that they would like to work on. The worksheet includes 17 items covering a variety of relationship areas, including autonomy, respect, mutual interests, and problem-solving. The worksheet can be helpful when couples are feeling negative about their relation and need a positive motivation to continue working on their interpersonal skills.
Possible uses in YPP:	Phases 3, 4, 5, and 6

(continued)

Table 7.3 CONTINUED

Title:	**Areas of Disagreement Checklist**
Description:	This worksheet is useful when couples are having a hard time identifying issues to discuss and you do not want to in the position of digging problems. This can help couples self identify disagreements to discuss so that they can develop their listening, expressing and problem solving skills. The worksheet asks respondents to indicate the magnitude of the problem and the length of time that the topic has been an issue so that you can help avoid making too much of small issues or getting pulled into really big issues. The worksheet covers 15 topic areas, ranging from money to substance use and issues of power. The worksheet may be helpful in Phase 3 as a prelude to the reflective listening exercise in Phase 3.
Possible uses in YPP:	Phase 3 (Reflective listening or problem solving)

Title:	**Areas of Change Checklist: Solvable Problems**
Description:	This worksheet is also useful for couples who are having a hard time getting started. It covers 16 common relationship issues that many couples hope to improve upon, including communicating more, spending time together, and expressing appreciation. The worksheet uses a scale from 1 to 5, with higher scores indicating a more serious problem. Results can be used as a follow up to individual and relationship goals identified in Phase 2 and as a prelude to several of the exercises in Phase 3.
Possible uses in YPP:	Phase 3 (Reflective listening exercise, expressing needs and feeling exercise or problem solving exercise)

Title:	Family map
Description:	The family map is designed to help couples share information about their families with the counselor (and each other). The goal of this worksheet is to help them begin to think about the roles they occupy and potential sources of support. It is often the case that the families of young couples are complex; drawing pictures of primary family members (using stick figures) helps the counselor to have a clear understanding of each partner's family structure.
Possible uses in YPP:	Phase 4, Phase 5

Title:	**My Support System**
Description:	Some couples may feel as though they have little or no support and need some help thinking about untapped resources in their social networks. This worksheet helps couples: 1) *identify individuals* who they can look to for support during the transition to parenthood; 2) identify the *type of support* they need or want from those people and 3) learn *how to request* support. The sheet is a concrete reference tool and can be useful as the counselor begins to develop a transition plan for the couple.

(continued)

Table 7.3 CONTINUED

Possible uses in YPP:	Phase 4, Phase 5

Title:	**Feelings Worksheet**
Description:	This worksheet is designed to facilitate constructive expression of feelings by providing a 'word bank' of varying emotions. The Feelings Worksheet can be used whenever either participant is having a hard time finding the words to express their feelings. This worksheet can help prevent you from putting words in the mouths of participants with limited vocabularies or who have a hard time naming how they feel.
Possible uses in YPP:	*All Phases*; Phase 3 (Expressing Needs and Feelings exercise)

Title:	**Acceptance Worksheet**
Description:	This worksheet helps partners "let go" of the small problems and complaints that generate conflict and learn to "pick their battles." The strategy is to help partners accept each others' quirks and learn to tolerate behavior that might be annoying but isn't harmful or a "deal breaker." The goal of this worksheet is to reduce unnecessary stress in the relationship and facilitate self-awareness.
Possible uses in YPP:	Phase 3

Title:	**What I like about you/What I like about us**
Description:	This worksheet helps couples identify and give voice to positive aspects of their partner and their relationship by answering 7 open-ended questions (i.e. You are good at_____; One of my favorite things to do together is_____). This worksheet is useful for couples that tend to be more hostile than warm; the exercise can help build relationship strengths during Phase 3.
Possible uses in YPP:	Phase 3

Title:	**Co-Parenting Planning Worksheet**
Description:	Couples often disagree about how to share parenting responsibilities. This worksheet facilitates discussion around 'division of labor' by listing some common parenting tasks (i.e. bathing and feeding, taking child to doctor's appointments, buying things for the child). Respondents are asked to indicate how frequently he/she will do each task (i.e. often, sometimes, rarely, or never) and how often his/her partner will do the task. Discussion following the completion of this worksheet should focus on facilitating cooperation (rather than arguing about discrepancies).
Possible uses in YPP:	Phase 5

PHASE 4: ROLE TRANSITIONS

8

IDENTITY AND PARENTHOOD

ALL ADOLESCENTS AND YOUNG ADULTS ARE IN A STATE of rapid role transition as their relationships evolve and they experiment with different identities. This age group is in the midst of renegotiating their relationships with their parents, some of whom may not appreciate their child's growing independence. Adolescents are also renegotiating peer relationships, becoming involved with romantic partners, and taking on more adult roles (Arnett, 2001; Erikson, 1980). This rapid role transition is often stressful because it involves juggling different sets of expectations and identities. Adolescents also expend a great deal of energy trying to figure out their own role-based expectations. It is often within the context of a specific role that an adolescent asks, "Who am I?" and "Who do I want to become?"

Table 8.1 PHASE 4: GOALS, TASKS, AND RESOURCES

Goals	Tasks
1. The couple begins to renegotiate their roles and interpersonal boundaries with family and friends. 2.The couple begins to present themselves as a family unit to their friends and family. 3. The couple feels more confident in their ability to integrate different roles and demonstrates a greater understanding of their respective role-related challenges.	1. Draw a family or social network map to launch a discussion about family and peer relations. 2. Role-play discussion with family and friends. 3. Work with the couple before a family meeting to be clear about what they would like to say and accomplish. 4. Meet with family members to facilitate the development of new roles and relationship boundaries. 5. Help the couple examine and redefine peer relations.
Additional Resources	
Family Map	

The process of identity development and the adjustment to adult roles is even more difficult for young parents because they are also trying to integrate these two new identities, being a parent and co-parenting partner (Feit et al., 2006; Frewin et al., 2007). As they struggle to figure out how to fulfill these new roles, they often feel stretched between conflicting expectations and desires, leading to "role strain" (see chapter 12 for a fuller discussion of this issue). For example, Chris wants to hang out with his friends, who are always asking him to play basketball or go drinking. This causes conflict with his partner, Mariana, who expects Chris to spend more time with her and get a job so that he can help support their baby. She resents that Chris is so unrestricted in his activities while she is stuck at home, eight months pregnant. Chris does not know how to manage the conflict between his desire to have fun with his friends and his desire to be responsible and supportive of Mariana. He worries that he is not cut out to be a father. This is a common dilemma for young parents, but if Chris and Mariana discuss it they may find common ground, which will make it easier for them to make compromises, temper their expectations, and support each other's wishes to have fun.

Some young fathers and mothers feel that some of the people in their lives are reluctant to acknowledge or accept them in their new roles. If their parents are angry, upset or disapproving, they may not fully support their son or daughter's shifting roles. For example, Richie knows his parents expect him to take responsibility for becoming a father, but they continue to treat him like the reckless, defiant 16-year-old he was last year. He wants to be responsible and wishes his parents would give him a chance. Meanwhile, his girlfriend's parents still regard him as a hoodlum because he was in juvenile detention last year. They have disapproved of him all along. His response to these negative expectations is to feel resentful and become withdrawn and sullen. This makes things worse because both sets of parents tend to see him as childish and unpleasant to be around.

Richie needs help finding the words to explain to his parents (and his girlfriend's parents) that he is working hard to become more responsible. ("I know you still see me as a kid, which is understandable, but I am working to become more of an adult.") Richie could help improve the relationship by asking for their support. ("It would be great—really great—if you could give me a chance to prove that I can do this, that I can be more responsible. Like, I could really use some help looking for a job.") Ideally, this would open a dialogue that would allow both sets of parents to be clear about their expectations and convey their support.

Friends and family are not always a source of support for young couples; they can be a source of conflict and stress. When a young man or woman has a history of unhealthy relationships with friends and/or family, he or she may need help finding a tactful way to set firmer boundaries. For example, if the young father's friends are gang involved or heavy drug users, the young mother may have legitimate concerns about her child's safety around these friends. She might appropriately put pressure on her partner to distance himself from negative influences that could land him in jail or put their baby in harm's way. Some young parents may need your help to understand the risks of exposing their child to a chaotic and potentially unsafe environment. Many adolescents and young adults are quite unaware of the risks or are unconcerned about them because they have grown accustomed to risks and/or they are risk takers. Some psychoeducation around how specific risks could affect an infant might be useful for re-orienting these young parents. As the YPP counselor, you can facilitate a discussion about how to protect their child and, if necessary, how to extract themselves from unhealthy relationships.

The primary goal of Phase 4 is to help couples negotiate their changing roles and, when appropriate, help them set healthy boundaries with peers and extended family members. Adjusting roles and relationships—even slightly—may be difficult at first, but over time, it is likely to garner respect from friends and family. The process can help the young parents to figure out what it means—for them—to become a family. Your job as counselor is to help couples use the interpersonal skills they learned in Phase 3 to communicate effectively with each other and with their friends and families about these shifting roles. Even when they are unsuccessful in their efforts to gather support and understanding from others, the co-parents will benefit from the process of working together. This process—in which the couple usually creates a plan for talking with their friends and family about becoming parents— is an exercise in growing up. The couple functions as a family unit and sends a powerful message that they are working hard to meet the challenges of parenthood together.

During Phase 4, some young couples may invite extended family members into sessions to work on specific concerns or conflicts. Some family members may see this as an opportunity for improving the lines of communication. Others may not want to participate. It is important for you to remain flexible. The young parents' parents—the grandparents—may be struggling to understand their new roles, too. Many young parents have a history of recklessness and wild behavior. Some grandparents may want to respect their children's transition to parenthood and adulthood but may worry about their readiness. They may have serious concerns about the well-being of their yet-unborn grandchild. Often, grandparents appreciate a forum that allows them to express their support and their concerns.

The YPP focuses on interpersonal skill building *before* bringing the extended family into the process because these multiple family sessions can be very challenging, particularly when emotions are raw and the couple's parents are meeting for the first time. Once the young couple has developed a fairly clear sense of themselves as co-parents, they can respond more positively to whatever challenges their parents may present in the session. More important, they will feel more comfortable asking for the support they need from their parents to cope with the stress of parenting. Working on what they might hope to accomplish in a family meeting can help each partner begin to independently revise and renegotiate their family roles, even if the couple is not able to meet with their extended family members.

In addition to helping young expectant parents manage role transitions within their families, Phase 4 can help the couple clarify their role in each other's lives now that they are expecting a child. If a young couple's progress through the YPP phases has gone reasonably well so far, they will have begun to solidify their co-parenting alliance. Regardless of their status as romantic partners, they have agreed to work together to provide their child with a safe, secure emotional environment. During Phase 4, couples are encouraged to discuss their expectations of each other and themselves both as parents and co-parents. Even if they disagree about their respective roles, they are likely to find common ground, and it is your job as the counselor to build upon this ground. Phase 4 typically requires one to two sessions (perhaps more if a family meeting is scheduled). There are two or three parts to this phase, which are outlined in the following.

PART 1: DRAW A FAMILY/SOCIAL NETWORK MAP

Ask the couple to draw a family diagram or "map"; use stick figures so no drawing skills are necessary. The map should include both of them (and their baby) and five to ten of the most important people in their extended family and social network. Let them define their family or social network in whatever way they choose. Give them 10 minutes to do this, explaining that the quality of the drawing is not important. Ask them to label everyone clearly (Tom, Older Brother; Jill, Maternal Aunt). If the couple is not comfortable making the map themselves, ask them to tell you about their family (who to include) and you can draw it for them. Having schemata of some sort will help to facilitate the discussion of roles and extended family relationships.

Step 1: Where Do They Fit?

Once the map is done, discuss how they—as a couple—fit into this network. Ask questions that will help them clarify the nature of each relationship and their position within the family, such as, "What is your role in your relationship with your mother?"

- How is becoming a parent going to change that role?
- Who in the family is likely to be most supportive of you as a parent?
- Who will help you take care of the baby?
- Who can help you find a job or a place to live?
- Who can you talk to when you are stressed out?

As the couple speaks about their relationships with different family members, draw lines between the stick figures and make brief notes describing their relationships. The goal of this exercise is to clarify the potential role of each family member in helping the couple make a successful transition to parenthood. Young men and women usually do not make full use of the people who are available to them for support because they do not recognize the possibilities. This activity highlights these possibilities. Although it is important to lead with a discussion of family strengths, some couples will identify family conflicts and focus on the lack of support they receive. Some will say their family relies on them; that they feel responsible for taking care of their parents and/or their siblings. Some may report feeling resentful or drained by their family. Some may need your help looking beyond their families for support. That said, young people often underestimate what their families are able to provide.

Step 2: What Relationships Do They Want to Change?

The next step is to identify how the couple would like their relationships and roles to be different. Ask questions that help the couple clarify how they would like to shift their position or role within their family system, such as:

- Which relationships could be improved?
- Does the expectant mother want to set firmer boundaries with someone?
- Does the expectant mother want her partner to set firmer boundaries with his family or friends?
- Does the expectant father want to be closer with someone?
- Which roles could be updated/renegotiated in response to the changing circumstances and growth?

A pregnant adolescent may need help expressing her appreciation for her own mother's ongoing support and also requesting that she let her work on co-parenting with the father of her baby... in their own way. The mothers of adolescent mothers—the grandmothers—often have a hard time respecting their daughter's position as a parent and their relationship with the young father. The grandmother may have ongoing concerns about her daughter's readiness to parent or the maturity of the father. An open, mutually respectful discussion can help the two of them constructively clarify these complex roles.

Family relationships can change, yet adolescents are often very pessimistic about this possibility. They are typically skeptical that their parents will listen to them or are capable of change. When such doubts arise, acknowledge that they might be right, but encourage them to consider the possibility that they might be surprised. Let them know that parents are often grateful for opportunities to discuss the shifting roles and are usually willing to adjust their own role if they are approached in a respectful way.

Step 3: Set the Stage for a Family Meeting

Next, help the couple set the stage for a positive family meeting, intended to support positive growth and healthy shifts in their roles and responsibilities. Introduce the idea that families tend to engage in the same behavior over and over again until someone says, quite deliberately, "Let's try something different." The goal is to help the couple make the first move toward having a more adult-like relationship with their parents (and other family members) and to do so using the communication skills they have learned.

If a young father would like to have a closer relationship with his own father, for example, you can help him think out loud about what he could say or do to reach out to make that happen. If he would like his mother to be less "in his business" or friendlier toward his girlfriend, help him find a way to ask for these changes without blaming her or putting her down. How could he ask for support in a way that will increase the likelihood of a positive response and outcome? Even if a couple does not want to invite family members to a session, such exercises can help facilitate positive discussions with family outside the context of YPP sessions.

Step 4: Role-Play a Family Meeting

Help the couple role-play making a request or a statement to a family member. Explain that knowing your message differs from choosing your words and saying them aloud. Role-play allows the couple to practice formulating their words over and over until they feel comfortable and their message is clear and polite. The key is to express honest feelings in a way that respects the listener. *Complete this exercise even if there is no plan for a family meeting, as it will bolster their capacity for communicating more effectively with their families outside of the YPP sessions.*

PART 2 (OPTIONAL): MEET THE FAMILY

Before the Meeting

If the couple invites one or more family members to a YPP session, do the following: (a) clarify what the couple hopes to accomplish with this meeting in order to manage expectations; (b) describe your role in the meeting (to help the couple request support or make a statement about shifting roles); and (c) consider calling and inviting family members to the session and explaining the session's goals. If the session is successful, family members should be drawn closer together and experience reduced tension.

During the Meeting

Keep the following points in mind:

- It is not appropriate to play the role of a family therapist or conduct a family therapy session. Rather, the goal is to help the couple ask their families for support.
- Act as a facilitator or moderator. For example, you should set the agenda, so the couple is able to start the meeting with a clear statement or request. This will help focus the discussion.

- If the couple feels that their families are not supporting their relationship, they may want to say something about how they want to work together to be good parents and hope they can rely on their families to support their efforts.
- If the potential for conflict is high, let the family know that you will give the "time-out" sign if you want someone to stop talking, and that you will interrupt when the topic is veering in a direction of blame or accusations.
- Assure the whole family that everyone will have the opportunity to talk during the meeting and that your job is to make sure this happens.
- At the end of the meeting, help the family come to some agreement about how they can work together to make sure the baby gets off to a good start. Refocusing on the baby will encourage everyone to join together and set aside personal issues and gripes.
- Wrap up the session by thanking each family member for coming and complimenting them on their contributions.

PART 3: PEER RELATIONSHIPS

Young men and women often complain about their partner's friends. Some feel that their partners spend too much time with friends. Some feel their partners' friends or family are a bad influence. Some common themes are as follows: (a) One partner feels that the other's friends pose a danger to the child because they are using drugs or are gang involved; (b) One partner is jealous or resentful of the other's friends for drawing him or her away from the relationship; and (c) One partner feels threatened by the other's old girlfriends/boyfriends. Although some of the jealousy you hear about may be caused by feelings of insecurity rather than legitimate concerns about faithfulness, it can be useful for couples to discuss setting appropriate boundaries with friends of the opposite sex.

Consider facilitating a discussion about how to reset peer relations now that the couple has a baby on the way. Young mothers and fathers struggle with renegotiating their relationships as they move into the very adult role of parenthood. It is safe to assume that most YPP participants feel deeply torn between having fun with their friends and committing more to the relationship and parenthood. As the counselor, approach this issue in a balanced way. On the one hand, having friends and outside interests, such as sports, school, and hobbies, is important to the emotional and social development of both partners. Becoming a parent requires a dramatic shift in priorities and focus, but it does not necessarily require giving up all social activities. On the other hand, it may be necessary for some young parents to curtail or discontinue youthful behavior, such as delinquency and drug use, which could interfere with their ability to function as a parent. A direct but nonjudgmental discussion of what social activities could negatively affect their child will likely lead to some realignment of peer relations and roles. The role-play activity described in the preceding section could be used to help young men and women practice what they might say to their friends.

Some young expectant fathers resist their partner's requests to set firmer boundaries with their friends because they are not ready to make this change. Many young men base their identities on their peer group; it can take some time for them to fully embrace their roles as fathers and co-parents. Unlike their partner, they do not experience the physical impact of the pregnancy and may not have bonded with the developing fetus. In may be useful to discuss the young father's feelings of being torn between different worlds and their conflicting desires. But be aware that some young mothers can be quite intolerant of any ambivalence about parenting in their partner, often demanding that they demonstrate their undivided and total commitment. Normalizing ambivalence is a first step toward integrating conflicting desires and finding a suitable and stable compromise. The important outcomes of Phase 4 are for parents to better understand why they are stressed by conflicting roles, learn to integrate their roles in order to reduce conflict, and develop an appreciation for the role conflict that the other partner is experiencing.

A Note About Traditional Fatherhood Roles

Many YPP fathers have highly traditional views of a male's role in parenthood. These young men do not want to be directly involved in changing diapers or bathing—especially with daughters—and tend to focus on becoming the primary provider. Unfortunately, young fathers are seldom able to find a job that allows them to fulfill this traditional role. When role expectations are out of sync with reality and not met, the couple is likely to experience stress and strain. These young fathers often benefit from broadening their perspective on fatherhood. You might use the problem-solving strategy outlined in Phase 3 to brainstorm different ways that they could fulfill their role as fathers. This can help the young couple loosen their preconceptions about what it means to be a mother or a father, allowing for a greater degree of role flexibility.

CHAPTER REVIEW

By the end of Phase 4, the couple has begun negotiating their changing roles, needs, and interpersonal boundaries with both family and friends. They may have met with family members to ask for support as they adjust to their new role as parents and/or have engaged in role-play exercises to facilitate discussions on adjusting peer and family relationships. The time has come to review the progress made and look beyond YPP, which is the focus of Phase 5.

9

PHASE 5: SUMMING UP AND LOOKING FORWARD

INTRODUCTION

PHASE 5 COINCIDES WITH THE END OF PREGNANCY and the beginning of parenthood. As young men and women approach the cusp of parenthood, they are understandably nervous and doubtful about their ability to meet the challenge. For many couples, this is a period of turmoil, uncertainty, and great stress. They are excited about the baby coming, but also nervous about their ability to take care of their infant and remain committed to each other. Pregnant teens are often scared about the physical process of childbirth. Because anxiety can lead to conflict, it is not unusual for couples to break up right before or after the delivery. At this point in the program, you should focus on supporting what is stable and secure. It is important to be calm, steady, and reassuring if and when disruptions occur.

The overall goal of Phase 5 is to help young couples summarize their gains and internalize a positive, co-parenting alliance. Doing so will help them feel more in control and more positively connected with each other. Table 9.1 highlights this phase's specific goals and tasks and the additional resources available. Phase 5 typically can be completed in one or two sessions, ideally shortly before the baby's birth. If the baby is born before the couple completes Phase 5, give them time to adjust, and then pick up where the counseling process left off (after checking in with them about their childbirth experience).

Table 9.1 PHASE 5: GOALS, TASKS, AND ADDITIONAL RESOURCES

Goals	Tasks
1. Summarize what the couple has gained from the intervention.	1. Underscore the couple's new interpersonal skills with concrete examples.
2. Help the couple "internalize" their co-parenting alliance and "identify" with the role of co-parent.	2. Explore with the couple potential future challenges.
3. Prepare for YPP "termination." Remind the couple that the counseling sessions will end after Phase 6 is complete.	3. Discuss the need to be aware of and to identify parenting support that the couple might need after the baby arrives.
	4. Discuss what it might mean to the couple for the therapeutic relationship to end.

Additional Resources
Forecasting Summary Worksheet
My Support System Worksheet
Preparation for Parenthood Action Plan Worksheet

GOAL 1: SUMMARIZE PROGRESS MADE IN THE YPP

- **Acknowledge individual progress.** Acknowledge each partner's efforts and accomplishments, using specific examples. For example, if the father has become better able to listen to his partner and can express himself without lapsing into blame or control, it will help him to have this reflected back. Be explicit in telling him you have noticed the progress he has made and provide a concrete example of what you have observed. Hearing this feedback from you will help him feel the weight of his accomplishment.

- **Acknowledge couple's strengths.** Commend the couple for what they have accomplished as a team and link their new interpersonal skills to parenting skills. Focus on and accentuate the positive, even when progress has been slow or erratic, for this helps reinforce the couple's positive co-parenting alliance.

- **Encourage the couple to set aside their struggles.** If they are struggling with feelings of distrust or betrayal, it might be useful to acknowledge that these issues remain a source of stress but also point out that it can be beneficial to set aside difficult issues during times of high stress. Putting them on the back burner can open the door for the couple to come together and focus on their child's birth. Point out that the skills they have developed, like listening and speaking with "I" statements, can help them build trust or heal old wounds…if they give themselves the space to do so.

- **Help the couple see the value of their relationship…no matter what their circumstances.** Remind the couple that their success in working together and supporting each other will help provide their child with a more stable, secure "home" no matter what difficulties they experience. Their *relationship* is their infant's "home," even more so than the apartment or house where they live. Also, remind them that their relationship is important, even if they break up, because working together to take care of their child will influence how their child experiences the world.

GOAL 2: INTERNALIZE A POSITIVE, CO-PARENTING ALLIANCE

Internalizing a constructive co-parenting alliance is a primary goal of Phase 5. But what does this mean? In general, internalization refers to the psychological process of absorbing experiences or relationships or values in the form of psychological constructs or schemas (Wertsch, 1985). Often unconsciously, these constructs function like personal roadmaps, helping to guide our expectations and responses as we approach new or difficult experiences. The process occurs through learning (e.g., assimilating knowledge and understanding) and socialization (e.g., identification).

Our internalizations are not necessarily positive. Some young parents have internalized views of themselves as bad, damaged, and incompetent. If we anticipate that we will fail and that our relationships will be disappointing, we will be more inclined to engage in behaviors that ensure failure and disappointment. One of the universal goals of therapy is to guide the internalization process so that clients develop more positive views of themselves and become more favorably predisposed toward others. Therapy seeks to replace maladaptive internalizations with more useful ones (Geller & Farber, 1993). If all goes well and a couple makes good progress in YPP, the internalization process will likely occur in the following, stepwise fashion.

(1) **Partners internalize the counselor's voice.** It is evident that the internalization has begun when a YPP participant starts making use of what she imagines her counselor might say or do. For example, a young mother might turn

to her partner in the midst of conflict and ask, "What would Amy suggest we do in this situation?" or suggest "Let's try doing that thing that Amy taught us to do when we start getting into this kind of conflict." Although Amy's guidance is not fully internalized into the young mother's self, such events suggest that the process is underway. If Amy's imagined advice is helpful and the process is repeated often enough, the young woman will begin to regard the advice as coming from within—as internal.

The therapeutic alliance—which we have emphasized throughout this book—is intended to facilitate this process. A mark of your success as a counselor will be your client's ability to create a mental image of you as a source of support and guidance during moments of stress or uncertainty. This will more likely occur if you demonstrate that you genuinely care about their well-being, provide useful input, and reinforce your appreciation of their progress and efforts to work together as co-parents. (The suggested exercises later in this chapter can help reinforce this internalization process.)

(2) **Partners see themselves and each other as cooperative co-parents.** The second step is the internalization of the "self" and the "other" as positive co-parents, who each have their child's best interests in their hearts. Couples who complete this step are better able to sustain a positive co-parenting alliance through whatever ups and downs occur in their romantic relationship. As partners go through this step, they will begin to do the following:

- Gain some understanding of what it means to be a positive co-parent.
- Believe in his or her own capacity to be a positive co-parent.
- Believe in his or her partner's capacity to be a positive co-parent. (As addressed earlier, it is possible for a young parent to distrust and dislike her partner romantically yet still believe in his capacity for positive co-parenting.)
- Identify with the role of co-parent.
- Recognize the value of negotiating and compromising.

Identifying oneself as a co-parent might conflict with the alternative identification as a single parent. Young mothers who grew up in mother-headed households may have internalized the idea that mothers have to do it alone and cannot depend on fathers as partners. Single motherhood is stressful, but many mothers would say that it is less stressful than co-parenting with an unreliable, dysfunctional father. For young mothers, the process of internalizing the self as co-parent might involve recognizing that despite the advantages of single parenthood, the advantages of co-parenting are worth the inconvenience of cooperating and negotiating. As the young mother and father begin to identify more strongly with the role of co-parent, they will recognize that putting effort into understanding the other's point of view and "putting up with" his or her tendencies is just part of parenting. This perspective is based in the belief that one's child will ultimately benefit from having a sustained and meaningful relationship with both parents.

(3) **Partners see themselves individually as positive parents.** This final step—internalizing the "self as a positive parent"—will not be complete until after YPP ends. It takes time for young parents to acquire enough experience with

their child to construct a stable positive internal image of "self as parent." Nonetheless, during Phase 5 you can begin to talk with both parents about the unique role they will each play in their child's life based on their personalities and their skills. This helps each partner think about what they can "bring to the table" as parents.

THE ROLE OF ATTACHMENT

The internalization process is affected by our attachment history. Young men and women who are securely attached to their own parents are well positioned to develop positive co-parenting relationships and create a secure environment for their child (Weinfield et al., 2008). Unfortunately, many young parents have grown up in unstable families, are insecurely attached to their own parents, and have developed dysfunctional ways to cope with their anxieties. It has been well established in the research literature that attachment security tends to be transmitted across generations so that securely attached parents are better equipped to raise securely attachment children (Weinfield et al., 2008). This raises the question of whether it is possible to be insecurely attached and provide a child with a secure home environment. The answer is yes, but it is not easy. Attachment-oriented researchers have found that a person who was insecurely attached can become more secure over time if he or she is lucky enough to develop a stable, positive, and close relationship with someone who is securely attached (Levy et al., 2006; Roisman et al., 2002; Simpson et al., 2003). This sore of "achieved" security often occurs with the help of a therapist, clergy, or a natural mentor who works with the insecure person to "separate from" and "let go of" past insecurities by becoming open to more positive relationships. The YPP is too brief to help young parents rework their primary attachments, but the goal of internalizing a positive co-parenting alliance is a step in that direction.

GOAL 3: PREPARE FOR YPP "TERMINATION"

Counseling sessions are designed to come to an end after Phase 6, so part of the counselor's role in Phase 5 is to prepare couples for this transition. As part of planning for this termination of services, you should work with the couple to facilitate the internalization of the positive co-parenting alliance (which you have been working on with the couple to create since they began the program!). The following activities may facilitate the internalization process and help the couple prepare for the birth of their baby.

(1) **Create something tangible to take away.** Help the couple create something concrete that they can hold onto as a sort of keepsake reminder of the work they have done to help provide their baby with a safe, secure foundation. For example, the couple could write a letter or make a video addressed to their unborn child, in which they tell the child what they want to provide as parents. In doing so, you can help focus the discussion on how they will work together to help their child feel loved and nurtured. The point of this exercise is not to create something for the child, but to create something for the parents to help them internalize their YPP experiences.

(2) **Make a plan for coping with expected challenges.** Help the couple identify what they see as the greatest potential challenges after the baby arrives; then

help them develop a plan so that they feel more prepared. For example, they may face decisions about living arrangements and child care. They may need to learn about safe sleep, how to feed an infant, bathe an infant, or change a diaper. You can approach this task as an opportunity to practice new communication skills and get ready for parenthood. There is a "Co-Parenting Planning Worksheet" in the YPP toolbox if you think using a worksheet would help structure or facilitate the discussion. Some couples resist planning for the unknown and this forecasting exercise is difficult. Many adolescents and young adults prefer to take it one day at a time, and in some ways their orientation is adaptive. It can be counterproductive to worry about things that are beyond one's control. However, forethought and planning can help young parents avoid some problems and prepare for other unavoidable ones. For example, not anticipating the need for birth control can result in an unplanned second pregnancy soon after the birth of the first child. Rapid repeat pregnancies and childbirth pose a health risk to the mother, add stress to the couple's relationship, and diminish both parents' abilities to adequately care for either child.

When couples anticipate and prepare for the future, they sometimes gain access to opportunities that might otherwise be lost: Pregnant teens may need to get on a waiting list to be eligible for school-based daycare; some colleges have support funds or scholarships for young parents; the couple may be in need of public housing and the waiting lists are often very long. Working with a couple to anticipate future "wants" and "needs" and develop an action plan will help them achieve some degree of mastery and control over their lives. Much of parenting involves (a) anticipating problems and avoiding them, and (b) anticipating opportunities and taking advantage of them. Forecasting the future is not intended to induce anxiety at a time when anxiety is running high already. The process can be handled in a way that is empowering rather than anxiety provoking.

Developing a parenting plan is especially important for young couples who still lack the skills to provide their infant with a safe, secure environment. For these young couples, the plan might focus on identifying additional services and resources. If you have serious concerns about a couple's readiness for parenthood, determine if the young mother has access to one of many state and federally funded home visitation programs, such as the Nurse Family Partnership program (www.nursefamilypartnership.org) or a parenting program designed for at-risk parents, such the Triple P-Positive Parenting Program (www.triplep.net).

(3) **Revisit the goals/strengths worksheet.** Add to, or fill in again, the sheet that you and the couple completed during Phase 1 of YPP. Discuss any goals that have changed, as a way to take stock of the couple's growth over the weeks or months of YPP participation. Even if the relationship between the couple is more strained than when they began the program—perhaps they broke up—it is still possible to take stock of what they have learned and what they are doing well.

AFTER THE BABY IS BORN

Finally, we strongly advise that you visit the couple in the hospital following childbirth to check-in and provide support (if this is allowed within the context of your practice). Meeting with a couple shortly after childbirth and while they are still in the hospital can be a powerful bonding experience that can contribute to them feeling cared for and appreciated by you. Ask first if they are OK with a brief visit—you just want to say hello and meet their baby. Couples are usually very open to having their YPP counselors (and care coordinators) visit them in the hospital. If your clinic provides them, bring a small gift of baby supplies such as baby blankets, diapers, and binkies. During the visit, let the couple know that you will give them some time and space to adjust before you follow up to schedule the final YPP meetings. Remind them that they may contact you any time in the meantime.

CHAPTER REVIEW

The following tasks should be accomplished by the end of Phase 5:

- The counselor and couple have summarized what the couple has gained from the intervention.
- The couple can identify future resources for family support and parenting.

The end of Phase 5 marks the beginning of a hiatus in the YPP program as the young couple prepares for childbirth and adjusts to parenthood. It can feel strange to step back at the moment when the couple feels most nervous; but if the YPP program has been successful, the couple will have internalized your helpful voice and begun to see themselves as competent. This break in counseling is a step toward wrapping up the program at the end of Phase 6. Given that they are just beginning a new phase in their lives, it is unlikely that the couple will experience a true sense of completion. However, it is possible to celebrate the marking of a major milestone. Always end with an acknowledgment of their effort and progress and let them know that they can (and should) call if a crisis emerges. We now turn our attention to Phase 6—the final phase of the program—which provides a few final "booster sessions" to reinforce learned skills and discusses the adjustment to parenthood.

10

PHASE 6: FOLLOW-UP CO-PARENTING SUPPORT

INTRODUCTION

THE GOAL OF PHASE 6 IS TO PROVIDE THE COUPLE with two or three "booster sessions" that (a) reinforce previously learned interpersonal skills related to providing their child with a safe, secure emotional and social environment, and/or (b) support the development of new interpersonal skills needed to address new co-parenting challenges. Follow-up also provides you with the opportunity to assess how the couple is managing as parents and to provide referrals to other programs or services if additional support is needed. This phase typically begins approximately one to two months post childbirth, after the couple has had some time to adjust following the initial shock of parenthood. They will still be in the midst of figuring out their co-parenting roles and responsibilities.

In some cases, a couple may want to meet with you earlier, shortly after childbirth, particularly if there is a crisis in their relationship or if they are having a very difficult time adjusting to parenthood. It is fine to meet with the couple sooner than one month post childbirth. Doing so does not undermine fidelity to the model. However, the goals and tasks of Phase 6 should be considered as *distinct* from crisis management support (which is discussed briefly in Chapter 11). You should try to be clear about whether you are engaging in crisis management or phase-specific YPP counseling, although we recognize that the distinction is not always entirely clear.

WHAT TO EXPECT DURING THE ADJUSTMENT TO PARENTHOOD

Some young couples transition smoothly to parenthood, particularly if they receive a high level of support from their extended families. In some cases, grandmothers take on a great deal of the child care and use the opportunity to mentor their daughter or "daughter-in-law". Some couples will report that all is well and they are doing fine. When this is the case, use the booster-session time to reinforce positive co-parenting skills, such as expressing support and reflective listening; it is not necessary to bring up problems. It can be helpful to revisit and revise the goals they set in Phase 2 or discuss how they could support each other as they pursue their individual goals related to work or school.

Most young parents feel somewhat stressed during the early stages of parenthood. It can be confusing to experience the thrill and joy of parenthood alongside the difficulties of a strained co-parenting relationship, the fatigue of sleepless nights, and the worries about supporting and caring for an infant. The interpersonal and coping skills the couple learned and practiced in YPP are put to the test during the early stages of parenthood, when they face new challenges.

Table 10.1 highlights the goals and tasks for Phase 6. The rest of this chapter details how you might go about meeting these goals. Phase 6 typically involves two to three sessions, which can be scheduled within the space of two or three weeks or spread out over two or three months, depending on the needs of the couple. At

Table 10.1 PHASE 6: GOALS AND TASKS

Goals	Tasks
1. Assist the co-parenting couple in re-assessing and re-prioritizing their needs as co-parents.	1. Explore their co-parenting experiences; what about parenting has been positive, challenging, or surprising?
2. Normalize the experiences of stress and adjustment as new co-parents.	2. Explore what coping strategies/ interpersonal skills worked best for them as a couple.
3. Reinforce positive parenting and co-parenting.	3. Determine (with the couple's input) if they might need new skills to cope with new challenges.
4. Develop new strategies for diminishing or managing conflict in highly stressed couples.	4. Develop (with the couple) a plan for meeting their goals.
5. Re-visit communication around family planning and reproductive health.	5. For high-conflict couples, focus on building positive communication skills or learn to set boundaries and minimize contact with each other.
6. Facilitate the closure of the therapeutic relationship.	

the end of this phase, you should wrap up a couple's participation in the program. In anticipation of this, start preparing the couple for the end of their YPP services at least two weeks in advance.

At this point, parenting is no longer a hypothetical situation. Phase 6 focuses on helping the couple adjust to the reality of having a child and being parents. Consistent with the program's emphasis on interpersonal strengths, it is best to focus on the couple's positive efforts (or intentions) as parents and co-parents. The overarching goal of this phase is to mobilize the couple's previously developed strengths to meet the challenges of parenthood and function well as co-parents. Although this positive focus is intended to be empowering, do not feel compelled to "cheerlead" or ignore problems. You may also help couples address their weaknesses as parents and co-parents and help them develop new skills as needed.

During this phase, most young parents experience changes in their relationships with their partners and their families. They are also adjusting their priorities and struggling to manage new responsibilities. In the two or three months since the end of Phase 5 and the beginning of Phase 6, the couple may have broken up or moved in together. There may be new partners involved with one or both of the co-parents, or they may be married.

The first priority is to assess how the couple has adjusted and set realistic goals for this brief set of follow-up sessions. Ideally, Phase 6 sessions will serve as boosters that support and reinforce the skills and positive intentions explored in earlier phases. However, some couples may be struggling with new issues related to co-parenting and parenting. Remember that YPP is not a parenting intervention; if a couple needs sustained parenting support, refer them to a reputable parenting class or program. There are many infant care classes offered through hospitals and clinics, possibly including the mother's OB/GYN clinic and the infant's pediatric clinic.

In Chapter 12, we will discuss how to conduct a post-YPP assessment to measure how well the program met the needs of your participants and your clinic. (Please jump ahead to Chapter 12 if you are interested in assessing couples at the beginning of Phase 6.) In that chapter, we only suggest target areas that you might consider assessing, such as: (a) intimate partner violence between co-parents; (b) risk for child maltreatment; (c) the quality of the co-parenting alliance; (d) the quality of the parent-child attachment; and (e) postpartum depression. Such measures can be used at the beginning of Phase 6 to gauge how well a couple is adjusting to parenthood and whether there are new areas of concern that require your attention.

It is also possible (and permissable within the model) to develop your own set of questions designed to assess how the couple is adjusting to parenthood at this point. It is often useful to ask broad, open-ended questions, such as, "Since it has been a while, please tell me everything about how you two have been feeling about your relationship since you've become parents? I really want to know what's been good and what's been hard." Open-ended questions can help the couple reconnect with you and tell you their most pressing concerns.

HOW DO YOU DIFFERENTIATE BETWEEN NORMAL POST-BIRTH TURMOIL AND MORE SERIOUS PARENTING CONCERNS?

If you determine that a couple is not experiencing any major problems and seems to be adjusting relatively well, it may be helpful to let them know it. Young parents do not necessarily know if they are doing well or poorly, and it can come as a relief to hear that whatever stresses they are experiencing are normal. They also may be reassured to know that they can use the skills they learned in YPP to help them cope with their stress and strain. However, some couples in YPP report abnormally high levels of stress and distress and may be at heightened risk for (a) a serious mental disorder, (b) intimate partner violence, or (c) child maltreatment. When working with these high-risk couples, it is important to name the problem and acknowledge whatever risks it presents. Most important, express your concern and let the couple know that you will work with them to address the problem, to help them prevent any harm from occurring.

Several new-parent stressors are listed in the following from least to most serious. Even common parenting stressors may impact young parents more severely than older parents because young parents may not have the coping capacities to take care of an infant for hours on end, day after day, or deal with the stress of having to provide financial support for a child. In addition, some young parents are quite isolated, living in poor housing conditions or impoverished neighborhoods with little support from their families (or partners). Be aware of these common issues, but keep in mind that this list is far from complete. Be attentive for stressors that are not listed.

- Worried about juggling responsibilities of parenting with work, school, and other responsibilities (normal concern)
- Increased bickering and arguing between co-parents or with extended family members (normal concern)
- Experiencing decreased quality of sleep, lack of sleep, and exhaustion (normal to moderate concern)
- Feeling down/depressed or feeling "baby blues" (normal for first two weeks; moderate concern after two weeks)
- Experiencing a rollercoaster of emotions; conflicting and simultaneous feelings about parenthood such as happiness, disappointment, fear, worry, and pride (normal to moderate concern)

- Feeling isolated because opportunities for social contact/time with friends and family has diminished (moderate concern)
- Feeling overwhelmed by needing to pay constant attention to the needs and caregiving of the baby (moderate concern)
- Not knowing what the baby wants or needs; having difficulty soothing the baby (moderate concern to serious concern)
- Not knowing what to do to support the baby's physical, emotional, and social development (serious concern)
- Worried about meeting the basic needs of self and baby (serious concern)
- Worried about not bonding with the baby (serious concern)
- Baby has chronic health problems and/or is not gaining weight (serious concern)
- Worried about hurting the baby or oneself (serious concern)

How you help a couple cope with any of these stressors will depend on the quality of their support systems, including their relationship with each other and their extended families. If the couple is managing relatively well and their stressors are less severe, your goal will be to help them use previously developed co-parenting skills to manage their stressors or to introduce new skills (drawing from Phase 3 in Chapter 7). The following is a list of tips for responding to parenting stress and distress.

(1) Normalize the difficulties and encourage the couple by highlighting what they are doing well for themselves, each other, and their infant. Help them give each other positive feedback for their small successes. This will help them feel more appreciated and increase the level of warmth between them.

(2) Next, with the specific stressors in mind, revisit the skills that the couple developed during Phases 3 and 4. Reintroduce exercises that are familiar and seemed to help in the past, such as stress management, reflective listening, or problem solving. This will remind participants that they were able to discuss and work through difficult issues in the past, which will help them feel more competent and capable of dealing with new stressors. For example, if a couple is feeling overwhelmed, you might say: "Let's identify a specific issue that is causing stress or conflict and see what we can do with it now. I am pretty sure that the two of you can use those skills you learned during the pregnancy to deal with this issue. I have seen you work together on some tough things in the past."

(3) If one or both partners are overwhelmed and exhausted, help the couple arrange ways to give each other a break from parenting duties. This might require a return to some of the relationship skills covered in Chapter 7 (expressing needs and providing support) so that either partner is able to ask for some relief, and the other is able to respond positively. Sometimes a break from parenting might involve one partner going out while the other stays with the baby, but sometimes it might be something more basic, like taking a nap or a long shower. Couples who are still romantically together may benefit from taking a break together if they can get a grandparent or a sibling to baby-sit. Introduce the idea that a little respite from parenting and time together (without the baby) can help them maintain a positive attitude about parenting and give them some time to "take care" of their relationship.

(4) Some couples may need to return to Phase 3 to learn new skills. Although it is difficult to dive back into skill building in a short time frame, it is best to get started as soon as possible if you determine that a couple could benefit from it. For example, some couples break up between Phase 5 and 6 and are now feeling very hurt and/or angry. If the hostility between them is intense, it may be prudent to teach the couple how to minimize communication for a while to avoid conflict and stay focused on the well-being of their baby (see Skill 9).

(5) Some couples may benefit from a brief return to Phase 4, to continue the process of re-defining roles and interpersonal boundaries with friends and family. Although extended family members and friends can be an important and natural source of support during the initial months and years of parenting, some young couples may not know how to make use of them. After you have worked with the couple to identify the areas in which they need support (e.g., mentoring, tutoring, transportation, babysitting, knowing how to take care of an infant), help them identify people in their network who could help. Young couples often resist asking for help for many reasons (pride, fear of rejection, embarrassment). You may need to convince them it is worth asking and guide them in how to ask. The most effective way to convince young parents to reach out and ask for help is to stay focused on the well-being of their child. As indicated in Chapter 8, it may be useful to ask extended family members to attend sessions so that you can facilitate a discussion and help the couple find the words to ask for the support they need.

If the couple is experiencing high levels of stress and/or distress and you are concerned about their risk for violence, maltreatment, or mental illness, use these booster sessions to work with them (and the care coordinator) to (a) come to a shared understanding of what additional resources are needed, and (b) make appropriate referrals for services that can assist with the identified stressor/need. This process can be quite difficult because the young couple may be terribly frightened about involving other service providers. Some may worry about getting into trouble with the law or having their baby taken away, and in severe circumstances, you cannot guarantee that this will not happen. But you can educate them that it is far better to seek help before a problem blows up, and you can coach them on how to ask for help in way that increases the likelihood of a supportive response.

COMMON ISSUES TO ADDRESS DURING PHASE 6 FOLLOW-UP

The primary goal of Phase 6 is for the new parents to use the skills they attained thus far to cope with the stressors they now face. It is difficult to script Phase 6, for a myriad of co-parenting and parenting issues may emerge. Although we cannot cover all of them, we can touch upon a few common ones.

1. Equitable Sharing and Dividing of Parenting Responsibilities

New parents often struggle with knowing how to divide and/or share the multitude of responsibilities involved in childcare. Before having a child, most young expectant parents were responsible primarily for themselves; now they are responsible for their child's physical and psychological well-being. Sharing that responsibility with the child's other parent can make the job easier or harder depending on the quality of their relationship.

Often, new parents feel that the arrangement is unfair in one way or another. For instance, many young parents divide responsibilities by following traditional gender roles; the mother attends to day-to-day childcare needs, and the father takes primary responsibility for earning money. Yet both partners usually feel so overwhelmed by their own responsibilities that they are unable to see or appreciate the other's contributions. A dialogue about the current division of labor may increase each parent's appreciation for each other's efforts and lead to a fruitful discussion about how they might share or divide more of their responsibilities. For example, some couples may realize that they are *both* trying to put the baby to sleep every night when it is more easily done by *one* parent (e.g., divide tasks); or they may realize that they both could be working, which would help with their financial difficulties (e.g., share the breadwinner role). Regular communication between partners about how they are experiencing their new responsibilities may involve the use of reflective listening skills (Chapter 7, Skill 2) and the positive expression of feelings/needs (Chapter 7, Skill 1).

When working with couples on the pragmatics (or fairness) of co-parenting, attend to each partner's personal, family, and cultural beliefs and values that inform or guide the division of responsibilities along gender lines. Remember that your goal is *not* for the couple to create an equitable division of responsibility that seems fair or appropriate to *you*. Rather, your goal is to help them work together to find a solution that feels right for *them* based on their circumstances and beliefs.

One way to help the couple address the division of labor is to ask both partners to discuss the other's strengths and how those strengths might contribute to meeting the baby's needs and their needs as a co-parenting couple. For instance, if the mother is identified as particularly patient and easygoing, she might be best equipped to soothe the baby when he or she is upset. If the father is a natural organizer, he might be the one to keep track of the baby's doctor's appointments and medical records. Referring back to the individual strengths (identified during Phase 2) can help set the stage for exploring links between each partner's natural strengths and the goal of working together as parents.

Another way to approach the issue of shared parenting is to focus on developing new parenting skills. For example, a young mother may be angry because her partner does not help with basic childcare. The young father may want to be helpful but is afraid or uncomfortable helping with basic childcare (or being alone with the baby). He is afraid he will do something wrong or do something that hurts the baby. Similarly, the mother may want to get a job and help earn money, but she cannot count on the father to help with childcare. In this situation, the father will need to learn about babies and childcare in order to increase his capacity for shared responsibilities. If they are able to do this, then the young mother may also be able to broaden the range of her parenting responsibilities.

2. Father Disengagement

One of the broad goals of the YPP (and this guide) is to keep fathers positively engaged in childrearing after a breakup has occurred. Based on our experience over the years, there are three primary reasons that fathers disengage from the co-parenting relationship and then from their children. First, the disappointment and strife between the parents becomes so difficult that one partner cannot tolerate it and cuts off contact. Second, the father has serious psychological problems that interfere with his ability to connect with his child or function as a responsible father. Third, the father feels inadequate because he does not know how to be a good co-parent or find an effective way to contribute to the well-being of his partner and child. We will explore each of these reasons for disengagement in more depth in the sections that follow.

When Disappointment and Strife Become too Difficult to Manage

Many of the exercises in Phase 3 of this guide are designed to reduce conflict and increase connection and understanding in the co-parenting relationship. This is particularly important, and more difficult, in the weeks and months after a couple has broken up. We know that when the relationship between co-parents is very stressful, a young mother may decide that the energy required to deal with the child's father is not worth the benefit of having him around. Similarly, the father may become motivated to detach in order to avoid contact and conflict with his ex-partner. For couples that have broken up, it will be important for you (together with them) to make a strategic decision; do you work with the couple to move past their disappointment and anger to re-connect as nonromantic co-parents, bridging their current divide through communication and understanding? Or do you forge a detente-like truce by helping them find ways to share parenting with minimal contact and communication in order to diminish conflict and stress? Couples who cannot communicate effectively on their own will likely appreciate having you serve as a sort of "referee" to help them work out some rules for managing their communications and clarifying their roles. Have specific agreements around hot topics (e.g., drop off and pick up) can help to reduce the intensity and frequency of future conflicts.

When a Father Has Serious Psychological Problems

Fathers who have a mental illness—such as substance dependence or a personality disorder—are often unable to sustain healthy relationships. They often disengage and disappear either because the conflict associated with the psychological problem becomes unmanageable or because they become too absorbed in meeting their own needs to attend to the needs of others. Young fathers with psychological problems are often unwilling to follow up on referrals for individual counseling, but sometimes the threat of losing contact with their child becomes a motivating factor for getting treatment or changing their behavior. It is appropriate to make a referral for individual counseling when it becomes apparent that either partner's individual psychopathology is interfering with co-parenting or parenting, as the YPP is not designed to address individual psychological disorders.

When a Father Feels Inadequate

Booster sessions are a particularly good time to address a father who disengages because he feels inadequate. Many young men have very narrow ideas about how they are supposed to contribute as fathers; these men typically focus on financially supporting their child and their partner. When they are unable to fulfill the "breadwinner" role, some feel badly about themselves and begin to disengage. Some become bitter and resentful and these feelings may spill into their relationships with their partner or the baby.

Of course, there are some things that a young man can do to increase his chances of finding a good job, such as staying in school and staying out of trouble with the law. Unfortunately, many young fathers have already dropped out of school and are in some sort of trouble. Many are racial and ethnic minorities who either are not eligible for work because they are undocumented immigrants or are being discriminated against by potential employers because they are persons of color. To make matters worse, when the economy is poor, jobs for young men (young, minority men in particular) dry up first. We have little control over many of these stressors. So what is a counselor to do?

The good news is that a lot can be done to help young fathers (and their partners) broaden their understanding of what is means to be a good father. One approach is to engage the couple in brainstorming sessions that expand the definition and characteristics of good fathering. When fathers use phrases such as "being there," it is important to ask what that means in a more concrete way. Next, get even more specific: Ask the young man what he could do this week that might help him feel better about his contribution as a father. Answers might include taking care of the baby while his partner goes out or gets some rest. They might also include taking clear steps to distance himself from a troubled past, getting into treatment for a substance abuse problem, or re-enrolling in school so that he can get a better job in the future. The important message is this: Young fathers can contribute to the well-being of their partners and children in many ways that are valuable and rewarding.

3. Parenting Issues

You may observe parenting behavior that concerns you and indicates that the couple needs some help with the basics of parenting. For example, a parent may not know how to read their infant's cues as to whether she or he is tired, hungry, or having digestive problems. The ability to read infant behavior requires some mix of interpersonal acuity, experience, and knowledge that many young parents have not yet developed. Other parenting basics that many young parents often need help with include: (a) how to feed their infant; (b) what to feed their infant; (c) how to ensure their infant is sleeping in a safe environment; (d) knowing when to take their infant to the doctor, including learning how to spot possible signs of sickness (such as dehydration and respiratory distress).

It may be difficult to know how to approach your YPP participant when you witness him or her engaging in parenting behavior that is potentially harmful or unhealthy. You might feel awkward offering advice, especially if it contains an element of correction. You might worry that the young parent will feel judged or criticized by you; most young parents are insecure about their parenting abilities and you do not want to undermine their confidence. To complicate things, you may not have the expertise to provide advice. Perhaps you just know when a decision—like filling a bottle with soda or putting the baby to sleep face down—presents a problem.

If you have the knowledge and skill to help with "on the spot" parent education, you should first ask the couple whether they would be open to being coached a bit on infant development and childcare. If you give the couple this choice, then it is less likely that any subsequent feedback you provide will feel intrusive or judgmental. Some young parents are quite defensive about their parenting because everyone seems to want to tell them what they should or should not be doing, or because they are filled with self-doubt about their abilities and want to prove that they can handle things on their own. Nonetheless, few are likely to say, "No thanks." Remember that adolescents and young adults want to do things independently of adult input. You will need to rely on the strength of the relationship that you have developed with the couple to find an approach that lowers their defenses and allows them to be open to learning.

On-the-spot coaching might suffice for some couples. For those who require more intensive parenting instruction and coaching, you will need to determine available parenting resources and assist in making the appropriate referrals. Alternatively, you may want to find a way to work through the infant's pediatrician or through the grandparents, especially if they are skilled in parenting and willing to help

The sort of parenting issues that we have discussed so far fall within the realm of inexperienced or poor parenting that does not require reporting to child protective services, but should not be overlooked or ignored. If a parent handles the child roughly or exposes the child to a chaotic environment in which people are drunk or using drugs, it makes sense to intervene more directly. You may witness or hear about parent behavior that is a red flag for neglect, endangerment, or abuse. If you believe that the child is in danger, you are required by law to make a report. In these cases, you should tell the father or mother that you are filing a report, explaining exactly why the behavior is of concern and what they can do to accomplish their goal in another way. This sort of discussion should always be presented as supportively as possible. In Chapter 11, we will discuss the issue of child abuse reporting in more detail.

4. Decreased Relationship Satisfaction

Researchers have documented that couples commonly experience decreased relationship satisfaction in the weeks and months following childbirth (Belsky & Pensky, 1988; Cowan & Cowan, 1988). The reasons seem obvious, given all that we have said up to this point. After the baby arrives, young mothers and fathers have little time for themselves and little time for each other. They have less sex, they go out less, they talk less, and they are exhausted. It makes perfect sense that their relationship suffers. Nonetheless, young couples may not see this so clearly and may benefit from knowing that their feelings of disappointment—feeling like something has been lost between them—is very common. This may not bring much comfort, but it may help them to know that as they adjust to parenthood their sense of loss and disappointment will pass. Moreover, there are concrete things they can do to help rejuvenate their connection, like find a babysitter so that they can spend time together—just the two of them.

5. "Baby Blues" or Postpartum Depression

Soon after childbirth, many new mothers experience the "baby blues." A woman may feel sad and irritable. She may worry about how well she is connecting with the baby or feel mentally and physically exhausted in a way that alarms her. These sorts of symptoms are experienced by many women in the first few days after childbirth and usually pass within a few more days (Howell & Yonkers, 2006). Although the experience can be disconcerting for the mother and father (*I am supposed to feel happy!*), they usually do not interfere with day-to-day functioning or the infant's health. However, in some cases the "baby blues" develop into postpartum depression, which is more intense and enduring. Postpartum depression is similar to major depressive disorder (Nydegger, 2006; Stewart et al., 2003), and is thought to be triggered by a dramatic shift in hormones combined with lack of sleep and increased stress. Women experiencing postpartum depression may report symptoms such as:

- Feeling overwhelmed and unable to keep up with life's demands
- Feeling sad or miserable
- Not looking forward to things with enjoyment
- Feeling inexplicably anxious or worried
- Blaming self when things go wrong
- Feeling inexplicably scared or panicky
- Being so unhappy that it is difficult to sleep
- Crying frequently
- Not being able to find humor in funny situations
- Having thoughts of self-harm or suicide

If a mother is experiencing several of these symptoms much of the time and the feelings negatively impact her ability to function and care for herself and/ or the baby, she is likely depressed and in need of treatment. It is not the role of the YPP counselor to diagnose or treat the suspected postpartum depression. However, the counselor may be in a unique position to (a) recognize postpartum depression, (b) educate the young woman and her support network (parents, guardians, partner) about postpartum depression, and (c) assist her in seeking medical and/or psychological attention (Gjerdergin & Yawn, 2007). Young women who have a history of depression are prone to postpartum depression. Recent evidence suggests that fathers may also be susceptible to postpartum depression and experience similar symptoms. It is thought that the trigger for postpartum paternal depression is the stress of parenting (including feelings of inadequacy) in combination with decreased relationship satisfaction, which is common in couples during the months following childbirth (Paulson & Bazemore, 2010).

6. Family Planning and Reproductive Health

Phase 6 provides a timely opportunity to re-visit issues of reproductive health and family planning. You may have discussed family planning with the couple during Phase 3 and can simply check in with them about their current practices and whether they have questions or concerns. You are encouraged to take the approach that was outlined in Phase 3 and focus the discussion on making a thoughtful decision about when, or if, the couple wants to have another child.

For couples who have remained in a romantic relationship with each other, this conversation can reinforce the importance of positive communication and joint decision making about when and how they will choose to protect themselves from unintended pregnancies and sexually transmitted infections. But what if the couple has broken up and one or both have become romantically and/ or sexually involved with other partners? Do you still have this discussion? We know that when young fathers have multiple children with multiple women, it has the effect of diminishing their involvement with some, if not all, of their children. Given the relatively high prevalence rate of multi-partner parenting among young adults, it makes sense to discuss family planning even if the couple is not together.

WRAP UP

It is likely that you will feel a special connection with every YPP couple that makes it all the way through Phase 6. You will have gone through a great deal together and hopefully you will have witnessed tremendous growth. Conversely, most YPP couples will feel a special connection to you and will likely be grateful for your guidance and care. It is not unusual for the last session to be an emotional, bittersweet experience. Still, it is important to wrap things up and bring the process to a close, even if both you and the couple feel there is more work to be done.

In this final session, it is important to be open and expressive about what you liked about working with them, explicit about the growth you have witnessed, and congratulatory about their successes—individually and as a couple. If there have been setbacks and failures, you can acknowledge these and let them know that you were glad to have helped them through their difficulties. As a final gesture intended to underscore the couple's hard work and accomplishment, YPP presents both partners with certificates of achievement (these are easy to design and purchase online). This often means much more to young couples than one might suppose, particularly if they have not completed or achieved much in their lives.

COMMON THERAPEUTIC ISSUES

11

Amy Kirby and the Young Parenthood Program Team

INTRODUCTION

YOU ARE NOW FAMILIAR WITH THE THEORETICAL AND PRACTICAL ASPECTS of counseling young, expectant co-parents through the Young Parenthood Program. You have studied the six phases of the YPP and are ready (or have begun) to engage and work with the couples. You may have already discovered that each co-parenting relationship is unique and requires you to be flexible, open, and responsive. This diversity keeps the work of YPP challenging and rewarding. Although it is important to treat each couple as unique, being aware of common themes and issues among young couples will help you be efficient in your YPP work.

This chapter presents six common therapeutic issues, themes, and dynamics that you will face when working with young co-parenting couples. Although we do not advocate using a "one-size-fits-all" approach, we believe in drawing upon the collective wisdom and experiences of others who have worked with young couples. It is worthwhile to consider how the particularities of each couple relate to general patterns of functioning common to young parents; it can be very useful when deciding how to respond to difficult interpersonal issues such as infidelity or violence. We believe that YPP counselors will be most successful when they blend their personal approach to counseling with established best practices.

HELPING COUPLES DEFINE THEIR RELATIONSHIP OR COPE WITH THEIR UNCERTAINTY

One of the interesting and perplexing things about working with young couples is that some do not know if they are a couple and some change their minds daily about their relationship status. Some young couples easily define their relationship in simple terms, such as boyfriend/girlfriend or fiancés. Others use terms that are more open to interpretation, such as "baby mama," "baby daddy," or "friends with benefits." Defining the relationship is complicated ("Are we together or not?") and can be the source of significant tension and distress (Guzmann et al., 2009). Partners often have different ideas about their relationship status, what they currently want from it, and what they hope will happen in the future. Because they are young, it is not unusual (or abnormal) for their thoughts and feelings to change from week to week. For some couples, it may be therapeutic to clarify that things are still up in the air and help them live with that uncertainty. From the beginning of YPP, you should track how both partners define the relationship and how their individual definitions and expectations impact the development of their co-parenting alliance. Create an open forum about this topic. Do not pressure them to define their relationship or come to an agreement about what it is or what it should be. You may introduce the idea that relationships continually evolve and change over time and that this is normal for young couples (Furman & Hand, 2008).

It may be important for each partner to specify his or her personal needs and wishes about the relationship. If one partner wants to be in a committed relationship, whereas the other wants to have a sexual relationship with the ability to date others, this can lead to significant conflict and distress. In such situations it can be useful to help both partners clarify their intentions, wishes, and boundaries. For example, one partner may need to say something like:

> I would really like to be in a committed relationship with you and I know you are not ready for that. I understand you are trying to make up your mind but in the meantime, I need to protect myself from getting hurt…so we cannot act like we are boyfriend/girlfriend if you are not committed to being in an exclusive relationship.

That said, not all couples need this sort of clarity. Some may be content with a high level of uncertainty about their relationship status. If that is the case, it is counterproductive to push the goal of clarifying boundaries. Other expectant parents cannot imagine being in a co-parenting relationship that does not also involve being in a romantic relationship. In their minds, the co-parenting and romantic relationships are intertwined and hard to separate. From the beginning of YPP, you should be clear with young couples that your work with them is about their co-parenting relationship regardless of what happens to their romantic relationship.

As clear as you may be about this distinction, some couples who break up will have a very difficult time differentiating between the co-parenting and romantic relationship. Some may feel that losing their romantic connection is equivalent to failing as a parent, whereas others will be relieved to hear (from you) that despite their uncertainty about what will happen between them as romantic partners, they can still work toward having a positive co-parenting relationship. For many couples this idea—that the romantic relationship and co-parenting relationship are distinct—might be the most therapeutic learning point of their involvement in YPP. With this in mind, you should emphasize that having a positive co-parenting relationship is not dependent on being together or even liking each other. If the status of their romantic relationship changes throughout the course of YPP (which is common), it may be important for you to reassure them that they are still capable of working together as co-parents.

COPING WITH INFIDELITY AND DISTRUST

Infidelity, although common among adolescents and young adult couples, almost always upsets both partners and is highly disruptive to their romantic relationship (Williams & Hickle, 2011). As discussed earlier, adolescent couples are not expected to make long-term commitments to romantic partners. In fact, infidelity is somewhat normative in the sense that adolescents often move from one relationship to the next without a breath between. The drama involved in getting together and then breaking up serves a developmental purpose; it helps adolescents learn what they want from their intimate relations. Nonetheless, when break-ups include infidelity, it can be tremendously painful and you should be prepared to help YPP participants cope with their intense feelings of betrayal, anger, and loss.

When infidelity occurs between adolescents or young adult romantic partners, the typical and perhaps "normal" response is to break up and move on.

When couples are having a child (or have a child), infidelity presents a very different sort of problem.[1] Finding a way to deal with infidelity is one of the most difficult challenges in YPP counseling because it is often accompanied by a profound sense of hurt and betrayal. Your role is to help them discuss their feelings constructively and help them find a way to move forward with their relationship as co-parents.

When counselors work through infidelity with adult married couples, they often explore the underlying causes and/or meanings of the infidelity, including each partner's individual contribution to the breakdown in trust and intimacy. However, this approach is unlikely to help YPP couples. It is best to keep it simple and remain focused on: (a) how to talk about the infidelity in way that does not make things worse, using skills outlined in Phase 3; (b) how the infidelity has affected their relationship and how they define it; and (c) how to heal the tear in their relationship and remain focused on their child. Even if you have a strong emotional reaction to finding out about the infidelity, remain neutral and use the skills outlined in Chapter 7 to support mutual listening and help diffuse overtly hostile interactions.

Snyder, Baucom, and Gordon (2013) have developed a practical, three-stage model of addressing infidelity with a couple that can be adapted for use with YPP couples. The stages are as follows.

Stage 1: Dealing with the Initial Impact

After it is revealed (or suspected) that infidelity has occurred, ask each young co-parent to express his or her feelings and manage his or her behavior by using the skills outlined in Phase 3. You may need to help them set limits on when and how they talk about the infidelity (so that they are not talking about it all the time), support the appropriate expression of needs and feelings, and help the couple use positive problem-solving skills as they begin to discuss what to do next, particularly if one or both partners wants to separate or break up. Often, the feelings are so raw that couples do not know how to talk about it without having huge blow-ups. You can help structure the discussion in the following way:

> "Often, when there has been cheating in a relationship, that cheating is always there in the back of each person's mind, even if they are not talking about it. It can be helpful for some couples to 'get it out there' so they can figure out a way to move on, whether that means moving on as a couple or as co-parents. I can help the two of you work through this one step at a time, in a way that is respectful and safe for each of you."

---

[1] The YPP is best suited to couples in which the male partner is thought to be the father. Sometimes this is not a certainty and questions of infidelity and paternity emerge as a major issue during the program. When this occurs, it is best to advise that the couple undergo a paternity test (when the child is born) because the uncertainty causes too much anxiety and conflict. Some couples remain together even after finding out that someone else is the father, but most young men quickly disengage if the paternity test is negative. Paternity questions usually emerge when there are persistent concerns about infidelity and trust. If a young man discovers that he is not the father of the baby, you should offer to help both partners express their feelings. The boyfriend typically feels betrayed, angry, and distraught about "losing" both his partner and his baby. The mother often feels very ashamed and upset about the impending loss of her partner. It is important to help the couple identify options for how to handle this situation.

Stage 2: Exploring Context and Finding Meaning

Once you are able to set up an emotionally safe context for a dialogue, you can help the couple discuss what the infidelity means for each of them and their relationship. Often, the couple's basic question at this stage will be, "Is the romantic relationship over?" Walk the couple through the steps of effective problem solving by helping them brainstorm several options for dealing with the infidelity, identifying the pros and cons of those options, finding something they can agree on, and identifying next steps. This is obviously easier said than done, and it may take weeks or months for a couple to agree on a solution. Nonetheless, your pragmatic approach will help them get through their intense emotional upheaval. Whether or not the romantic relationship is over, the couple will benefit from talking about how to forgive and build trust as co-parents. It may help to inject some hope by framing their decision in terms of their health as a couple and as co-parents. Even if you doubt the outcome of their decisions, you can still help them feel positively about the decision-making process.

Stage 3: Moving on

The couple may need your guidance as they try to figure out how to move forward as co-parents. Whether they break up or remain together, couples will wonder, "Where do we go from here? How do we do this?" Forgiveness is an important part of the integrative model (Snyder et al., 2013), in which it is suggested that forgiveness can occur without reconciliation. This model promotes a realistic approach to forgiveness; rather than emphasize total forgiveness, it helps couples set limits on how much they allow negative feelings to define or dominate their relationship. That said, this phase might include coaching the unfaithful partner on how to listen and respond in a non-defensive way to the hurt feelings of his or her partner, which may linger for a long time. You may also want to coach the "hurt" partner on expressing his or her feelings about being betrayed without being belligerent or punitive. There are several models available to help couples work through the steps of forgiveness and rebuilding trust after infidelity (Gottman, 2011; McCullough, 2001). Although it is beyond the scope of this chapter to outline these models, helping couples move on requires a high level of skill and it is worth the time to consult the clinical literature.

Case Examples

In the following section are three case examples of couples facing the issue of infidelity under different interpersonal circumstances, followed by YPP counselors' responses.

Couple 1: Past Infidelity—James and Alicia

James and Alicia have been together off-and-on for almost two years. Alicia is three months into her pregnancy. Part of the reason for the instability in their relationship is Alicia's infidelity. During one of the counseling sessions, James says that Alicia has cheated on him three times and he is worried that she will do it again. James states that he saw some numbers that he did not recognize on her cell phone. Alicia claims that she has only cheated twice, and those were "one-time deals," which were not serious, and the numbers on her phone were just people from school. She says she has been faithful for the past six months, and that she is very committed to James and the baby. Despite Alicia's attempts to reassure James, their conversation becomes increasingly hostile as she tries to defend herself while he cites more evidence supporting his suspicions.

Couple 2: Present Infidelity—Carlos and Elena

Carlos and Elena miss their scheduled appointment with their counselor. Later, Elena calls the counselor crying and says that Carlos has been cheating on her with a girl she thought was her friend. Elena says her relationship with Carlos is over and that she never should have trusted him in the first place. She says she does not want to come to the counseling sessions any more because she "never wants to see Carlos again!"

Couple 3: Suspicions—Phil and Erin

Phil and Erin have been together for seven months. Phil claims that he has never cheated on Erin, and never would. Erin, however, is constantly accusing him of cheating. For example, she says he was supposed to be home from work at 6:00, and did not get home until 8:00. Phil says he had to work overtime and promised he is not cheating. When they are out together, Erin sometimes yells at Phil for supposedly looking at other girls. Phil says he usually does not even notice other girls. These types of interactions occur regularly until one day Phil snaps, "Maybe I should cheat on you so it will be real!"

These three couples present different sets of challenges, but share the common element of mistrust in the relationship. In James and Alicia's case, the mistrust is grounded in past infidelity that has not been resolved. For Carlos and Elena, the present situation has damaged their trust in one another and feelings are still very raw. For Erin and Phil, there is a fundamental mistrust even though it is possible that no one has been cheating. As with Carlos and Elena, infidelity may undermine a couple's willingness to participate in YPP. Helping the couple come back to the table will be difficult but potentially crucial to salvaging the co-parenting relationship.

Therapeutic Applications

Couple 1: James and Alicia—Applying the Three-Stage Model

If you were working with Alicia and James, you might apply the three-stage model to address the infidelity.

Stage 1: Dealing with the Initial Impact You might help Alicia to take responsibility for her behavior (and apologize for the hurt it has caused) by directly addressing James's feelings of hurt and distrust. Because this couple has chosen to remain together, James will likely need a heavy dose of reassurance and time before he can trust Alicia again. It may be useful for you to acknowledge common emotional reactions to infidelity, such as wanting to retaliate, to increase controlling behavior, or to engage in ongoing hostility. While normalizing these reactions, point out alternative ways of coping, such as asking for reassurance (building trust) and learning to forgive.

Stage 2: Exploring Context and Finding Meaning Begin by explaining to James and Alicia that how they cope with infidelity will affect their goals as co-parents. If they were married adults, you might explore longstanding marital problems, such as a lack of sexual intimacy or having grown apart. Because they are so young, it is more appropriate to acknowledge that although cheating is common in couples their age, they will need to decide for themselves, as individuals and as a couple, what sort of relationship they desire. This incident can lead to a conversation about how to create stability, trust, and intimacy. You can use the reflective listening exercise to help James and Alicia discuss how they would like to improve their relationship. It may also be helpful for James to tell Alicia what she can do to help him feel more trusting.

Stage 3: Moving On Throughout the process of exploring the impact of infidelity on their relationship, it is important for you to commend Alicia and James (and couples like them) for hanging in there as co-parents and remaining committed to their child despite significant bumps in their romantic relationship. You can help them choose how they want their relationship to move forward and then outline specific steps to move in that direction. It will be important for both partners to state whether they want to rebuild trust, recognizing that doing so will require different things from each of them. For Alicia it might mean responding to James's hurt feeling and suspiciousness with understanding and without defensiveness; for James it might mean choosing to accept Alicia's words of reassurance and recognizing that he cannot control her behavior…only his own. As they move through the program, help the couple find concrete ways to build trust through communication and acts of compassion.

Couple 2: Carlos and Elena—Modifying the Three-Stage Model
With Carlos and Elena, the primary concern is how to get them in for a session together, which they are likely to resist. You may need to meet with each of them individually to talk about the value in having a joint session and to figure out how to make it emotionally safe. Once the couple is together, you should address the fact that their relationship may have changed, but that they will always be parents together. You should be upfront about the fact that you are not going to try to get them back together or take sides. The first step will be to help them disentangle their former romantic relationship from their future co-parenting relationship.

You can use the three-stage model to help the couple work through this. If the couple clearly wants their romantic relationship to end, you may not need to spend much time in stage 2. If this is the case, spend the bulk of your time with them marking the end of their relationship and providing a safe context to express feelings of anger, betrayal, regret, loss, and so on. If this proves to be too difficult, consider shifting to problem solving and discussing the practical issues of how to communicate about the child.

Be open to the possibility that Elena and Carlos could change their minds about what they want. It is possible that once you start helping them break up, they will get back together, which will require you to recalibrate your approach. Because young couples are quick to break up and quick to forgive, you should maintain a neutral and nonjudgmental stance regarding such decisions. Any opportunity to continue to model and encourage positive interactions and healthy communication will benefit the couple, even if they do not stay together in the long run.

Couple 3: Phil and Erin—Instead of the Three-Stage Model
When one partner suspects that the other is cheating, it is easy for counselors to get caught up in sifting through the evidence. Counseling should not become an investigation and it is not your job to help determine a partner's innocence or

guilt. Instead, focus on helping the suspicious partner discuss his or her anxieties; help the suspected partner respond to those anxieties; and help the couple come up with a plan for moving past the distrust. In the case of Phil and Erin, there may be unresolved feelings from previous relationships or family issues that feed into Erin's suspicions. Perhaps anxiety about being pregnant and fears about losing Phil amplify her suspicions. Understanding Erin's anxiety can help Phil take the accusations less personally. With some guidance, he may be more effective in reassuring her. With support, Erin can communicate her feelings in a way that is less attacking or accusatory. If Phil is actually cheating, it will eventually emerge; in the meantime it is best to presume innocence.

PARENTHOOD AND THE CHALLENGE OF IDENTITY DEVELOPMENT

One of the major developmental tasks of adolescence is to develop a "useful" identity, defined as a coherent and continuous sense of oneself and a relatively secure sense of belonging within a social setting. Achieving this sort of identity will help a young man or woman navigate his or her way into adulthood without drifting too far from what is personally most important and meaningful. A strong sense of identity is like an interpersonal anchor: It helps stabilize relationships (Harter, 1990; Kroger, 2012).

Achieving a solid but flexible and adaptive identity can be a tremendous challenge for some adolescents, particularly those who live in a context in which resources and opportunities are scarce and the future looks bleak for many adults. In addition, becoming a parent changes the way most people see themselves, their roles, and their responsibilities. For many YPP couples, the compounded challenges can seem overwhelming. Given their stage of life, expectant adolescents or young adults are constructing their identity as parents before they have a solid sense of their identity in any other realm of experience (Shade, Kools, Weiss, & Pinderhughes, 2011). "Normally" developing adolescents are expected to be moody, impulsive, fickle, and self-absorbed because these moods are regarded as part of the developmental process. When young people become parents, these otherwise "normal" behaviors that go hand-in-hand with identity development are often viewed as irresponsible and selfish.

Identity development tends to be easier for young mothers than for young fathers. This is not to say it is easy or less significant for them. However, the roles and responsibilities of mothers tend to be more clearly defined and accessible in our society, regardless of age or marital status. Most young women have more parenting support available, provided by their families, their prenatal clinic, their schools, and so on. When a woman becomes pregnant, friends, family, and colleagues tend to rally around to support the adjustment, particularly if she is having her first child.

Young fathers have fewer supports in place. The world does not rally for young fathers as it does for mothers. Becoming a father requires developing a new identity (e.g., "I am a father and have a child who depends on me for . . ."). A number of factors will influence how a young man constructs his identity as a father. These include his maturity, job security, education, family support, cultural and societal expectations regarding fatherhood, and the availability of appropriate role models. When a young man does not have access to the tools he needs to be a good father, such as the education he needs to obtain a good job or the skills to care for an infant, he will doubt his ability to fulfill the "breadwinner" role (Frewin, Tuffin, & Rouch, 2007; Kiselica, 2012; Tuffin, Rouch, & Frewin, 2010).

Some young men have a very difficult time accepting fatherhood and the responsibility for their child's well-being. It is overwhelming for them and they may cope by trying to avoid reality. They might keep their distance or act in ways that create distance, get into conflicts with their partner, or get into trouble with the law. When this happens, everybody loses: The mother loses a co-parenting partner, the child loses his or her father, and the father suffers a tremendous loss of self-esteem. A young man's self-doubts about fatherhood can lead him to give up or reject the fatherhood role. If a young man does not feel ready for fatherhood and is not receiving the support he needs to get ready, his anxiety can be overpowering and his sense of failure can be profound and demoralizing.

When a young father is unable or unwilling to step into the fatherhood role, the co-parenting relationship can quickly deteriorate, making it even more difficult for the young father to identify with this role (Henley & Pasley, 2005; Kiselica, 2012; Olmstead, Furtis, & Pasley, 2009; Tuffin, Rouch, & Frewin, 2010). For these reasons, it may be important for you to use YPP sessions to help a young man begin to formulate (and feel comfortable with) his identity as a father. Most young fathers receive little support in the development of their identity as a father, and it may be useful to spend some time helping him talk with his partner about what being a father means to him—even if this discussion feels a bit awkward and uncertain. As their counselor, you can help the young father define his role in a way that feels less daunting and more reachable.

It is our experience that most young men want be involved in childrearing and become positive role models for their children, but often do not know how to accomplish that goal (Parra-Cardona, Wampler, & Sharp, 2006). For many young men, the day-to-day tasks of childcare (e.g., diaper changing, feeding, bathing, holding, comforting, teaching) feel foreign and uncomfortable, particularly if they do not live with their child. Most young men were not taught caregiving skills and do not know where to begin when it comes to caring for an infant or child. Many fear doing something wrong or inadvertently hurting their child, but may not share these fears with the child's mother or professionals working with them. This may be brought to your attention in Phase 6 when the young mother complains that her partner is not helping enough or spending enough time with her and the baby. The young man may tell you that he is not feeling able to be the kind of father he wants to be. Although most counselors recognize that fathers can fill a wide range of important roles beyond being the breadwinner, many young men have very rigid views about fatherhood. Although we cannot examine all the complexities of identity development in this guide, counselors should know that disruptions in identity development are common among adolescents/young adults in general and young expectant parents in particular. As a young man's personality emerges in your sessions (he demonstrates how he is playful or gentle or a hard worker), help him connect who he is as a person to who he can be as a father. It can be useful to comment on how he might make use of his personal strengths in his role as parent and co-parent.

INTIMATE PARTNER VIOLENCE

As a counselor working with young couples you should be prepared for the possibility of aggressive and/or violent behaviors between them; this behavior is typically referred to as intimate partner violence (IPV). Intimate partner violence is more prevalent among adolescents than adults (Halpern, Oslak, Young, Martin, & Kupper, 2001; Messinger, Davidson, & Rickert, 2011). Additionally, an unplanned pregnancy increases the likelihood that IPV will occur. The intense personal and interpersonal stress that accompanies an unplanned pregnancy and parenthood increases strain and conflict in a relationship (Goodwin et al., 2000; Mohllajee et al., 2007), which raises the risk for IPV (Campbell et al., 2009; Cunradi et al., 2002; Jain et al., 2010; McLanahan, Garfinkel, Reichman, & Teitler, 2001).

Different levels of aggressive behavior occur among young couples, including (a) yelling, screaming, belittling, and name calling; (b) throwing objects or kicking walls; (c) slapping, pushing, shaking; or (d) punching, choking, or worse. It is not unusual for aggression and violence to be reciprocal among adolescent couples, committed by both partners against each other. It is our experience that some young couples who engage in aggressive or violent behavior do not recognize it as a problem. Their definition of an unacceptable level of violence is rather high, in part because they have grown up in a youth culture that is endemically violent. Some couples believe that as long as the male partner is not physically assaulting the female partner, then they do not have problems with IPV. Additionally, young couples often do not regard verbal aggression or even pushing or slapping as true violence.

Low levels of IPV do not pose an imminent danger to either partner or their child, but can lead to significant stress over time or escalate quickly as stress increases. As such, even low levels of IPV should be addressed immediately. Often, the most effective way to address IPV concerns with young couples is to discuss how aggression and violence can negatively affect their infant's development. You may need to educate the couple about the ways this can harm their baby, including:

- Emotional harm and stress on the child from observing hostile interaction between parents
- Unintended or accidental physical harm that could occur to their child
- The negative impact of violence on parenting—parents are not able to attend to the needs of their babies when they are embroiled in violent conflict with their partners
- The possible emotional harm that would occur if the child were removed from their care because the child was found to be in danger by the Child Protective Services (CPS) authorities

Depending on the couple and the circumstances, you will need to determine the most appropriate way to relay your concerns about IPV. Below are three example statements a counselor might use.

"It can be [upsetting/damaging/scary] for a child to see and hear their parents fighting. A lot of people believe that a baby won't remember, but your baby can sense when you are upset, and this does affect [him/her]. Babies become overwhelmed by intense negative feelings and will either start to cry or sort of shut down when it is too much for them to handle . . . Even if they do not seem upset, we know that beneath the surface they are feeling very stressed. This level of stress is not good for their developing brains. Also, when parents are very upset or feeling scared, it is almost impossible for them to concentrate or focus on the needs of their baby. Even if the baby doesn't quite know what is going on, this kind of behavior can definitely affect [him/her]."

"I know you both want your baby to be safe and secure. One way to make sure of this is to be safe and secure in how you treat each other. What you are describing right now has me concerned that you are not always safe or secure together. Let's figure out a way to change the situation for you and your baby."

"When there is this type of physical fighting or behavior between you, somebody could become concerned that your child isn't safe. Sometimes people make calls to Child Protective Services for this type of thing between parents. Sometimes children have to live with other people to stay safe when their parents have this going on between them. Let's work on preventing anything like that from happening by helping you find better ways to work out conflicts and disagreements."

As a YPP counselor there are two questions related to IPV that require careful consideration: reporting and assessing/addressing.

When Do I Report Intimate Partner Violence?

Intimate partner violence should be reported to CPS or the police if you believe it could be harmful to the fetus (or the infant). Underage adolescents who are victims of IPV should also be reported to CPS. For example, if an 18-year-old expectant father is hitting his 16-year-old pregnant girlfriend, his behavior is a form of child abuse.

How Do I Assess/Address Intimate Partner Violence?

Within the context of YPP, you might include a clinical assessment of why IPV is occurring, exploring individual factors (lack of empathy, hostile personality), the interpersonal conditions (grew up with domestic violence), and the patterning of aggressive/violent behavior (couple does not know how to de-escalate their conflicts). This assessment may include gathering information about the following:

- Nature and severity of the behavior (i.e., name calling daily, punching walls once in a while, pushing and hitting weekly)
- Direction of the aggression/violence (i.e., from her to him, from him to her, they both act aggressively with each other)
- Situations likely to trigger the aggression/violence (i.e., money issues, when she talks to other guys, when he stays out with his friends, job/school stress)
- How the aggression/violence generally ends or dissipates (i.e., he leaves to cool off, she wears herself down, she cries and he apologizes, someone else steps in, they do not talk to each other for days, they break up for a little while)

After assessing for potential harm, identify what can be done to prevent future violence. What constructive behaviors could be used to replace the violence? Some young people engage in violence impulsively and prevention involves learning to self-regulate. Some young people use violence or threats of violence to control their romantic partners. This strategy sometimes works, because partners comply and the violence is self-reinforcing. As a YPP counselor, ask yourself (and perhaps the couple you are working with), "What purpose is being served by this violent or aggressive behavior?" And then, "What is a better, healthier way to accomplish that goal?"

Your role is to teach aggressive/violent couples to use healthier, safer ways to handle their stress, anxiety, anger, jealousy, and so on. Most of the communication skill building exercises that are part of YPP (Phase 3) will assist couples in stopping aggressive/violent behavior from continuing or preventing it from happening in the first place. It should be noted that some violent/aggressive couples might need a higher level of intervention than you can provide with YPP. You should refer these couples to appropriate treatment programs. In some cases, you may need to refer the pregnant woman to a shelter for victims of domestic violence.

By highlighting the impact of the IPV on their child, as well as their relationship with each other and their families, you can help motivate them to address the issue. The best way to "treat" IPV is to catch its early warning signs, before it begins. Based on research (Florsheim, McArthur, Hudak, Heavin, & Burrow-Sanchez, 2011), we believe it is often possible to identify couples who are at significant risk for engaging in physical violence simply by assessing their verbally aggressive behavior, such as shouting, name calling, or threats. This behavior is particularly worrisome when one or both partners appear to lose their empathetic connection with the other. For example, when one partner only wants revenge or the satisfaction of punishing the other. One of goals of the YPP is to help hostile couples minimize their hostile, aggressive exchanges and increase their warmth and capacity to listen and remain connected during difficult moments.

WORKING WITH INDIVIDUAL PARTNERS

The primary purpose of YPP is to help young parents strengthen their co-parenting relationship, and we believe that the most productive way to accomplish this is to work with the partners together. However, there are times when it is necessary to work with each partner individually. You may strategically decide to separate the couple because of significantly hostile and unproductive conflicts you do not feel you can manage when they are together. In other cases the decision will be made for you, when one person does not show up for a counseling session or the couple refuses to meet together. In these cases you will need to decide whether to insist on meeting together or "go with the flow." Generally, we advise that you do what is necessary to (a) maintain safety and (b) keep the momentum moving forward. When meeting with partners individually, keep the following in mind.

Do Not Take Sides When meeting with one partner individually, stay in tune with your role as the counselor for the co-parenting couple and resist the temptation to slide into the role of individual counselor. You may have to work especially hard not to take sides or not *appear* like you are taking sides simply because you are engaging in active listening with one parent. You may need to remind both partners that meeting individually does not shift the focus of sessions away from the co-parenting relationship.

Gently Challenge Them to Take Responsibility When meeting with an angry young man or woman in individual sessions, you can challenge them about their role in the conflict, and ask each to consider how he or she might act and react differently to help create a better co-parenting relationship. These individual sessions can be an opportunity for each partner to reflect upon their conflict with the other, and gain insight into their own behavior. Listen empathically to the perspective of each partner, but be careful to prevent either partner from thinking that your *understanding* of their perspective and concerns equates to *siding* with them against the other.

Work to Bring the Partners Together as Co-Parents When appropriate, bring the discussion back to the goal of getting the couple to meet together and work on developing healthy and productive ways of communicating. Regardless of whether you are able to bring the couple into a joint session, you can work toward helping them develop the skills to negotiate a positive co-parenting relationship on their own. For some couples, YPP is about planting seeds for future growth.

CRISIS MANAGEMENT

A crisis is defined as a situation that deserves immediate attention in order to protect the well-being of the young parents and their child. Many young expectant parents will have such a crisis during the time you are working with them (and some will have more than one) because young expectant couples tend to live high-stress lives. They may get kicked out of school, evicted, deported, or arrested. They may be abused or become suicidal and you will need to respond. As a counselor, you should think about how to respond to these crises from two different perspectives: (a) what you should do to assist and support the young parents, and (b) how you can use the crisis to help the couple learn to either prevent or cope with future crises.

Counselor Response to Active Crises

It is important for you to be prepared for anything and remain calm when a crisis emerges. Your response can have a strong impact on the working alliance between you and that partner or couple. If they do not feel you are taking their crisis seriously, they may believe that you do not really care or understand and the counseling process may get stuck. If you overreact, the parent in crisis—who is looking to you to provide a reasonable and balanced response—may not trust your ability to help him or her through the situation. If the crisis is addressed with concern and respect, and in a calm and rational manner, the young parent is likely to feel heard and able to move forward in the counseling process and refocus on the co-parenting relationship.

When helping young expectant parents manage their crises, it is best to have a systematic approach because it can help you to remain calm, even when everyone else is in a panic. There are various models of crisis intervention that use a step-by-step approach (James & Gilliland, 2013; Roberts & Ottens, 2005). Most of these models promote basic goals: assure safety, decrease risk, help stabilize the situation, and determine next steps to resolve the crisis and underlying cause. In many instances, some collaboration with the care coordinator and/or a referral to an outside agency will be necessary to adequately address the crisis. The following are general guidelines for responding to crises when providing YPP:

- **Stay calm.** Do not further inflame the situation with your own anxiety.
- **Gather additional information** from the couple or individual partner about the situation. Understand the facts (as much as possible) as well as the emotions of the situation.
- **Be nonjudgmental.** A parent may be embarrassed to report a crisis to you because mistakes were made or poor judgment was used.
- **Explain that safety is your first priority** and that you will take whatever action is necessary to ensure it. If necessary, call 911 or other relevant authorities.
- **When possible, do not make decisions alone.** As appropriate, consult with your clinical supervisor, clinical team, caregiving adults, and the couple's other service providers.
- **Once the immediate risk is addressed or reduced, problem solve the situation** with the participant(s) by examining options, alternatives, and coping strategies for resolving the situation.
- **Devise a clear plan with the participant(s)** that includes concrete steps for the near future (today, tomorrow) and the more distant future (next week). Help them define some modest goals and schedule check-in times. This plan might include involving parents or other adult providers.

Examples of Crisis Scenarios

The following are three crisis scenarios we have encountered during YPP counseling sessions with a brief summary of the crisis response. Please remember that in a crisis situation there is generally not just one correct response. Many contextual factors will play a part in how you respond to a particular crisis.

> **Intimate partner violence.** An expectant 17-year-old came to a YPP session alone and reported that the 20-year-old father recently shoved her against a wall and choked her when they were arguing. She stated that this was not the first time this had happened.
>
> The counselor gathered additional information about past, similar situations, the couple's current status, and the young father. The counselor determined with the young mother that there were realistic threats to her safety and the well-being of the baby.
>
> The counselor talked with the young mother about informing her grandmother (with whom she lived) about these threats from the father so that the grandmother could support her efforts to remain safe. The young mother was scared to tell her grandmother, but decided it was the right thing to do. With the counselor's support, the young mother told her grandmother after the session ended. The grandmother was concerned and was a key factor in devising a safety plan for the young mother in which she would not be left alone in the home; other precautions would be put in place to provide a protective buffer between the young mother and the young father. The counselor consulted with the clinical supervisor and determined that a CPS call would be made to report the young father's alleged behavior as a risk to the expectant mother and the unborn baby. The counselor followed up with the young mother and her grandmother to keep them informed of the CPS report process and to assist with additional aspects of resolving the risk, including linking the young mother to care coordination resources relevant to domestic violence

victim support and safety. The counselor also attempted to contact the young man and offer him individual counseling. Unfortunately, he disappeared and did not make use of YPP counseling. The counselor worked with the young mother to transition out of YPP to more appropriate individualized services.

Homelessness. An 18-year-old father, who had been kicked out of his parents' home and had been living at a friend's house, reported that he could no longer stay at his friend's place, nor would the young mother's family allow him to stay with them. He told the counselor that he had no place to go after the session ended.

The counselor spent time getting more information from the young father to fully understand the situation and the immediacy of his needs. The counselor then contacted a program care coordinator to assist him with finding a shelter resource. The young father, the counselor, and the care coordinator worked together to determine a plan of action and found him a short-term shelter beginning that night. The young father had a number of questions for the shelter staff that he was not sure how to ask. The care coordinator accompanied him to the shelter, helped him talk with the shelter staff, supported him in asking questions, and helped him arrange his stay. The counselor and care coordinator followed up and worked with the young father to devise a plan to secure more permanent housing and to explore options in the interim. The care coordinator continued to work with the young father until a more permanent housing option was identified and the situation stabilized.

Suicidal talk. A 16-year-old pregnant teen and her 17-year-old partner came to a YPP session. The father reported that he was concerned about his partner; she was irritable and withdrawn and lately had spent all of her time sleeping. He said it seemed like more than just crankiness and tiredness from the discomforts of the pregnancy and that he did not know how to make her happy. Through further exploration, the young woman revealed that she was tired of the drama between her and her partner, overwhelmed by the thoughts of being a mother, and sometimes thought everyone would be better off if she just "ended it all."

The counselor commended the young man for appropriately expressing his concerns and for his desire to support his partner. With the couple's permission, the counselor excused the expectant father from the session for a while and completed a suicide risk assessment with his partner (see Fowler, 2012 for a good discussion of the assessment process). The counselor reviewed the completed risk assessment with a colleague and determined that there was no imminent risk. However, he was concerned enough to call the young woman's mother and ask her to come in to plan for her daughter's safety. The counselor devised a safety plan with the pregnant teen, her partner, and the young woman's mother. All agreed to help ensure her safety while efforts were made to address the underlying stressors. The counselor provided all three with information about crisis mental health resources in their community.

Once the counselor calmed things down and ensured that the young woman was safe, he discussed the next steps to help her handle her feeling of being overwhelmed. A plan was devised including steps to: (a) use YPP skills to reduce the amount of the drama in the couple's relationship; (b) connect the pregnant teen with care coordination and individual mental health services; and (c) have the young woman and her mother consult with the medical clinic to rule out any current medical issues impacting her mood. Additional care coordination services were accessed to assist the young couple in feeling more prepared as parents and to obtain baby care items that they were concerned about being able to afford. The plan included regular check-ins to monitor the young woman's physical and emotional safety.

Crises as Learning Opportunities

After a crisis situation has been resolved, it can be useful to circle back and discuss what was learned and what could be done the next time a similar crisis arises. In addition to preparing YPP clients for future crises, a counselor can play an important role in modeling healthy and positive types of responses to crisis situations. The ways in which you remain calm, sensitive, and thoughtful in your response can help them adopt a similar approach to problem solving and decision making when handling future crises.

PERINATAL LOSS

Some young expectant couples experience perinatal loss through miscarriage or stillbirth. A miscarriage—which can occur anytime during the pregnancy—can be a significant tragedy/trauma even if the pregnancy was unplanned or initially unwanted (Maker & Ogden, 2003). Young couples can become very confused by the range of emotions following a perinatal loss, which can include grief, anger, sadness, relief, and self-doubt. Although such a loss affects both young mothers and fathers, they typically experience different types of reactions and emotions (Rowlands & Lee, 2010; Vance, Boyle, Najman, & Thearle, 2002). The very fact that they have dissimilar reactions can result in more confusion and some misunderstanding.

For instance, it is not unusual for young mothers to grieve openly and outwardly, showing their emotions through crying and sadness. By contrast, young fathers typically grieve more privately and internally, sometimes taking on the appearance of anger or indifference (Swanson, Chen, Graham, Wojnar, & Petras, 2009). Family, friends, and even medical and social service professionals often view perinatal loss as a mother's issue. Do not dismiss the experience of the young father; make a point of acknowledging that the mother and father may have different ways of feeling loss and sadness. The father might feel he needs to take care of or support his partner through the loss, in the meantime neglecting his own feelings. You can help create a forum for both partners to express their grief in ways most comfortable for them.

Studies on the adjustment of parents after perinatal loss indicate that supportive, informal (family, friends, partners) and formal relationships (medical providers, service programs, religious communities) are important to helping parents successfully get through their experiences of grief and loss (Rowlands & Lee, 2010; Vance, Boyle, Najman, & Thearle, 2002). Young parents need to be allowed to grieve in their own ways and not feel pressured to get over it or move on too quickly. Even well-meaning support systems can place this kind of pressure on young parents. As the counselor, you might have an opportunity to help guide the young couple's support systems regarding the best ways to support the couple. For example, you can reassure families that it is normal for the mourning process (in whatever way a young man or woman is experiencing it) to take some time, but that each person will have his or her own timeline for this. At the same time, you can also help families recognize the signs of depression so that they can be aware of when to seek help for mental health concerns.

Young expectant parents who have experienced perinatal loss are at increased risk for having a repeat pregnancy in a short period of time, especially when they lack support and opportunities to resolve their feelings of grief and loss (Coard, Nitz, & Felice, 2000). It may be helpful to explore their thoughts and feelings about another pregnancy, so that they can cope with their pain without feeling pressured to get pregnant right away. This can be an opportune time to help a young couple explore what another pregnancy would mean for them at this stage of their life and help them become more deliberate about when to have a child. If appropriate, provide some education about how it may be emotionally and physically best to wait awhile before trying to have another child. An exploration of family planning similar to that described in Phase 3 may be appropriate here.

Tips for Working with Perinatal Loss

Here are some important practical tips to consider when working with a young couple that has experienced perinatal loss.

- Err on the side of assuming this is a significant loss for *both* partners.
- Conduct an informal assessment of how each partner is experiencing and adjusting to the loss.
- Keep in mind that one or both partners may have ambivalent feelings about the loss (grief and relief), which can lead to feelings of guilt. Educate the couple that it is normal for them to be feeling a variety of emotions and that it is not unusual for them to have these feelings for quite awhile.
- Shift the focus of YPP from co-parenting to the adjustment and grieving process regarding the loss of the baby.
- Encourage the couple to use the healthy communication skills they may have learned/begun to learn to support each other's experience of loss and grief.
- Collaborate and consult with other involved professionals, including medical providers and care coordinators; make appropriate referrals to additional supportive services.
- Educate the couple that they cannot expect to experience their loss in the exact same way and that it is OK for each of them to need different things while working through their grief.
- Give them opportunities to explore how the loss is impacting them and to express to each other how they are feeling and what they need.
- Carefully explore whether they are thinking about another pregnancy in the near future and discuss the couple's family planning needs.

Some young parents may not report significant feelings of grief following a perinatal loss, and for others the grief may be brief. Do not push them to express feelings they may not feel; it's possible that they are dissociating from the experience and need time before they are ready to experience their grief. You role is to acknowledge that it is ok to feel grief and let them know that they should not be surprised if a sense of loss comes up at a later point in time. Sometimes one partner experiences grief more significantly than the other. When this happens, you may shift toward being more individually focused on the needs of that young parent who is more upset. Some couples break up after a miscarriage, which can exacerbate their sense of loss. When this occurs you may want to shift to an individualized focus and hold individual sessions to address each former partner's grief (regarding the loss of baby *and* relationship).

SUMMARY AND RECOMMENDATIONS

The list of therapeutic issues presented in this chapter is by no means exhaustive. It summarizes the most common issues we have encountered when providing YPP counseling. At times these issues can seem to have the potential to derail your YPP work and undermine your efforts to reach phase specific goals. It is important to avoid seeing these issues as interference. For some couples, one of these issues may be the primary focus of YPP. By staying attuned to the core needs of the co-parenting couple, you create opportunities for growth and development.

The common therapeutic issues you encounter may be similar to those described earlier or may be quite different and unique. How you respond will depend on a number of factors, including the policies and procedures of your organization, the resources available in your community, the specific dynamics of the couple and their family, the surrounding community and social systems, and your level of comfort and training. As you may have noticed, some of the most important counselor responses to these types of issues involve counselor support, facilitating positive communication skills, and drawing upon the strengths of the young mother and father. Whatever your response, it is important to remain attentive to the ethical matters, safety concerns, and the importance of delivering the YPP with integrity and fidelity to the model.

12 CLINICAL ASSESSMENT AND PROGRAM EVALUATION

INTRODUCTION

IN TODAY'S WORLD, IT IS ESSENTIAL THAT MENTAL HEALTH AND PUBLIC HEALTH PROFESSIONALS systematically evaluate their programs and their work with individual clients. It is expected that we are actively engaged in demonstrating that our programs "work" and improving their effectiveness because we are accountable to our consumers, our funders and our community partners. There is no doubt that the assessment of individual couples and the evaluation of programs are time-consuming and costly processes to implement and manage. Collecting data from YPP couples and evaluating that data requires resources that are often in short supply in clinical and educational settings. However, saving costs by not engaging in these processes may be penny wise and pound foolish if programs are cut because of a lack of outcome data. For this reason alone, assessment and evaluation systems are worth the investment. This chapter will orient you to the steps involved in completing the clinical assessment of YPP couples and using your assessment data to evaluate whether the YPP is meeting the needs of your community and clinic/agency.

At the end of any significant endeavor, it is healthy to stop and reflect upon what was gained or learned from the experience, how to make the most of it, and what we might do differently given the opportunity to do it all over again. In the world of social and mental health services, this sort of reflection is woven into our training and professional practice. As we engage in clinical work, we routinely identify goals, track progress, assess outcomes, and seek input. This reflective process helps us: (a) refine our treatment models; (b) hone our clinical techniques; and (c) facilitate better outcomes for clients (Osofsky, 2005). The practice of reflection can also help us make general program improvements by helping us track what works (and what does not) among groups of couples.

In this chapter we distinguish between "clinical assessments," which we define as assessment processes that focus on the functioning of the individual couple, and "program evaluations," or processes that focus on the functioning of the program itself. For the most part, clinicians and program evaluators operate in parallel universes, despite the fact that their activities can be mutually supportive. Throughout this chapter, we emphasize how the data collected as part of the YPP counseling process can also be used for the purposes of YPP program evaluation. We highlight how the specific tasks involved in clinical assessment and program evaluation can be aligned to help achieve the overall goal of improving the quality of co-parenting support services. The first part of this chapter describes how to assess the outcomes of YPP participants as part of an overall YPP clinical assessment strategy that we introduced in chapter 5. We then provide a general outline for evaluating YPP within the context of your clinic, agency, or school, utilizing the data collected as part of the clinical assessment process.

Clinical assessments and program evaluations are complex endeavors that cannot be adequately described in a single chapter. We encourage you to make use of other resources that focus specifically on the topic of clinical assessment (Goldfinger & Pomerantz, 2010; Simmons & Lehmann, 2013) and program evaluation (Mertens & Wilson, 2012). Our goal is not to instruct you on the development and implementation of an assessment or evaluation plan. Rather, we will introduce you to some of the primary issues involved and provide some basic guidelines for implementing an assessment strategy and an evaluation plan.

THE CLINICAL ASSESSMENT PROCESS

At the beginning of YPP counseling, you identified each couple's strengths and weaknesses and developed a plan to help them meet their goals as co-parents. This assessment process involved gathering information from both partners about their current circumstances, their family relationships, and their relationship with each other (see chapter 5). As you moved through the six YPP phases, you documented session activities, progress made, and challenges faced and/or overcome. Now it is time to document each couple's overall progress and developmental gains. It may also be appropriate and helpful to provide recommendations geared toward supporting the couple's growth as co-parents.

Generally, the post YPP assessment process includes three steps. First, re-administer baseline assessment measures. This step is necessary in order to determine whether positive or negative changes have occurred on key measures of functioning. For example, we recommended that YPP counselors administer the CADRI to obtain a baseline assessment of a couples' capacity for expressing positive feelings and their risk for engaging in aggressive and/or violent behaviors. Re-administering the CADRI will help you identify if a couple is reducing specific negative behaviors and increasing positive behaviors. The recommended post program questionnaires are listed in Table 12.1.

Second, calculate your fidelity to the program. In chapter 5, we provided you with guidelines about how to track your YPP activities throughout the six phases. This information will be used to calculate your "fidelity score." For our purposes, we define fidelity in terms of two fundamental components: adherence to the YPP protocol and perceived helpfulness. As indicated in the next section, fidelity is an important component of program evaluation (McHugh, Murray, & Barlow, 2009; Shoenwald et al., 2011). It can also be a useful part of the clinical process by helping clinicians stay on task when using a structured intervention (Mazzucchelli & Sanders, 2010). Programs such as YPP allow for some flexibility but require counselors to remain true to the fundamental structure and focus. Significant deviations from protocol will likely diminish the effectiveness of the program. If the program was not administered as intended and your results are not what you hoped for, you will be unable to discern if your disappointing findings are due to inadequacies in the program or in its delivery.

We developed a simple strategy for measuring fidelity to the YPP model based on a formula that incorporates the following elements: (a) completion of specific program activities; (b) dose of "treatment"; and (c) perceived program helpfulness. There is a fidelity-tracking worksheet in the Appendix to assist you in calculating fidelity scores. Phase-specific checklists will help you track counseling activities and session-specific helpfulness and are administered to participants at the end of each session.

Third, measure participants' functioning in parenting-related areas of functioning. After the last session, you should schedule a time to administer selected "outcome" and post-assessment measures to gauge parents' functioning in areas such as co-parenting attitudes/behavior, parenting attitudes/behavior, parenting stress, and reproductive health behavior. In Table 12.1, we recommend several established measures to use in this assessment. These measures were selected based on the following: (a) the background research demonstrating their validity and reliability; (b) their readability, which is essential for adolescent and young adult populations; (c) their capacity for capturing important outcomes relevant to the focus of YPP counseling. These measures have been tested and retested in diverse samples and have been found to be both valid (accurately measures what it intends to measure) and reliable (consistent in its measurement). Having psychometrically sound measures will help you feel more confident in the accuracy of your findings.

The measures described in Table 12.1 can help you determine whether a couple is at high risk for parenting and co-parenting dysfunction, including attachment problems, intimate partner violence, child abuse, and/or high levels of parental stress. They will also help you identify a couple's strengths in key areas of parental development, such as nurturance and cooperation. Generally, these measures will help you gauge whether a couple is more or less healthy, although it is important to remember that definitions of health can vary across population and communities (Sussman, 2004; Unger, 2001). You should be cognizant of cultural variations in what constitutes healthy co-parenting and parenting among the communities you serve. In addition to these measures, we recommend using a measure of birth control use to assess the effectiveness of the family planning module (see chapter 7) and a measure of birth outcomes to test whether the YPP has impacted pregnancy risk (e.g., low birthweight, prematurity).

Filling out questionnaires can be tedious and potentially intrusive when questions are highly personal and the process seems bureaucratic. If you structure the data collection process to be friendly (provide comfortable seating, privacy, and

---

Table 12.1 RECOMMENDED POST PROGRAM ASSESSMENT MEASURES

A. Measures to Be Re-administered (previously administered in Phase 1)

Drug and Alcohol Abuse. The *CRAFFT* is a recommended screening tool for identifying drug and alcohol abuse concerns (Knight, Shrier, Bravender, Farrell, Vander Bilt, & Shaffer, 1999). It is designed for use with youth under the age of 21 and recommended by the American Academy of Pediatrics' Committee on Substance Abuse. It is short (six items) and reliable and can help you determine if a longer conversation about drug and alcohol use is warranted. The CRAFFT and instructions for its use can be accessed through the following website: http://www.ceasar-boston.org/clinicians/crafft.php.

Intimate Partner Violence/Relationship Conflict. The *Conflict in Adolescent Dating Relationships Inventory* (CADRI; Wolfe, Scott, Reitzel-Jaffe, Wekerle, Grasley, & Straatman, 2001) is a recommended questionnaire for assessing both positive and negative behavior between intimate partners. The measure focuses primarily on the negative behaviors, but includes some questions regarding positive approaches to addressing disagreements. The introductory section about dating history may not be necessary during a YPP assessment, so consider dropping that part. Ask each participant to focus on his or her relationship with the co-parenting partner specifically, even if the co-parents are not together as a romantic couple or they are dating other people. This measure, along with information regarding its development and validation, was published in *Psychological Assessment, 13*(2), 2001.

(continued)

General Mental Health. The *Youth Outcomes Questionnaire: Self Report* (YOQ—SR; Ridge et al., 2009) is recommended as a quick and easy way to assess social, emotional, and behavioral symptoms. For YPP participants who are 18 or over, there is an adult version called the Outcomes Questionnaire (OQ). These instruments are brief measures of mental health that can be used repeatedly with participants and are sensitive to changes in functioning over time. The YOQ and OQ are not in the public domain but are inexpensive and can be purchased at http://www.oqmeasures.com. If cost is a factor, there are several symptom checklists/screening devices that are in the public domain, such as the Strengths and Difficulties Questionnaire (Goodman, 2001; http://www.sdqinfo.com).

Perceived Stress. The *Perceived Stress Scale* (either 4 or 10 items) is a recommended tool for assessing the degree to which situations are appraised as stressful (Cohen, Kamarck, & Mermelstein, 1983). This brief measure can be easily used to track perceived stress over time. The PSS-4 and PSS-10 can be found at the following website: http://www.psy.cmu.edu/~scohen/scales.html.

Resilience. The *Child and Youth Resilience Measure—Short Version* (CYRM-12; Liebenberg et al., 2013) measures resilience in youth at three levels of experience (individual, family, and community context). The CYRM manual defines resilience as being comprised of three capacities: (a) the capacity of individuals to navigate their way to resources that sustain well-being; (b) the capacity of individuals' physical and social ecologies to provide those resources; and (c) the capacity of individuals, their families, and communities to negotiate culturally meaningful ways for resources to be shared. The 12-item version of the CYRM is based on the longer 28-item, original measure (Unger & Liebenberg, 2011). Both versions have been found to have adequate content and construct validity, test-retest reliability, and internal consistency. The CYRM-12 can be obtained from the primary author (Dr. Linda Liebenberg, Co-Director of the Resilience Research Centre, at Dalhousie University, Halifax, NS Canada; linda.liebenberg@dal.ca).

Trauma Symptoms. The *Screen for Posttraumatic Stress Symptoms* (SPTSS; Carlson, 2001; Caspi et al., 2007) is a 17-item brief screening measure designed to identify people with high levels of posttraumatic stress symptoms. Items closely match the DSM-IV criteria for PTSD and are written in simple language making the instrument suitable for use with a wide variety of populations. One of the advantages of the SPTSS is that trauma symptoms are not asked in reference to a specific event, which allows it to be used with individuals who may have experienced multiple stressful events. The SPTSS has been found to have adequate psychometric properties (Caspi et al., 2007).

B. Parenting Measures (not previously administered)

The *Paternal Postnatal Attachment Questionnaire (PPAQ) and Maternal Postnatal Attachment Scale (MPAS)* (Condon & Corkindale 1998; Condon et al., 2008) are 19-item scales that have been used to assess parent-infant attachment. The PPAQ has the following three subscales: (a) patience and tolerance; (b) pleasure in interaction; and (c) affection and pride. The MPAS subscales are as follows: (a) quality of attachment; (b) absence of hostility; and (c) pleasure in interaction. Participants respond to items on a scale that ranges from 1 to 5. So far both measures have been found to have adequate psychometric properties. This measure is available in the public domain and can be obtained by contacting the author (Dr. John Condon, Flinders University, Adelaide, South Australia; john.condon@flinders.edu.au).

The *Parenting Stress Index—Short Form* (PSI; Abidin, 1990, 1997) is recommended for measuring levels of stress directly related to parenting and co-parenting The PSI is designed to assess (a) the child's stress-related characteristics (adaptability, acceptability, demandingness, mood, distractibility, hyperactivity); (b) the parent's stress-related characteristics (depression, attachment, restriction of role, sense of competence, social isolation, relationship with spouse, health); and (c) general life stressors. The PSI is widely used in parenting research and has been found to have good psychometric qualities. This measure is available through Psychological Assessment Resources.

(continued)

Table 12.1 CONTINUED

The *Child Abuse Potential Inventory—Short Form* (CAPI; Milner, 1994) assesses for the presence of parental attitudes that increase the risk of child abuse. This self-reporting measure assesses several dimensions of child abuse potential, including: distress, rigidity, unhappiness, problems with child and self, problems with family, and problems with others. The CAPI uses a true/false format and items are weighted on the basis of their predictive value. Sample items include "Children should never be bad" and "Many things in life make me angry." Generally, the CAPI has been found to have sound psychometric properties, including internal consistency, construct validity, concurrent validity, and predictive validity (Ammerman, Kolko, Kirisci, Blackson, & Dawes, 1999; Haskett, Smith, Scott, & Fann, 1998; Milner, 1994). This measure is available through Psychological Assessment Resources.

The *Parent Behavior Checklist* (PBC; Fox, 1994) can be used to assess a co-parent's nurturing behaviors and tendency to engage in punitive physical and verbal discipline with their child. Participants rate each item on a 4-point frequency scale (4 = almost always/always, 3 = frequently, 2 = sometimes, 1 = almost never/never). The Nurturing scale contains 20 items measuring specific parent behaviors that promote a child's psychological growth ("I read to my child at bedtime."). The Discipline scale contains 30 items that assess the parent's tendency to engage in verbally and physically punitive behaviors (spanking, verbal threats, hitting, or slapping). From a representative sample of 1,140 mothers, Fox (1994) found that the internal consistency for the Nurturing and Discipline scales were acceptable (alpha = .82 and alpha = .91, respectively). Test-retest reliability correlations were .81 for the Nurturing scale and .87 for the Discipline scale. This measure is available through Child Development Media, Inc.

C. Co-Parenting Measures (not previously administered)

The *Co-Parenting Planning Worksheet*. We created a measure of co-parenting activities, based on questions from the *Fragile Families and Child Well-Being Survey* and the *Who Does What* (Cowan & Cowan, 1988). This measure includes questions regarding the frequency of several co-parenting activities, such as playing, changing, bathing, and so on. Respondents are asked to indicate the frequency that each parent (self and other) will engage in a listed activity (Often, Sometimes, Rarely, Never). This measure is available in the YPP Toolbox.

The *Co-Parenting Relationships Scale* (CRS: Feinberg et al., 2012) was developed to assess a four-domain model of co-parenting based on Feinberg's theoretical work on co-parenting. The four domains of co-parenting are: childrearing agreement, co-parenting support and/ or undermining, division of labor, and joint management of family dynamics. The CRS includes seven subscales: Co-parenting Agreement, Co-parenting Closeness, Exposure to Conflict, Co-parenting Support, Co-parenting Undermining, Endorse Partner Parenting, and Division of Labor. The subscales can be scored separately or combined to yield an overall co-parenting score. There is both a long and brief version of the CRS (35 vs. 14 items), each with a 7-point response scale (0 = not true of us, 6 = very true of us). Both versions demonstrated acceptable reliability, stability, and construct validity. This measure was published *Parenting: Science and Practice*, 12(1), 2012.

---

snacks) and clearly explain the reasons for collecting all this information, most young people will be more interested and invested. Many of the questionnaires included in our list of recommended measures focus on problem behaviors. This can be off-putting for some young people, who may feel judged. However, if they feel you are asking about their problems because you want to help, the experience can strengthen the therapeutic alliance.

Although we provide suggestions about what measures to include in your pre- and post-assessments, you should not feel constrained by our recommendations. You may have your own ideas about how to measure co-parenting skills, communication skills, or stress levels, or you may be interested in an outcome not covered by our recommended measures. Moreover, new and better measures of psychological and interpersonal functioning continue to be developed, tested, and disseminated. Ultimately, you should design and implement an assessment strategy that works for you, your clinic/institution, and your clients. The measures described in this manual provide an overall assessment framework, outlining the primary domains for evaluation purposes.

WRITING THE YPP SUMMARY REPORT

After a couple has completed the follow-up assessments, your final task is to write a relatively brief YPP summary report that documents their progress and makes recommendation for further growth. There is no singular correct format or style for writing a program summary. The report should be long enough for the reader to obtain a fairly clear understanding of the couple's basic background, current circumstances, strengths, and challenges. In most cases, it should also include a short set of recommendations to support continued growth. Brevity is important; if the summary contains too much detail or is too long, other professionals may not read it. Generally speaking, your final task as a YPP counselor is to succinctly describe the young couple's greatest strengths, biggest challenges, and highest priorities as co-parents and parents. A suggested template for writing YPP summaries is provided in Table 12.2.

Table 12.2 TEMPLATE FOR YPP SUMMARY REPORT

1. **Background**. Briefly orient other professionals to the basic facts of the young couple's life and circumstances, and include the following:

   a. Description of the couple at program completion, including their age, racial or ethnic identity, current education, work status, economic status (poverty; food security), living arrangement, and relationship status

   b. Description of the pregnancy outcome, including infant's gender, health status at birth (weight, gestation age), birth complications and/or developmental concerns

   c. Psychosocial status of both partners, including involvement with other services or systems including mental health services, parenting classes, court involvement, job trainings, and educational support programs
   Note: Because we do not diagnose psychiatric disorders or learning disabilities as part of the program, we avoid using diagnostic language when discussing psychosocial history or current concerns.

   d. Social and contextual issues/support, including family support and/or conflict, and (if relevant) peer and neighborhood relationships

   e. Description of YPP to orient the reader to the goals of the program and the scope of services received

2. **Progress and Outcomes**

   a. Brief, to-the-point description of the strengths and risk factors of the couples' relationship. Focus on the top two or three factors that will be most relevant to other providers. At the couple level, this might include the level of warmth and stability in the relationship. At the individual level, this might include a description of personal traits relevant to positive co-parenting and parenting, such as empathy, listening, and stress management/self-regulatory skills. Include some information about outcomes. If outcome scores are included (such as PSI or CADRI scores), succinctly interpret them for the reader.

(continued)

Table 12.2 CONTINUED

b. Description of the couple's progress toward identified personal and relationship goals within the context of the YPP. This might include the development of communication skills, their capacity for problem solving or stress management, or their ability to manage conflict and contain hostility. It is best to describe both progress made (e.g., couple demonstrates an increased ability to interrupt hostile exchanges by using the reflective listening strategy) and areas for further development (e.g., both partners continue to feel very insecure about their relationship, which often leads to conflicts focusing on jealousy and distrust).

c. Care coordination progress/outcomes. If care coordination support was provided, the summary report should include (a) progress throughout care coordination services, including goals accomplished; and (b) description of both partners' coping and self-advocacy skills.

3. **Primary recommendations**, including activities to maintain gains, further develop skills and strengths and/or address ongoing concerns/problems

a. Individual development: No more than three priority recommendations for each partner (e.g., empathy development, job training, identification with parenthood).

b. Co-parenting skill development (e.g., reduction in hostile exchanges and improved listening skills)

c. Parenting skill development (e.g., sensitivity to infant cues; conflict management skills)

d. End with a constructive summary statement that is encouraging and pragmatic, optimistic, and actionable.

WHY BOTHER WITH CLINICAL ASSESSMENTS?

As this point, you may be thinking that this process sounds time consuming and labor intensive. Is it worth the investment? Recognizing that our approach to assessment goes beyond what is typically done in practice settings and many clinic settings, we believe there are several good reasons for this level of investment, outlined as follows.

The assessment process can help couples understand themselves better. The assessment process can help provide structure and add meaning to a YPP couple's experience. The day-to-day lives of a young, expectant couple are often confusing and overwhelming and they may (appropriately) look to you to help them make sense of their experiences. At times, your role is like a narrator who reflects a couple's story back to them, helping them recognize unifying themes and shared goals. Other times you are like a guide who helps them stay on track and focused on their primary goal to become good co-parenting partners. The clinical assessment process is designed to help you fulfill both of these important roles. It provides you with the opportunity to reflect upon the couple's interpersonal behavior from session to session and find ways to help them move toward their goals. Communicating with couples about their progress, their accomplishments, and their struggles will help facilitate the internalization process discussed in Phase 5. Your efforts to understand their stories and goals will help them become more reflective about themselves and each other.

Assessments are useful to other professionals. Clinical assessments help communicate important information about your clients to other professionals, such as teachers, psychiatrists, and court officials. The value of the information you provide will be greatest if you are able to summarize a couple's strengths and weakness, progress and setbacks in a way that can facilitate growth.[1]

Assessments are necessary for institutional accountability. Clinical record keeping is essential to the accrediting agencies responsible for ensuring that clinics and schools are using best practices. Once you complete your clinical notes and reports, these documents become part of the medical or educational record, which may follow your clients throughout their lives. It is important to remember that you have little control over who reads your reports or how other professionals will use them. For this reason, you should remain mindful that your record keeping is about the most private and intimate aspects of your clients' lives. Although you should be clear and direct about your most significant concerns (e.g., ongoing relationship violence, severe substance abuse problems), you should also strive to include your positive observations, such as progress made and notable strengths.

Assessments can dovetail with program evaluations. Clinical assessments can be used to help you evaluate how well the YPP is meeting the needs of the populations you serve. If you administer the same assessment measures to all YPP participants in your clinic or school, you can pool the data across couples to: (a) determine if most couples are making meaningful gains as co-parents and parents; (b) help identify which components of the program are most effective for the populations you serve; and (c) understand why some couples seem to do better than others. We believe it is possible to align the goals of clinical assessment with the goals of program evaluation so that these two processes are mutually supportive. In the next section, we elaborate on this idea of linking assessment and evaluation in greater detail.

THE PROGRAM EVALUATION PROCESS

Program evaluation is defined as the systematic assessment of prevention or intervention processes and outcomes for the sake of providing timely and useful information about the impact of programs, contributing to the improvement of program delivery, and assisting in decision making about continued program support (Rossi et al., 2004). Just as there are different approaches to clinical assessment, there are different approaches to program evaluation, which means you will need to determine which approach is best for you, your clinic, and your community. This will depend on the questions and issues you are most interested in addressing.

For example, if your goal is to demonstrate that couples who participate in YPP do better than couples who do not receive co-parenting counseling, then you will want to conduct a randomized treatment-control study, comparing YPP participants to a "control group" condition. This design is the best way to address the

---

[1] When you write your YPP summary, you will inevitably convey personal information about both partners. As such, you should be careful about releasing this information to others without obtaining a signed release of information form from both partners. For example, a young father's probation officer may request information about the progress he made during YPP. In addition to needing the young father to sign a release of information form, you may also need the young mother to sign a release form if your summary contains personal information about her. Alternatively, you could cleanse the document of the mother's personal identifying information, which might be difficult.

basic question of whether the YPP works for your client population. However, randomized clinical trials are very expensive/labor intensive and difficult to implement in community settings. Alternatively, if you want to demonstrate (more simply) that YPP "helps" those couples who complete the program, then you would need to define what you mean by "helps" by setting benchmarks for success and then tracking what proportion of couples reach that mark. For example, you might propose that couples who complete YPP will report a 50% reduction in the occurrence of intimate partner violence and will raise the level of paternal involvement in shared parenting by 30%. This approach to program evaluation is oriented toward determining whether YPP participants demonstrate improvements in their functioning and/or reach their goals.

You may also want to determine why YPP is more effective for some couples than others. Sometimes the explanation is fairly simple, such as when different outcomes are due to differences in the number of sessions completed. However, sometimes understanding different outcomes is more complex, such as when differences are due to the quality of program administration (related to differences in counselor skills) or perhaps social or psychological differences among couples. Because there are many different approaches to program evaluation, it will be important for you to clarify what you hope to learn and what is the best way to ensure that you will be able to answer the "program evaluation questions" you are asking.

THE CENTERS FOR DISEASE CONTROL AND PREVENTION MODEL OF PROGRAM EVALUATION

As indicated, we encourage you to educate yourself about the different approaches to program evaluation. In this section, we illustrate how you could use one commonly used framework to design and implement a program evaluation strategy. The Centers for Disease Control and Prevention (CDC) has developed a six-step model for systematically investigating the "merit, worth or significance" of public health programs, which can be found and downloaded at http://www.cdc.gov/eval/framework/index.htm. One of the many things we like about this model is that it emphasizes the importance of community engagement throughout the evaluation process.

APPLICATION OF THE CENTERS FOR DISEASE CONTROL AND PREVENTION MODEL TO THE YOUNG PARENTHOOD PROGRAM

Step 1: Engage the Stakeholders

In the case of YPP, stakeholders can be defined quite broadly to include: (a) the population receiving YPP services (expectant mothers and fathers and their families); (b) clinic or school staff who provide support or ancillary services; (c) community partners who refer young couples to the program and/or provide additional services in support of the program; or (d) fatherhood advocates. One reason to engage stakeholders in the evaluation process is to find out what outcomes are most important to them. Because YPP has a broad focus (improved communication skills; positive co-parenting alliance) there is a wide range of outcomes that could be identified and targeted. As you engage different stakeholders, you are likely to find that they want different things; school staff may want to keep young parents enrolled in school; clinic staff may want to ensure healthy birth outcomes; young couples may want to strengthen their relationship; and you may be interested in addressing issues of trauma. Although some of these issues are not central to the focus of YPP, it is possible to address each of these issues and add measures to assess impact over time.

Step 2: Describe the Program

Describe the program, focusing on expected outcomes. Although much of this work is done—this book describes YPP—every counselor or program administrator should specify *why* he or she chose YPP and what he or she hopes clients will gain from participating. This step will help you clarify how the YPP fits within the context of your agency's mission. Articulating *how* the YPP is expected to support positive outcomes among your clients (or within your community) is an important part of your own program description.

The CDC recommends constructing a logic model to help clarify the intended goals of the program, the employed activities for achieving those goals, and the overall assessment strategy for tracking progress and outcomes. A logic model is a tool for clarifying the logical (if-then) relationships between each component or phase of program implementation, including the inputs (resources needed, implemented activities), the outputs (the utilization of resource/activities), and the expected outcomes and impacts. Specifying these relationships can help guide the evaluation process. Program evaluators often use logic models to help outline their evaluation plans and clarify goals (Miller et al., 2001; Rossi et al., 2004). For example, you may expect that by implementing YPP activities (trainings, outreach, recruitment), couples will become engaged and participate in YPP sessions (outputs), which will lead to positive co-parenting outcomes (impact). Figure 12.1 presents a sample logic model for YPP that may help you construct your own plan for implementing and evaluating YPP; the logic model in Figure 12.1 could be easily revised to address questions specific to your community or organization.

Step 3: Focus on Evaluation Design

Next, design the evaluation procedures. This means deciding: (a) what measures to use; (b) when to administer them; and (c) how to administer them in a way that assures that high-quality data will be gathered. The questionnaires listed in Tables 5.3 and 12.1 are included because we believe they measure important aspects of individual and interpersonal functioning related to positive co-parenting. That said, it is always worth considering other measures as new measures become available.

Before you invest in a particular assessment strategy and design, you should be clear about what you are trying to learn from the data you plan to collect. This sort of clarity will not only help you get the answers you need, it will also provide motivation for everyone involved. Collecting data simply for the sake of collecting data often feels like a waste of time and can be demoralizing in a busy clinic setting when time is short. If everyone understands why they are being asked to fill out questionnaires or track their activities, they will be much more likely to engage in the evaluation process. As indicated earlier, we believe it also makes sense to coordinate the parallel processes of clinical assessment and program evaluation by identifying measures and implementing procedures that can serve both purposes. We have selected measures that could be used to track the progress and outcomes

Outputs

Inputs and Preliminary work	Activities	Participation	Outcomes -- Impact Short	Medium	Long
Inputs: Assemble project team and identify key stakeholders Plan meetings to enhance community engagement and cross-systems collaboration for successful recruitment and program implementation **Preliminary work:** Convene meeting with key stakeholders to identify primary objectives and develop an evaluation plan Select measures for pre and post YPP assessments Consult with community experts about adapting the YPP model to address local needs	Train clinical staff in the YPP model Develop protocols for assessments, referrals, etc Invite/recruit young expectant couples to participate Administer assessments to all participants prior to initiating services Provide co-parenting counseling to interested co-parenting couples Provide care coordination services or facilitate access to case management programs	Maintain retention in YPP through continuous outreach Measure fidelity to the YPP program model using agreed upon measures Measure level of engagement among YPP couples using agreed upon measures Maintain engagement of couples in YPP services for minimum number of sessions Refer to outside programs and agencies as appropriate Conduct post program assessments	Support development of positive co-parenting skills Decrease/prevent high levels of life stress Decrease/prevent depression Decrease/prevent trauma related symptoms Decrease/prevent intimate partner violence Increase levels of co-parenting warmth and support. Improve coping/resiliency skills	Set "benchmark" indicators of program success: 1. Positive paternal and maternal attachment to infant 2. Positive co-parenting relations 3. Reduction in intimate partner violence/hostile conflict 4. Low to moderate levels of parenting stress 5. Increase positive paternal involvement in child rearing	Support healthy child development Increase access to community resources for young parents Imbed co-parenting services in clinics and schools

Assumptions

- With encouragement, fathers will engage in co-parenting support sessions
- Clinic staff from the partnering sites will assist with recruitment

External Factors

- Different cultural values regarding co-parenting and parenting
- Socio-economic barriers to effective co-parenting and parenting
- Health disparities in birth outcomes.

FIGURE 12.1 **Logic Model for the Young Parenthood Program**

of individual parents as well as overall program effectiveness. This can be helpful when explaining the value of assessment to your stakeholders who may have very different ideas about why and how the YPP is worthwhile.

When selecting measures, be strategic by focusing on those aspects of psychological and social functioning that will reveal what you need to know about: (a) individual level risk and protective factors related to co-parenting; (b) whether the program is having its intended effect (on interpersonal and individual level development); and (c) how well couples are functioning as co-parents at some logical point after they have completed the program.

Because parenthood is such a complex developmental process, it is likely that you will be tempted to administer more measures than is reasonable or possible. The risk of asking too many questions is twofold. First, many questionnaires focus on the negative aspects of the young parent's life because most screening instruments ask about symptoms or stressors or problems. Too many negative questions in one sitting can be overwhelming and demoralizing; a very negatively focused assessment procedure may deter some couples from participating. Second, when the assessment process is very long and arduous, young people are less likely to want to continue in the program, thinking it will require too much of their time or be too difficult. Before adding new questionnaires to the assessment/evaluation protocol, consider these factors.

It is also important to think strategically about when and how to administer questionnaires. We typically assess couples at three points in time: (a) just before beginning YPP, which is usually in the second trimester of the pregnancy; (b) about six months post-childbirth, when most couples are past the initial turmoil of early parenthood (which can obscure program effects on co-parent functioning); (c) between 18 and 24 months post-childbirth—at the beginning of toddlerhood—which allows us to assess parenting during a time that tends to be fairly stressful for most parents.

Step 4: Gather Credible Data

This step involves developing processes for collecting data in a manner that assures that (a) participants are comfortable with data collection procedures and (b) data are collected in compliance with ethical and professional standards. Make sure that everyone involved in gathering data has been properly trained and demonstrates the skills needed to collect and manage data. For example, the quality of questionnaire data can depend on how the instructions were administered and whether the participant is able to read and comprehend the questionnaire. Once the data are collected, it will need to be scored or coded. Data processing can be a labor-intensive process, and it is easy for missteps (lack of cultural sensitivity in data coding) or mistakes (data entry errors) to occur. When mistakes or missteps occur, the credibility (and validity) of that data is undermined. Thus, it is imperative that your data systems are set up in way that ensures the proper handling of data.

The CDC model emphasizes that if the data are not seen as credible among stakeholders, the entire endeavor could be called into question. This is an important point, underscoring the need to keep stakeholders informed regarding data collection and management procedures. A vital component of credibility is the responsible use of data. Evaluation data often get put away and shelved forever. This is unfortunate because it is quite possible that the data contain information that can help an agency establish credibility, obtain funding, and improve the program.

Step 5: Justify Your Conclusions

This step involves analyzing the data collected, interpreting the results, and using the findings to address your original set of questions (or goals). Many agencies and school systems find that analyzing their data and obtaining meaningful results is the most challenging part of the evaluation process because it requires some familiarity with statistics and access to statistical programs. Often, even simple questions lead to complex data sets. Drawing meaningful results out of complex data is as much an art as it is a science. Optimally, you will want to work with a statistician who understands the nuances (and potential messiness) of program evaluation data.

One of the complicating features of YPP data is that a mother's and father's data are interdependent. That is, a young father's co-parenting behavior will affect his partner's co-parenting behavior and vice versa. This means that when you evaluate program effects on a young father's co-parenting behavior (or parenting behavior), you will need to account for (or control for) the effects of her behavior on him and his behavior on her. It is possible that whatever impact the program is having on the father's behavior is mediated by program effects on the mother's behavior (Ngu & Florsheim, 2011). Missing data is another common problem; questions were skipped or sessions were missed or one partner dropped out of the program. These examples are intended to help readers (who are nonstatisticians) anticipate problems and complications that they will encounter but will be unlikely to manage on their own. Fortunately, most data analysis issues, including interdependence and missing data, can be solved relatively easily with the assistance of a competent statistician.

If your questions are clear at the outset, a good statistical consultant will be able to identify an analytic approach that will "answer" those questions and deal with whatever problems emerge along the way. If your results do not provide the answer you wanted, it is usually worth considering secondary or alternative questions/hypotheses. For example, if you find that YPP is not preventing or reducing intimate partner violence as you had hypothesized, consider examining differences between subgroups of couples, perhaps stratified by level of risk for violence. This would allow you to refine your original hypothesis and examine if the program is more effective for couples who are at lower levels of risk than for couples who are at higher levels of risk.

After obtaining your results, you need to interpret their meaning and then justify your conclusions. Explaining positive findings (the program works) is much easier than justifying negative or mixed findings because there are many more explanations for why programs fail than for why programs succeed. Although it is important to make sense of disappointing or complex findings, remember that you can undermine the value of your findings with lengthy, convoluted explanations. Sometime the best approach is to engage your stakeholders in the interpretation and justification process; raise questions rather than provide answers. Different stakeholders may interpret the findings in very different ways; some will see program benefits where others see failure. The process of interpreting results involves reaching a consensus regarding the program's success and logical next steps toward program improvement.

Step 6: Ensure Use and Share Lessons Learned

Ensure that findings are put to good use and the lessons learned are shared with stakeholders and other interested parties, including participants (they are often very interested), agency staff (it helps them to appreciate the value of the program they have been helping to support), funding agencies, and other practitioners and researchers (through the publication of journal articles). Your findings will likely hold implications for program improvements, particularly those that address the specific needs of the populations you serve and know best. YPP is not intended to be a finished product; it is new and innovative and requires further development and enhancements. Again, it is important to include stakeholders in any discussion about how to use program evaluation results to improve YPP in your agency.

CONCLUSION AND INTEGRATION

Engaging in the systematic evaluation of programs and practices is essential to our professional integrity and necessary to improve outcomes. Although our hope is to demonstrate our success in supporting positive co-parenting, we must be prepared for the possibility that some couples (or populations) may not benefit from the program, despite our best efforts. When our programs do not function as we hoped or an individual client does not benefit from our efforts, consider the lessons learned and the implications for program improvements. For example, consider the following.

When Co-Parenting Counseling Fails for Individual Couples

We have worked with several young expectant fathers who were severely antisocial, meaning that they had little capacity for empathy and were highly invested in manipulating others (including their partners) to meet their own needs. Some of these young men had histories of aggressive behavior and were heavily involved in substance use and criminal activities. In the vast majority of these cases, the co-parenting outcomes for these couples were not positive, sometimes ending with violent break-ups and police involvement. In some cases, YPP counseling seemed to bring some of the problems to the surface; as the young mothers learned to express their feelings and needs more directly and set firm interpersonal boundaries, the young fathers became more frustrated and angry. Over time, some of these antisocial young fathers drifted away (to find other partners); some of the young mothers began to restrict their involvement in order to protect themselves and their children. Despite the fact that program goals were not met (these couples did not function well as co-parents), we found that in most cases, the young mothers developed a set of skills that helped them refocus their attention away from a dysfunctional relationship and toward the goal of building a healthier life. Our inability to help these young fathers—despite significant effort—was often enlightening for their partners; sometimes our "failure" to change these young men seemed to give the mothers the strength and security to end the relationship and move on.

When Co-Parenting Counseling Is Not Effective for Your Client Population

At the level of program evaluation, we have found that YPP works better for young fathers than young mothers, particularly with respect to parenting outcomes (Florsheim et al., 2012). That is, the program appears to help young fathers become more positively engaged with their children but the effects on maternal involvement (parenting) are weak. This finding makes some sense because young fathers have few natural supports to help them with parenting. For many of these young men, the support we provided was all they received, aside from their partners' support. By contrast, young mothers tend to receive support from their extended family. This means that it is easier to demonstrate a measurable effect of the program on young fathers than young mothers. Nonetheless, the finding that YPP did not demonstrate a measurable impact on maternal stress or maternal parenting behavior inspired us to make modifications that would enhance the effectiveness of the program for young mothers. Several revisions to the program were made, including the addition of Phase 6 and the Stress Reduction module in Phase 3. The finding that previous versions of YPP failed to fully meet our expectations contributed to the development of the revised program presented in this guide.

There is a great deal to be learned from the obstacles (and even the failures) we encounter because they force us to acknowledge limitations, make improvements, and consider alternatives. Sometimes this might mean referring a couple to another program or modifying the YPP approach to meet the particular needs of a specific group of young parents. As counselors and program developers, we are naturally prone to be invested in our own methods and biased toward believing that our efforts to help others will be effective. Therefore, it is important to employ strategies for assessment and evaluation that will support our objectivity and diminish our biases. A well-designed assessment/evaluation plan not only keeps us honest about the value and fitness of our program, it also provides us with the information we need to best address the needs of the clients and communities we serve.

CULTURAL ADAPTATION AND THE YOUNG PARENTHOOD PROGRAM

13

Sheri Johnson and the Young Parenthood Program Team

INTRODUCTION

NOW THAT YOU HAVE READ ABOUT THE YPP INTERVENTION in detail, and become familiar with many of the techniques and activities to promote positive co-parenting, you may be wondering, "Will this work for the young people I serve in my agency?" You may be thinking about whether this approach makes sense given the range of issues that young expectant couples likely need to address during this critical window of opportunity. Perhaps you have also considered whether counseling, derived largely from Western and European worldviews about mental health and well-being, is relevant for pregnant and parenting adolescents from diverse cultural backgrounds. That is, do talk therapy approaches fit well with the ways in which people from a variety of social and cultural traditions view the process of growth and change necessary to transition into the role of a parent? Is it universally accepted that promotion of a positive co-parenting alliance, by engaging in couples-focused, skill-building activities, is the best or the right thing to do?

We have discussed the value of recognizing cultural identities, experiences, beliefs, and practices that may impact the effectiveness of the Young Parenthood Program. We have emphasized the importance of counselors' ability to practice cultural humility, which includes both self-reflection (regarding our own values and biases) and effort to learn as much as possible about the health and beliefs of people from diverse cultures. Evidence suggests that these skills can strengthen the therapeutic alliance, and may contribute to positive outcomes. In addition, the YPP's flexible approach allows counselors and young people to focus on the most relevant and personally meaningful aspects of the intervention, while still adhering to the overarching theory and approach. As such, the YPP offers an intervention framework for young expectant parents from a variety of social and cultural backgrounds that can lead to beneficial health outcomes for young co-parenting partners and their children.

Yet, despite the emphasis on cultural humility and the flexible nature of the YPP, a growing body of literature indicates that more is needed to maximize the effectiveness of interventions delivered in diverse communities across the United States today. The YPP is a research-supported preventive intervention. Demonstrated efficacy in increasing interpersonal competence, reducing intimate partner violence, and increasing father involvement in white and Latino (primarily Mexican-American) couples suggests that further dissemination is warranted (Florsheim et al., 2012). But, does the existing evidence mean that the YPP is equally beneficial for young couples from the Menominee Indian Tribe of Wisconsin, or for young African-American co-parents in the rural South, or for Dominican-American couples in a large Northeastern city? What about a Vietnamese-American young co-parenting dyad living in California? In what ways are all of these couples like the young people who participated in YPP in Utah? In what ways do their cultural orientations, practices, and beliefs differ? How do the economic and social contexts for these young couples affect their decisions related to co-parenting?

CHAPTER AIMS

This chapter focuses broadly on questions related to how to fit the YPP to the social and cultural context of diverse co-parenting dyads while maintaining fidelity to essential components of the empirically tested intervention. These questions are rooted in an ongoing discourse among prevention and intervention scientists and practitioners interested in identifying strategies to improve outcomes for the increasingly diverse adolescent population in the United States. Determining what works, for whom, in what conditions, is essential. Given these questions, the chapter aims to:

(1) Describe definitions, frameworks, themes, and constructs related to cultural adaptation of evidence-based interventions.
(2) Summarize relevant evidence supporting cultural adaptation.
(3) Identify a range of strategies to culturally adapt interventions.
(4) Apply cultural adaptation theory to YPP.

Support for development of interventions aimed at strengthening the co-parenting alliance has increased as social scientists and practitioners have recognized the dramatic shifts in family formation processes that have occurred since the 1970s (McHale et al., 2012). Simultaneously, knowledge regarding early childhood brain development grew exponentially and the importance of creating safe, supportive, and stable environments for young children became both a health and an economic imperative (Eckenrode et al., 2009). Yet, preventive interventions designed to strengthen "fragile families" have yielded mixed results (Cowan et al., 2010). The populations studied thus far include primarily adult low-income, racial and ethnic minority men and women, which allow us to learn about the efficacy of these interventions for a diverse sample of parents. However, the majority of well-studied family-strengthening interventions have not specifically been designed to meet the developmental needs of young adolescent co-parents (McHale et al., 2012). As such, it is unwise to assume that the impacts of interventions developed for adult co-parents could be generalized to teens and emerging adults.

We are not aware of any other preventive intervention specifically designed to match the developmental and relational context of adolescent co-parenting dyads. Building Strong Families (BSF), a group-formatted, psycho-educational intervention for unmarried parents with newborns, was successful in enrolling young African-American and Hispanic parents (72%). Approximately 40% of couples had one member who was 21 years old or younger. Unfortunately, no overall intervention effects on couples' relationship quality, co-parenting, or father involvement were demonstrated—although for couples in which both parents were African American, relationship quality improved at 15 months (Cowan et al., 2010). Fagan

(2008) developed a group intervention for unmarried adolescent fathers, aged 15 to 25. Fathers who participated in a co-parenting curriculum self-reported increased engagement with their babies, compared with fathers who were randomly assigned to a childbirth class. However, the young mothers were not a focus of this group-based intervention.

Thus, the YPP fills a unique gap in this rapidly emerging field. The YPP incorporates a strengths-based approach to fostering relationship skill development to enhance adolescent mothers' and fathers' abilities to provide a warm, supportive family environment for their child, regardless of whether the romantic connection between the couple is sustained. Because the efficacy of the YPP has only recently been demonstrated (Florsheim et al., 2012), efforts to pursue a cultural adaptation of the program are just getting underway.

Some would argue that replicating the YPP with a larger sample of young couples, without any attempt to make cultural adaptations to fit YPP with the values, beliefs, or practices of specific cultural groups, is the logical next step in program development. If comparable results emerge, it could be reasonably asserted that YPP is appropriate for broader dissemination (APA, 2008). This line of reasoning is most consistent with researchers who emphasize fidelity as the key to achieving larger-scale impact. This approach tilts toward a universal understanding of how human beings function. From this perspective, in order for us to know what works across diverse populations, we must develop and test the same or similar models across groups, using good outcome measures that can be validly transported across settings.

Other researchers adopt a highly localized, culturally specific approach to program development and testing, arguing that we need to build our models from the ground up with community participation so that what emerges will reflect the needs and values of the people served. From this relativist perspective it is folly to impose a model developed in one context onto another and expect that it will work, unless the contexts are very similar. Although the universalists might argue that this localized approach will yield too many models and programs that are not generalizable, the relativists are unlikely to be much bothered by this critique, as they believe that models are built from the ground up. For example, the Healing of the Canoe project was developed by the Suquamish Tribe in the rural Puget Sound area of Washington with a high level of community involvement. The program aims to prevent alcohol and drug use and teach youth how to navigate through life without being pulled off course by alcohol or drugs, with culture and tradition serving as both anchor and compass (Thomas et al., 2009). Although the program may not be generalizable to other populations because it draws from locally identified values and practices, its strength lies in the fact that it is grounded in the community and reflective of Suquamish culture.

Of course, some scholars and practitioners seek a compromise position somewhere between these two extremes. For example, we believe that the evidence supporting the efficacy of the YPP with couples in Utah does not necessarily suggest that the YPP will be effective for all young expectant couples, particularly those living in qualitatively different circumstances. Indeed, if the goal is to create a program that is generalizable and transportable, it makes sense to assume that some adaptations will be needed. However, in order to hold on to the core principles of the model, it also makes sense to be conservative about the depth and breadth of modifications made, at least in the beginning.

If we tested the YPP on a sample of mainland Puerto Rican adolescents, we would need to set some criteria for concluding whether the program was comparably effective. For example, if participation rates were similar to participation rates in the Utah samples, could we conclude that the structure of YPP intervention (i.e., 10 to 14 weeks of face-to-face counseling with case management support) fits well with mainland Puerto Rican norms and beliefs about successful young parenthood? Or, would it also be important to demonstrate that improved outcomes for young parents were achieved? Absent improved outcomes, would an adaptation of the YPP be warranted? These are some of the difficult questions that practitioners and research scientists face. We do not provide definitive answers regarding a right approach, but we encourage readers to intentionally consider these issues as they provide services to expectant young couples from diverse cultural and social backgrounds. As we seek to test the effectiveness of the YPP, a fundamental task is to demonstrate that it can help young parents across diverse ethnic, social, and economic groups, with relatively minimal or modest modifications. Unfortunately, when and how to make these modifications is not entirely clear so it is advisable to consider the tension between "fit" and "fidelity" as it pertains to the work you do with young couples from diverse cultural and social backgrounds.

This chapter differs from earlier sections of the manual in that it is less focused on how to implement the YPP and geared more toward broader "what if" and "now what" questions. It is not intended to provide a step-by-step approach for adapting the YPP, but rather begins to address thorny issues that readers will encounter as they consider implementing the YPP in real-world settings. Questions like, "What if the communities I serve are oriented more toward the extended family system than the couple dyad?" and, "If I've had difficulty engaging young people in face-to-face counseling, will they come to 14 sessions of the YPP?" may have surfaced as you read earlier sections of the manual. This chapter situates those kinds of questions in the context of an ongoing professional and academic dialogue about the benefits and challenges of implementing evidence-based interventions at scale. Additional in-depth study of the cultural adaptation literature is recommended before embarking on efforts to adapt YPP or other preventive interventions.

HUMANISM AND CULTURE

Humanistic theories posit that there are universal needs shared by all people. Theory and practice is grounded in respect for the person and acceptance of his or her subjective experience. Humanistic therapists explicitly seek to respect each client's culture, values, and the freedom to make life choices that reflect an innate capacity to be psychologically healthy (Norcross, 2010). There is a strong emphasis in most humanistic therapeutic approaches on appreciating the client's personal story. Narrative therapy, built from humanistic theoretical constructs, has been practiced across cultures for centuries (Katz, 1993).

The YPP incorporates humanistic theory into both the assessment and intervention approach. Therapists are highly focused on helping young people learn how to tell their stories to each other and how to listen to one another empathetically. These skills are expected to build the co-parents' capacities to work together to provide a nurturing environment for the child. Thus, the theoretical underpinnings of the YPP make it particularly suited to application with diverse expectant young parents. Despite the strong emphasis on understanding and appreciating cultural influences within humanistic theory, many scholars argue that further tailoring of interventions may be warranted, because the ways that people across cultures strive to meet needs for safety, security, and relational satisfaction, and the tasks that are prescribed by values and social norms, also differ. Thus, helpers must be attuned to the unique cultural and social orientations that clients bring. Groups of people with a common set of experiences, beliefs, explanatory models, and practices may approach the negotiation of major life events or developmental responsibilities in similar ways. Shared social norms and values influence many types of behavior.

Individuals may identify with multiple groups or cultures simultaneously, and may reject discrete aspects of culture as she or he constructs a unique worldview. In addition, the salience of various cultural identities may vary according to context (Pedersen et al., 2008). Moreover, identity development across the life-course allows people to bring various aspects of culture into varying levels of focus and emphasis at different times (Cross et al., 2012; Helms, 1994; Rumbaut, 2005). Essentially, culture is a complex, dynamic force influencing human behavior and decisions in a myriad of ways. As such, it is important to recognize the sameness among us, while paying equal attention to the ways in which our cultures, experiences, and worldviews differ. Efforts to actively challenge cultural encapsulation—the tendency to define reality according to one's own set of cultural assumptions (Wrenn, 1985)—must be part of every practitioner's work. Sue, Ivey, and Pedersen (1996) have described this balance in the following way:

> We are both similar and different at the same time. No matter how different another person is from you, there is always some degree of similarity. No matter how similar the other person is to you, there is always some degree of difference. If either similarities or differences are overemphasized, you will get into trouble. If you overemphasize diversity and differences between people, you end up with stereotyped, disconnected categories that tend to be hostile toward one another. If you overemphasize similarities, you rob persons and groups of their individual identities.

In addition, it is critical to actively undo socially constructed views of certain groups of people as inferior or superior. Examination of our assumptions regarding the behaviors, beliefs, and values of groups of people based on outward physical appearance and social group assignment (i.e., race/ethnicity) is essential to unpacking commonly held negative biases that impact our ability to provide effective care. Finally, recognizing that societal structures and policies create conditions that can both hinder and promote well-being is important. This is especially true for people currently in the nondominant group in the United States. Young, racial and ethnic minority men are particularly disadvantaged in contemporary society, and the consequences for young families and children are well documented (Smeeding et al., 2011; Tach & Edin, 2011). Researchers in political science and sociology have demonstrated that joblessness, incarceration, and under education are a lethal combination of forces impacting young men and their children. Despite common aspirations among people from majority and minority groups regarding parenthood, family formation, and marriage, the prospects for success are much dimmer for low-income young men and women of color (Tach & Edin, 2011).

Individuals, nested in family, community, and societal contexts (Bronfenbrenner, 1979) are sometimes constrained, and at other times supported in making healthy behavioral choices. This is true for young expectant parents who we seek to engage in the YPP. Understanding social and economic variations, and adapting our interventions to reflect and leverage cultural norms, beliefs, and practices, is part of the work of cultural adaptation. Even though the YPP is built upon a humanistic framework that intentionally seeks to honor the individual's experience within his or her own culture, it is important to critically evaluate outcomes for different groups of young expectant couples and to consider adaptation of the intervention in order to maximize effectiveness and positive outcomes for young families.

WHERE TO BEGIN? COMMUNITY ENGAGED RESEARCH CONTINUUM

Practitioners and researchers continue to discuss whether it is feasible to adapt interventions for the myriad number of cultural groups that exist in the United States alone. Moreover, cultures are dynamic and ever changing, making it even more complicated to keep up with prevailing attitudes, beliefs, and norms. Yet, a robust movement toward community-engaged research—defined as "the process of working collaboratively with and through groups of people affiliated by geographic proximity, special interest or similar situations to address issues affecting the well-being of those people"—is well underway (CTSA Consortium, 2011). This movement, toward equalizing the input of community members who have knowledge about both the assets and problems that affect their health and well-being, strongly supports an increased emphasis on developing culturally adapted interventions.

Like the process of cultural adaptation, community engagement in program development (CTSA, 2011) can also be conceptualized as a continuum, based on the quality and level of involvement with the population or group being served. The community engagement paradigm is relevant to cultural adaptation because researchers and practitioners who wish to culturally adapt a program such as the YPP must also engage the community at some level.

At one end of the continuum, researchers and program developers do not engage the community in the process of program design, but rely on the community to help conduct outreach to those they wish to serve, providing information about the intended activities to establish communication channels. This level of engagement is often utilized when the focus is on making use of previously tested models of intervention and maximizing recruitment into an intervention. At the next level, community members are consulted about a proposed project. Feedback regarding program elements or approaches may be solicited with the goals of tailoring recruitment and retention strategies, and building connections between program providers and potential participants. Further along, community members become involved more directly in program delivery, so that a component of participation is introduced, which is expected to increase cooperation. Yet another level of engagement entails collaboration with members of an affected community, such that members contribute to identifying priorities, developing and testing solutions, and communicating results. Last, the highest level of community engagement brings community members and practitioners/researchers together as equal partners. Community members decide what is needed, what resources are available, and what solutions are best suited to the particular health concern. At this end, interventions developed from the ground up are focused on congruence with the lived experience, cultural orientation, and value system of a particular group. Probably the best known approach for building interventions from community-identified priorities is Community Based Participatory Research (CBPR; Israel, 2005).

The continuum of community engagement, from outreach to shared leadership in the development of interventions, encompasses a range of potential points of entry in working with diverse communities and cultural groups (CTSA, 2011). Some experts in the field advocate for more culturally relevant and community-driven interventions using a CBPR approach. They believe that in order to make progress toward reducing racial and ethnic health disparities in particular, a shift toward community identification of priorities, needs, assets, and solutions is required (CTSA, 2011). Our humanistic approach respects the uniqueness of cultures and communities, but as a model the YPP is more top down than community driven. Nonetheless, we recognize that if the model is to have a sustainable impact, we must demonstrate its value and relevance to the specific communities we hope to serve.

WHAT IS CULTURAL ADAPTATION?

Cultural adaptation has been defined as "systematic changes made to a protocol so that features of the culture and language of particular groups are considered as part of the treatment" (Bernal, Jimenez-Chafe, & Domenech Rodriguez, 2009). Other definitions highlight similar concepts, and also emphasize the client's context, and the importance of increasing compatibility or congruence between the intervention and the client's worldview, to positively influence the expected outcomes of the intervention (Bernal et al., 2009; Castro et al., 2010).

Numerous models, frameworks, and guidelines for cultural adaptation of evidence-based interventions are now accessible in the psychotherapy and counseling literature (Bernal & Domenach-Rodriquez, 2012). Bernal and Domenach-Rodriguez identify 12 published descriptions of cultural adaptation. Although each has some unique features, or is guided by a particular theoretical orientation, many commonalities exist in the models, frameworks, and guidelines published for adapting evidence-based interventions to specific cultural groups. For example, many of the frameworks include formative and summative phases, where data are collected regarding local norms and values and pilot work is done to test culturally adapted interventions to help shape future iterations of the treatment protocol. Several models emphasize the value of developing a conceptual framework for guiding the adaptations, based on hypothesized links between cultural and psychological processes. An important element that cuts across most models is the incorporation of input on intervention content from local stakeholders and experts, via various engagement strategies. As suggested earlier, many of the models direct attention to the process of balancing fidelity to the original intervention, with fit for the population who will receive it. The models also share a common focus on improving outcomes via cultural adaptation. Many emphasize attention to provider characteristics as well as treatment process and content in order to maximize relevance, acceptability, and validity for diverse clients (Bernal & Domenach-Rodriguez, 2012).

A more in-depth description of one model used in both practice and research context is instructive. Domenach-Rodreguez and Wieling's Cultural Adaptation Process Model (CAPM), developed in 2004 has three phases—setting the stage, initial adaptations, and adaptation iterations. In the first phase, collaboration between the intervention researcher and a cultural adaptation expert is established. The collaborators utilize the available scientific literature to evaluate the fit of the proposed intervention for a specific cultural group. Meetings with local stakeholders follow, to gauge priorities, needs, and interest in the proposed intervention. This is augmented with additional community needs assessment activity. The second phase includes work to identify appropriate outcome measures, and a two-step process to adapt the intervention. The first adaptation (a priori) is completed using data collected in Phase 1 assessment activity. Then, a post intervention adaptation occurs, based on lessons learned. Finally, in the third phase, research/practitioner teams evaluate whether additional adaptations are needed, and whether the original intervention may be improved by incorporating changes discovered during the adaptation process (described in Bernal and Domenach-Rodriguez, 2012). As you will read later in this chapter, the CAPM was utilized to inform early stages of the cultural adaptation process of the YPP. There are many models and frameworks to select from, some of which are more complicated and labor intensive than others. Before deciding on which is best, researchers are urged to evaluate what is necessary to conduct a valid test of their model and what resources they have available for the adaptation processs.

WHAT IS THE EVIDENCE SUPPORTING CULTURALLY ADAPTED INTERVENTIONS?

Several recent evaluations of culturally adapted interventions (CAI) demonstrate the importance of strengthening the evidence-based toolkit available to practitioners by adapting existing prevention and psychotherapeutic interventions. Griner and Smith (2006) conducted one of the first meta-analyses of CAIs that included both prevention-oriented studies and studies of interventions focused on clinically diagnosed populations. Findings clearly supported the effectiveness of culturally adapted interventions; an effect size of d =. 45 was reported, which is considered a moderate level of effect. Of the studies included, the vast majority (84%) described adapting interventions to better incorporate cultural values and concepts from the group served. Large percentages of the studies reviewed utilized therapist/client matching by ethnic group (61%) and by preferred language (74%). Those studies that reported that interventions were provided to clients in their primary language (other than English) were twice as effective as studies that did not utilize this element of cultural adaptation. Studies that had higher numbers of Latino participants and larger proportions of older subjects also had greater effect sizes. Griner and Smith concluded "culturally adapted interventions resulted in significant client improvement across a variety of conditions and outcome measures" (Griner & Smith, 2006).

Two more recent meta-analytic studies that combined results from racial and ethnic minority patients who participated in 59 and 64 studies, respectively, demonstrated that cultural adaptations of existing evidence-based interventions for psychological disorders are more effective than the original unadapted intervention protocols (Benish et al., 2011; Smith et al., 2011). The effect size for culturally adapted interventions evaluated in Benish and co-workers (2011) was d =. 32 and in Smith and colleagues (2011) the effect size reported was d =. 46. Although these two meta-analyses included only studies that utilized psychotherapy to reduce suffering, distress or illness, and excluded studies that focused on prevention, the results are still applicable. Because YPP utilizes many features of traditional or bonafide psychotherapy (Wampold, 1997), including a tailored therapeutic relationship, incorporation of psychological processes, and a manual to guide therapists, it is reasonable to consider these meta-analytic results as supporting evidence for pursuing adaptations of preventive interventions.

ARE CULTURAL ADAPTATIONS NEEDED?

Psychologists and mental health providers from a variety of other disciplines adhere to codes of ethics that explicitly recognize the importance of understanding the cultural orientation of those we seek to serve (APA, 2010). Competency standards for delivery of care to individuals from varying cultural, social, and economic backgrounds have been established (APA, 2002; USDHHS, 2013). In addition, formal definitions of evidence-based practice in psychology include direct reference to integrating "the best available research with clinical expertise in the context of patient characteristics, culture and preferences" (APA Presidential Task Force on Evidence Based Practice, 2006). Therefore, although the YPP has established a strong evidence-based track record through two randomized control trials, questions and opportunities remain in order to increase its effectiveness for young people from a variety of backgrounds and who embrace a range of cultural identities.

Individual practitioners, supervisors, and program managers are not expected to undertake comprehensive adaptations based on the introductory nature of this chapter. However, we do expect that the issues covered will prompt counselors and service providers to consider whether YPP is contextually relevant, to reflect on what adaptations might be warranted, and to utilize evaluation strategies described elsewhere in this volume to monitor and decide when a formal adaptation is appropriate. In addition, through the practice of cultural humility, we expect that counselors and supervisors will invest time and resources in implementing some elements of cultural adaptation in service delivery with couples. Details about the specific elements of cultural adaptation are described later in this chapter, which includes the following steps: (a) provide YPP in the preferred language of clients; (b) consult with community leaders regarding local history, culture, and social conditions; and (c) engage young parents to gain their insights regarding strategies that could enhance the relevance of YPP for their peers.

WHAT TO THINK ABOUT NEXT: HOW MUCH CULTURAL ADAPTATION?

As indicated earlier, cultural adaptation is situated along a continuum, from surface to deep structural changes, allowing for increasing or decreasing levels of cultural specification. Resnicow and colleagues (1999) defined surface cultural adaptations as those that involve changes in materials or activities that address observable and superficial aspects of a target population's culture (i.e., music, food, clothing). This might be achieved by arranging office environments in ways that reflect the cultural values, history, and pastimes of the people that are served. Displaying typical artwork, playing waiting room music associated with certain cultures, and including signage and informational materials in the primary language spoken by intervention participants are some examples of surface structure adaptations. For some programs, incorporation of staff training and supervision to address issues of cultural competence is considered a step toward cultural adaptation. Generally, these approaches put the onus of responsibility on the provider and organization to build the capacity to deliver effective services to program participants from diverse backgrounds.

A cultural adaptation of the YPP that includes surface-level program modification to the process of engaging couples seems like a logical first step. Programs might prioritize hiring administrative support staff who speak multiple languages, who live in the neighborhoods in which participants are recruited, and who are committed to serving young parents. Although hiring people who look like or speak the same language as participants is important, one should not assume that these staff are not in need of supervision and training. It is the combination of clinical skill and insider knowledge about the culture and community that will yield respectful and sensitive care tailored to each unique couple. With the right organizational environment, a balance between professionalism and cultural sensitivity can be achieved.

By contrast, deep structured adaptations involve changes based on cultural, social, historical, environmental, and psychological factors that influence health behaviors in ways that are more fundamental and linked to shared social norms about behavior. Deep structural adaptations require researchers and practitioners to incorporate multidisciplinary perspectives from sociology, history, political science, anthropology, and psychology to best understand the explanatory frameworks that individuals bring into preventive interventions. For example, if a young urban African-American woman has grown up in a social milieu in which most families are multigenerational and include both biological and nonbiological kin, then focusing on strengthening the co-parenting relationship between mother and father may be regarded as incongruent with cultural practices, social norms, and expectations.[1] In fact, Gaskin-Butler and co-workers (2012) report that among a sample of pregnant, unmarried first-time African-American mothers (mean age = 20.7), the majority of participants reported expectations of a multi-person co-parenting system that includes the maternal grandmother, father, and other relatives. Collectivist ideology, in contrast to a more individualistic ideology, is associated with many non-Western cultures (Pederson, Crether, & Carlson, 2008). This suggests that a deeper level of cultural adaptation would define co-parenting more broadly to include other family members who contribute to childcare.

Cultural adaptations are needed because: (a) Few studies of existing evidence-based interventions report outcomes by group; thus it is not clear whether everyone is benefiting equally from available preventive intervention services; and (b) Most evidence-based interventions have not included sufficient numbers of individuals from diverse cultural backgrounds to assure that the

---

[1] For some readers, a broad generalization about Western and non-Western culture strikes a negative chord. Indeed, you might be thinking, "This is not unique to African Americans or other national groups. European-American ethnic cultures also value extended family systems." Or you might think it is unwise to lump so many diverse histories and cultures together, and assign them to seemingly opposing worldviews. These concerns are understandable, and again remind us to avoid reductionist thinking and embrace complexity in an effort to appreciate the way that culture impacts the work we do (Sue, 1998).

findings are applicable or generalizable to these populations. Despite the lack of available science to determine whether it is reasonable to conclude that current evidence-based interventions are appropriate for diverse groups of people living in the United States, data regarding utilization of mental health services by racial and ethnic minorities suggest that we are not adequately addressing needs or improving health outcomes (Alegria et al., 2002; USDHHS, 2001).

Researchers and practitioners struggle to decipher the right ingredients needed to effectively engage members of cultural groups with distinct health beliefs, practices, and histories that vary from the dominant, European and Western culture of the United States. Although young expectant women and men report many similar values, desires, and goals for their relationship and children's futures, the path to achieving that vision is sometimes different. Moreover, the obstacles along the way, because of social and economic conditions that often vary with racial and ethnic status, can erect significant obstacles.

Research studying the trajectories of unmarried women, men, and their children recently concluded that policies to strengthen fragile families should:

> Support the three Ts: Treat early, Treat often, and Treat together. Although many fragile families break up in the years after their babies are born, most of the parents are together at the time of the birth and most have high hopes for a future together. Services to fragile families at this "magic moment" should be immediate, intense, and focused on the couple in their role as cooperative parents. (Executive Summary, *The Future of Children*, 20(2), Fall 2010)

In addition, research findings from the Fragile Families and Child Well-Being study suggest that community-based programs that focus on building relationship skills among at-risk parents and include mental health components are needed. These findings suggest that young people typically engaged in YPP are likely to benefit from its focus on communication, relational competence, and development of a warm, supportive, and stable environment for children. However, the modality, content, and process of an intervention to best fit the cultural and socioeconomic circumstances of young couples is not prescribed in the recommendations regarding fragile families. Opportunity to tailor interventions, based on knowledge of the preferences, beliefs, and values of segmented groups of young parents (i.e., Island Puerto Ricans, first-generation Vietnamese immigrants) exists within these broad recommendations.

In fact, results from government-funded marriage and relationship education programs for lower income couples are quite mixed, leaving some room for optimism, but also challenging practitioners and researchers to continue efforts to identify what works. Interestingly, questions and opposing interpretations of results regarding the effectiveness of these programs for racial and ethnic minorities are currently being debated (Hawkins et al., 2013; Johnson, 2012, 2013). In two of the recent interventions focused on building relationship skills among low-income and/or racial and ethnic minority men and women, African-American and Hispanic couples were initially more likely to benefit than whites, but these effects disappeared over time. In one program, negative effects among African-American couples were reported. Although scholars agree that the recruitment and retention of minority and low-income couples into these programs has been effective, disagreement about whether continued investment is warranted is strong. Some see the modest, but short-term (15 months) positive effects of marriage and relationship education programs as evidence for further development and testing of these approaches (Hawkins et al., 2013). Others suggest that the evidence is weak and that funds used to support marriage and relationship education programs are being diverted from more effective family-strengthening approaches that reduce poverty, such as Temporary Assistance to Needy Families (Johnson, 2013).

These concerns about whether interventions that focus on building relationship skills are the right investment are serious, given the association between racial and ethnic minority status and low socioeconomic status in the United States. Many argue that directing policy and resources toward poverty reduction represents a better long-term strategy to improve outcomes for young parents and their children. This chapter will not resolve long-standing debates, but it is important for practitioners, supervisors, and program managers to be cognizant of the competing issues. As is the case in many complex health and social policy debates, we do not yet have definitive answers about which way to go. It may be wise to advocate for "both/and" rather than "either/or" at this point. That is, support for relationship education programs, such as the YPP, is warranted alongside investments to increase high school graduation rates, create transitional jobs, and implement living wage policies. The YPP's dual focus on couples counseling and case management recognizes the importance of addressing factors at the individual, couple, family, and system level that are likely to contribute to the development of a successful co-parenting alliance and to result in better outcomes for children born to young parents.

The evidence for cultural adaptation of evidence-based interventions is strong, but a clear roadmap has yet to emerge. Pursuit of surface structure adaptation will not address fundamental differences in health beliefs, social norms, and family process among the various cultural groups living in the United States today. Yet, recognizing that there are many overlapping cultural values, there is some justification for incorporating surface level adaptations into our program and practice tools. When evidence emerges that surface level adaptations have not yielded adequate results, or when negative impacts are discovered, deep structural adaptation and/or development of interventions through approaches like Community Based Participatory Research is warranted.

HOW CAN EXISTING INTERVENTIONS BE CULTURALLY ADAPTED?

Culturally adapted interventions utilize existing evidence-based interventions as a base and then incorporate varying levels of community engagement to best fit the intervention to the cultural context of intended participants. Several examples illustrate the process of adapting evidence-based interventions to specific groups. Nicolas and Schwartz (2012) reported on lessons learned for adapting a cognitive behavioral treatment for black Caribbean youth. The authors utilized the Ecological Validity Framework (Bernal, 2006) to adapt a well-researched depression intervention—the Adolescent-Coping with Depression Course (ACDC), which has been adapted for Puerto Rican adolescents as well. The project integrated community engagement strategies with cultural adaptation processes. Through a series of four focus groups with Haitian-American adolescents, the treatment developers collected data about how depression symptoms are manifest among Haitian adolescents and what barriers exist to recruitment and retention. In addition, the adolescents reviewed the treatment manual for the ACDC and provided written feedback and verbal comments regarding the fit of ACDC content to the adolescent's own experience. Selected quotations from adolescents who participated in the focus groups amplify the importance of undertaking the adaptation process.

> In one group, a boy (age 15) said, "I did not see anything at all in the book that came close to Haitian culture." A girl (age 16) said, "Actually I don't think that there was anything in the manual that looked like the culture of many of my friends either, and they are not Haitians." Another girl (age 15) said, "When I was reading the direct sections, I felt like someone was just talking down to me, like I did not know anything at all. We are young, not stupid." Data from the focus groups was utilized to develop an adapted version of the ACDC, which is now undergoing a second round of reviews prior to being tested with depressed Haitian adolescents.

Other intervention researchers also provide detailed accounts of the cultural adaptation process. Lau (2012) reported on her experience in adapting parent training programs for Chinese immigrants. Using the Selective and Directed Adaptation Framework (Lau, 2006), which focuses on efforts to improve engagement and outcomes, a three-phase process integrated quantitative and qualitative data from Chinese immigrant parents and Chinese bilingual, bicultural clinicians to guide the adaptation of the evidence-based Incredible Years intervention. The primary concepts of evidence-based parent training were presented to clinicians in three focus groups, and feedback regarding the cultural acceptability and relevance for Chinese immigrants was solicited. Clinician's provided valuable insight into the match or fit between standard parent training models and the social context of Chinese immigrant parents. For example, reactions to the concept of utilizing child-directed play as part of a parent training intervention yielded the following responses from two bicultural clinicians:

> Clinician 1: "Play generally isn't something that Asian parents and their kids do, it's not hierarchical...there's a proper position of the parent and the child so that following the child doesn't fit." Clinician 2: "Culturally, this kind of play is almost nonexistent. It's not seen as something that's beneficial. The Chinese culture is more achievement oriented. So everything has to have educational value." (Bernal & Domenach-Rodriguez, 2012, p. 137)

Based on the data collected, the treatment developers concluded that an adapted intervention needed to address possible concerns about cultural incongruence by focusing on therapeutic process elements, including the working alliance between parents and therapists. They hypothesized that efforts in this realm would improve engagement. In addition, the adaptation process attended to therapeutic content, ultimately augmenting the original nine session Incredible Years intervention with five additional sessions that addressed culturally relevant stressors for immigrant Chinese parents and challenges that were identified in learning new skills. This adaptation represents a balance between fitting the model to the population and fidelity to the original model.

Results reported by Lau and co-authors (2011) indicate that the adaptations produced positive results. The retention rate for parents was 83% across the

14-week intervention. Parents who received the intervention reported lower levels of negative discipline and increased positive school involvement with clinically referred children, when compared with waitlist controls. Children also showed significant decreases in both internalizing and externalizing behavior problems. Further study of the adaptation is being pursued to better understand which components of the cultural tailoring process are most important to achieve outcomes (Lau, 2012).

HAS THE YPP BEEN CULTURALLY ADAPTED?

In this section, we describe preliminary work to culturally adapt YPP to better fit the local culture and socioeconomic context of African-American adolescents in Milwaukee, Wisconsin. The descriptive account provides examples of some of the theoretical issues surrounding cultural adaptation of evidence-based interventions described in previous sections of this chapter.

Funding awarded in 2010 from the Office of Adolescent Pregnancy Programs, Adolescent Family Life Program created an opportunity to test the YPP with a new group of adolescent expectant parents. The two prior studies that tested the efficacy of the YPP intervention enrolled predominantly white and Latino (primarily Mexican-American) youth, because of the population demographics in Salt Lake City, Utah. Questions about whether YPP would work with adolescents who are negotiating the transition to parenthood in a different cultural, social, and economic milieu needed to be answered.

The Milwaukee Young Parenthood Study (MYPS) sought to implement a cultural adaptation (Resnicow, 2000) that was aimed primarily at optimizing recruitment and retention of young African-American couples. We were open to modifying how the program was to be delivered, but maintaining fidelity to the original model was held as a priority (including the focus on couples-based co-parenting). Several elements of Domenach-Rodriguez's (2004) CAPM were incorporated. The MYPS team understood that deep structural adaptations might need to be considered in future projects, based on lessons learned. As a result, the team proceeded with a mostly top-down approach that included (a) review of the YPP by a local expert in culturally competent service delivery, (b) engagement with community leaders and experts serving African-American youth and families, (c) elicitation of feedback from African-American pregnant and parenting males and females via focus groups, and (d) development of staff training on cultural humility. The Evaluator and Project Director reviewed all of the qualitative and quantitative measures that were used to measure YPP outcomes, and made some additions to the protocol in order to gather information from participants about aspects of the ecological context that may be more relevant for urban African Americans (such as perceived discrimination and views of the opportunity structure). Several interesting findings emerged from the process. The following sections focus on two of the four elements of the adaptation process: feedback from community leaders and experts and focus groups with youth.

Feedback from Community Leaders and Experts

Ten community leaders and experts were invited by the MYPS project director and evaluator to participate in a group discussion focused on testing YPP with African-American expectant couples in Milwaukee. Invitations to participate in the discussion were based on (a) experience providing services, broadly defined, to African-American youth and families, and/or (b) experience advocating for African-American youth and families. A multi-sector group of experts attended a 90-minute facilitated dialogue. Extensive written materials were provided in advance, including (a) the full YPP Counselor Manual, (b) a synopsis of the essential theoretical and program elements of YPP, and (c) a summary of central considerations in cultural adaptation, based on Bernal's ecological validity framework. A consultant from the local community, with expertise in social marketing, assisted with developing the discussion guide and facilitated the conversation. The MYPS staff, including the project director and evaluator, participated primarily as listeners and note takers.

Several important insights regarding the fit between the YPP intervention and local African-American history, culture, and context emerged. First, the discussion participants voiced questions regarding the value of a top-down approach to culturally adapt an existing intervention. They cautioned the MYPS team about the pitfalls of a research-driven versus community-driven process to assess local needs and develop effective programs. One expert noted that we should "allow community to shape this program; don't have the program shape the community." Another participant highlighted the importance of local culture, stating, "In relation to the YPP program, it feels as if we are trying to put a square peg in a round hole; make the program fit for African American families when it was not created with their values/beliefs at the core." The second theme that emerged related to the intersection of culture and socioeconomic status. Several participants emphasized that diversity within the African-American culture—across generation, gender, and socioeconomic status—merits critical attention and consideration. Last, the expert panel members questioned whether YPP adequately incorporated an understanding of the structures and dynamics of African-American families in Milwaukee. Similar to concerns raised by Chinese-American therapists in Hwang (2012) regarding cultural expectations and values related to hierarchical boundaries between youth and parents, local African-American experts cautioned that YPP's focus on the co-parenting dyad may clash with cultural norms.

Youth Focus Groups

Three focus groups to assess the need and acceptability of YPP, and to gather input regarding methods to optimize recruitment and retention, were held with self-identified African-American expectant and parenting adolescent mothers and fathers. Participants were recruited through community-based organizations and were facilitated by the same community consultant who led the facilitated dialogue with community leaders and experts. The consultant also assisted with development of the focus group guides. The project director was present for the focus groups, which were recorded and transcribed. The MYPS program manager and evaluator each reviewed the focus group transcripts for major themes. Four primary topics emerged from the discussion.

First, participants encouraged MYPS staff to highlight the intervention's focus on the child as a tool for enhancing recruitment. Second, young people emphasized the importance of employing caring, respectful counselors and staff. They cautioned against staff interacting in an overly scripted manner. One young person stated, "Come straight forward—throw the book out the window." Third, they highlighted the benefits of a genuine alliance between young people and service providers to maximize retention. "Call to check on us sometime, when you know somebody cares, it's gonna motivate you." Two themes suggested the need for deep structural adaptation. Focus group participants suggested that MYPS staff consider incorporating gender-specific individual and/or group sessions as a way of promoting better understanding of the perspectives of expectant mothers and fathers. Similar to Fagan's (2008) approach described earlier, adolescents in the focus groups indicated that some topics might need to be discussed among mothers and fathers separately in order to foster readiness to engage in productive dyadic communication. The adolescents in Milwaukee noted that a key to maintaining engagement of expectant fathers in YPP would be the ability to connect young men with jobs and resources. Fourth, pride emerged as a critical construct in several of the participants' reflections about what would make YPP work in Milwaukee. One youth commented, "Feed their [fathers] pride" and another added, "Make the young father think about [his] pride," explaining that the program can help young fathers show their partner's family that he is *trying* to make it work.

Some, but not all, of the themes and suggestions identified by community experts, leaders, and young people have been integrated into the MYPS manual, which is consistent with the third phase of the CAPM model, in which adaptations process findings inform the original interventions. Whereas some of the suggested adaptations could be incorporated into the program without diminishing the core components of the model (outlined in chapter 2), other suggestions would have required a more fundamental revision of the model, which would have defeated the purpose of testing *this* model with a new sample of young expectant parents. For example, based on the feedback provided, we adapted the model to engage extended family members more fully, depending on each couple's preferences and needs. In addition, the introduction of cultural humility as a guiding framework for YPP practitioners grew from input from both community experts and young people, who reinforced our appreciation of the importance of a therapeutic working alliance, and highlighted a set of skills that may enable counselors, young people, and their families to forge productive bonds. Finally, the revised model emphasizes the role of economic and social disadvantage as a risk factor/stressor, which may affect couples' relations and parenting.

We enrolled a small number ($N = 52$) of expectant couples in a randomized control trial of YPP in Milwaukee (MYPS) and are currently analyzing results. Preliminary findings suggest that recruitment of couples into the intervention in Milwaukee was more challenging than recruitment in Salt Lake City. In Milwaukee, 50% of couples who were randomly assigned to participate in the YPP intervention actually agreed to participate (recruitment into intervention), and 60% of those couples completed the intervention through Phase 5 (retention). In Salt Lake City, 79% of couples assigned to the intervention were retained (Florsheim et al., 2012). These differences in the interest and/or willingness of young couples to participate in the YPP intervention may be a sign that further adaptations are warranted. However, analysis of follow-up and outcome data is most critical in determining intervention impacts and next steps in the adaptation process.

CONCLUSION

This chapter set out to (a) define cultural adaptation, (b) present a rationale for cultural adaptation of evidence-based interventions, (c) highlight frameworks and guidelines currently utilized to adapt existing interventions, and (d) describe early efforts to culturally adapt YPP. We provide a basic level of information for readers, but do not expect it to sufficiently equip clinicians and program managers with all of the tools needed to embark upon a thorough process of culturally adapting YPP to fit the local context in which you serve and support young expectant parents. Nonetheless, the ideas presented in the chapter may nudge your thinking and motivate efforts to make surface level adaptations. For example, hiring staff that can deliver YPP in the preferred language of your clients is an important surface level adaptation that can be prioritized. Assuring a physical environment that includes cultural artifacts and décor that reflects the populations you serve is feasible in most cases.

As governments, community-based organizations, and practitioner leaders come to full appreciation that the United States will be a "majority-minority country" within the next 30 to 40 years, interest and emphasis on community engagement as a key strategy for translating research into practice is growing (IOM, 2013). Many resources now exist to assist communities, researchers, and practitioners who are acting in earnest to promote health for all, and reduce health disparities. It is important to recognize that successful community engagement includes knowledge, skills, and art. As mental health practitioners, we have a leg up in many ways, because our clinical training requires that we practice self-reflection in order to foster therapeutic rapport and engagement. Many of us have chosen this profession because of a passion and commitment to providing care and support to marginalized groups of people. The culture of mental health practitioners has resources and assets that help us to attend to the unique, individual characteristics of those we serve. Yet, we are challenged, like other helping professions, to examine and question the prevailing paradigms, and to critically evaluate and improve our profession in an iterative manner. We must commit to learning "how to design new programs and, if warranted, modify existing ones to properly support parents of different ages and in diverse racial and ethnic groups" (McHale et al., 2012). We hope that this chapter provides a solid beginning, or validates a path already followed.

OTHER HELPFUL RESOURCES

(1) Community Tool Box: http://ctb.ku.edu/en/default.aspx
(2) Guidelines on Multicultural Education, Training, Research, Practice, and Organizational Change for Psychologists, American Psychological Association: http://www.apa.org/pi/oema/resources/policy/multicultural-guidelines.aspx
(3) Native American Center for Excellence: http://nace.samhsa.gov/Resource Library.aspx?search=youth
(4) Principles of Community Engagement, Second Edition: http://www.cdc.gov/phppo/pce/
(5) Report of the 2005 Presidential Task Force on Evidence-Based Practice Ronald F. Levant, EdD, MBA, ABPP, President American Psychological Association: http://www.apa.org/practice/resources/evidence/index.aspx
(6) Research Evidence into Action for Community Health: *http://www.centreforreach.ca:82/reach_public/Pages/research_tools.aspx*

CULTURAL ADAPTATION TIPS

(1) Know the demographic characteristics of young parents in your local area.
(2) Review existing community needs assessments to identify local priorities, assets, and resources.
(3) Engage adult and youth stakeholders to learn about programming needs for young expectant parents using focus groups or town hall meeting formats.
(4) Partner with academic institutions that can assist with a rigorous adaptation approach for YPP.

THE YOUNG PARENTHOOD PROGRAM TOOL BOX

The following worksheets and exercises have been developed for use in the YPP intervention. You should use your clinical judgment in determining whether or not toolbox resources will benefit each couple, depending on their particular needs. It is helpful to familiarize yourself the materials/worksheets in the toolbox prior to beginning counseling with your first YPP couple.

WHAT DO YOU KNOW ABOUT EACH OTHER?

Adapted from Gottman, 1999

Read each statement and place a check mark in the appropriate TRUE or FALSE box.

I can name my partner's best friends.	True ☐	False ☐
I can tell you what stresses my partner is currently facing.	True ☐	False ☐
I know the names of some of the people who have been irritating in my partner's life.	True ☐	False ☐
I can tell you some of my partner's life dreams.	True ☐	False ☐
I can tell you about my partner's basic philosophy of life.	True ☐	False ☐
I can list the relatives my partner likes the least.	True ☐	False ☐
I know my partner's favorite music.	True ☐	False ☐
I can tell you the most stressful things that happened to my partner as a child.	True ☐	False ☐
I can list my partner's major hopes in life.	True ☐	False ☐
I know my partner's current major worries.	True ☐	False ☐
I can tell you in detail my first impression of my partner.	True ☐	False ☐

Gottman, John M. (1999). The marriage clinic: A scientifically based marital therapy; Pp. 456. New York: W.W. Norton & Company, 1999

AREAS OF STRENGTH CHECKLIST

Adapted from Gottman, 1999

- Circle the things below that are strengths in your relationship

- Check the box next to the things that you would like to work on in your relationship

- It is OK to both circle an item (a strength) and check it (something to work on).

	This is something we should work on
1. We have very good communication.	☐
2. We have a good sex life.	☐
3. We allow one another a lot of independence.	☐
4. We help each other out.	☐
5. We have good relationships with our families.	☐
6. We have similar ideas about how to have a good time and enjoy life.	☐
7. We are good friends.	☐
8. My partner gives me no reason for feeling jealous.	☐
9. We are very good at helping each other to reduce stress.	☐
10. I feel respected by my partner.	☐
11. I feel cared for by my partner.	☐
12. I feel confident that we could handle any problem that might come along.	☐
13. I feel secure in this relationship.	☐
14. We agree on issues related to children.	☐
15. We have a lot of fun.	☐
16. My partner knows and understands me.	☐
17. I have all the independence I need.	☐

Gottman, John M. (1999). The marriage clinic: A scientifically based marital therapy; Pp. 456. New York: W.W. Norton & Company, 1999

AREAS OF DISAGREEMENT CHECKLIST

Adapted from Gottman, 1999

This form contains a list of topics that many couples disagree about. We would like to get some idea of how much you and your partner disagree about each area. In the first column please indicate how much you and your partner disagree by placing a number from 0 to 100 next to each item. A zero indicates that you don't disagree at all and 100 indicates that you disagree very much. In the second column, please write down the number of years, months, weeks, or days that this has been an area of disagreement.

For example:

We disagree about...	How much?	How long?
Alcohol and drugs	90	2 months

This indicates that alcohol and drugs are something you disagree about very much and that this has been a problem for about 2 months.

We disagree about...		How much?	How long?
Money			
Communication			
Families			
Sex			
Religion			
Having fun			
Friends			
Alcohol and drugs			
Children			
Jealousy			
Emotional expression			
Issues of power			
Independence			
Handling stress			
Other:			

Gottman, John M. (1999). *The marriage clinic: A scientifically based marital therapy.* New York: W.W. Norton & Company, 1999

AREAS OF CHANGE CHECKLIST: SOLVABLE PROBLEMS

Adapted from Gottman, 1999

Circle the issues below that represent areas in your relationship that you think require some change. If that area is only a small problem circle a "1", if it is a very serious problem, circle a "5". Use the other numbers to indicate if you feel the problem is somewhere in between.

	Small Problem → Serious Problem				
1. I would like us to talk to each other more.	1	2	3	4	5
2. I would like able to do more things on my own or with friends.	1	2	3	4	5
3. I would like it if we spent more time together	1	2	3	4	5
4. I would like our relationships with our parents to improve.	1	2	3	4	5
5. I would like to have fewer problems with my jealousy.	1	2	3	4	5
6. I would like to have fewer problems with my partner's jealousy.	1	2	3	4	5
7. I would like my partner to have fewer problems with alcohol and drugs.	1	2	3	4	5
8. I would like us to have more friends in common.	1	2	3	4	5
9. I would like us to talk more.	1	2	3	4	5
10. I would like my partner to show more physical affection toward me.	1	2	3	4	5
11. I want us to go out on more "dates" together.	1	2	3	4	5
12. I want us to make love more often.	1	2	3	4	5
13. I would like to receive more appreciation for what I do.	1	2	3	4	5
14. I would like us to agree more about saving money.	1	2	3	4	5
15. I would like it if our lives were less chaotic.	1	2	3	4	5
16. I would like it if we had fewer disagreements about spending money.	1	2	3	4	5

Gottman, John M. (1999). The marriage clinic: A scientifically based marital therapy; Pp. 456. New York: W.W. Norton & Company, 1999

CONFLICT START-UP

Read each statement and circle whether you feel it is true or false for your relationship.

My partner is often very critical of me.	True	False
Arguments often seem to come out of nowhere.	True	False
My partner thinks I feel picked on too much.	True	False
I seem to get blamed for most things.	True	False
My partner says things that are mean and hurtful.	True	False
My partner acts like he or she is smarter or better than me.	True	False
I have just about had it with all this negativity between us.	True	False
I feel disrespected by my partner.	True	False
I just want to leave when conflicts occur.	True	False
I think my partner can be totally irrational.	True	False

FAMILY MAP

The first goal of the family map is to help both of you (and your counselor) get a clear idea about who are the most important people in each other's family. You family might include your biological relatives, your stepparents/siblings, and other people who are "like family," but not really related biologically or by marriage. Include both your families, putting you and your baby in the middle of the page. The second goal is help the two of you think about whom you can go to for support, particularly around issues of parenting. You do have to draw everyone in your family and you do not have to draw actual pictures. A box can be used to represent a male member of the family and a circle can be used to represent a female. You can fill in the box or circle with the name of the person.

Father of Baby's Family	Mother of Baby's Family

MY SUPPORT SYSTEM

Who is in my support system?	What do I need/want from them as support?	How do I contact them and ask for help? (consider listing phone numbers, etc.)

FEELINGS WORKSHEET

People experience a variety of emotions or feelings every day and everyone has different ways of expressing how they feel. Sometimes we have trouble finding the right words to explain how we feel. Learning how to express how we feel in a clear way helps us to communicate better with each other. Below is a list of common emotions. Use this to help your find the words to tell your partner how you feel. Feel free to use the blank boxes at the bottom to add your own words.

Annoyed	Scared	Embarrassed	Peaceful
Angry	Nervous	Excited	Resentful
Worried	Happy	Frustrated	Satisfied
Bored	Ecstatic	Hurt	Comfortable
Disgusted	Content	Jealous	Interested
Thoughtful	Anxious	Lonely	Relieved
Sad	Ashamed	Loving	Overwhelmed
Distracted	Confused	Motivated	Suspicious
Surprised	Determined	Proud	Energetic

ACCEPTANCE WORKSHEET

Some of you may be familiar with the "serenity prayer" which goes like this: "God, grant me the serenity to accept the things I cannot change, the courage to change the things I can, and the wisdom to know the difference." Even if you are not religious, this prayer can be useful in thinking about how to accept ourselves and how to accept each other…when acceptance is the wise thing to do.

Learning to accept your co-parenting partner—including their faults—can be helpful, regardless of your status as a couple. The following exercise involves thinking about and evaluating your own undesirable behaviors and those of your co-parenting partner. How important is it to change the behavior(s) that you've identified? Are these behaviors hurtful or just annoying? Can you learn to live with it? Is it worth fighting about? These are all questions to think about as you try to 'let go' of different quirks and reduce stress in your co-parenting relationship.

Thinking about yourself

Write down one behavior that you would like to change about yourself:

_____

_____

_____

How important is it to you that you change this behavior?
(1 = not very important, 10 = very important) _____

How hurtful do you feel that this behavior is to your partner?
(1 = not very hurtful, 10 = very hurtful) _____

Could you learn to accept or tolerate this behavior?
(1 = unacceptable, 10 = can live with it) _____

Bonus question: What purpose does this behavior serve?

_____

Thinking about your co-parenting partner

Write down one behavior that you would like to change about your co-parenting partner:

_____

_____

_____

How important is it that your partner changes this behavior?
(1 = not very important, 10 = very important) _____

How hurtful do you feel that this behavior is to you?
(1 = not very hurtful, 10 = very hurtful) _____

Could you learn to accept or tolerate this behavior?
(1 = unacceptable, 10 = can live with it) _____

Bonus question: What purpose does this behavior serve?

_____

Discussion question: Can this exercise help you separate the problems or issues that you really want to change from the problems or issues that you can probably just let go and stop arguing about?

WHAT I LIKE ABOUT YOU/WHAT I LIKE ABOUT US WORKSHEET

Please fill in the sentences below related to your co-parenting partner and your relationship with him/her. Feel free to use the word bank provided, or come up with other positive, constructive words to fill in the blanks.

WORD BANK

Happy	Inspired	Secure
Energetic	Joy	Amazed
Excited	Loving	Silly
Amazed	Motivated	Fun
Comfortable	Peaceful	Happy
Content	Proud	Wanted
Hopeful	Satisfied	Proud

You make me feel _____.

Our relationship makes me feel _____.

A characteristic I admire about your personality is _____

_____

_____.

You are good at_____.

I knew I wanted to be in a relationship with you when _____.

One of my favorite things to do together is _____.

I like when you_____.

CO-PARENTING PLANNING WORKSHEET

Below is a list of common parenting responsibilities. Thinking about yourself and your partner, please indicate how you will share or divide these responsibilities:

	Often	Sometimes	Rarely	Never
Take your child to his/her doctor appointments				
You will do this	3	2	1	0
Your Partner will do this	3	2	1	0
Get up in the night to feed or soothe your child				
You will do this	3	2	1	0
Your Partner will do this	3	2	1	0
Buy necessary things for your child				
You will do this	3	2	1	0
Your Partner will do this	3	2	1	0
Earn money to buy items or contribute financially for your family (baby stuff, groceries, rent)				
You will do this	3	2	1	0
Your Partner will do this	3	2	1	0
Change diapers				
You will do this	3	2	1	0
Your Partner will do this	3	2	1	0
Put clothes on your child				
You will do this	3	2	1	0
Your Partner will do this	3	2	1	0
Clean the room/home				
You will do this	3	2	1	0
Your Partner will do this	3	2	1	0
Make bottles for your child/feed your child				
You will do this	3	2	1	0
Your Partner will do this	3	2	1	0
Give your child baths				
You will do this	3	2	1	0
Your Partner will do this	3	2	1	0
Put your child to bed				
You will do this	3	2	1	0
Your Partner will do this	3	2	1	0
Take your child to day care (if you use one)				
You will do this	3	2	1	0
Your Partner will do this	3	2	1	0
Play with your child				
You will do this	3	2	1	0
Your Partner will do this	3	2	1	0

INSTRUCTIONS

The fidelity check consists of 3 components: 1) dose, 2) completed program activities, and 3) session helpfulness.

1) Dose is quantified as whether the counselor provided a minimum number of sessions for each phase. Counselors will receive a '1' if they did not meet the minimum number of sessions and a '2' if they met or exceeded the minimum.
2) Critical program activities for each phase are listed below. Counselors receive a '1' if none of the phase activities were completed, '2' if some (but not all) items were completed, and '3' if all items were completed.
3) Session helpfulness will be assessed via participant self-report. Participants will be asked a helpfulness question after each session; MOB and FOB responses will be averaged after each phase is complete to generate a 'helpfulness couple score' for each phase.

PHASE 1
FOR PARTICIPANT USE

Please rate how this session helped you and your partner work together to take care of your baby. Please respond honestly. We want to use your feedback to make the program better for you and others.

Session 1, Date: _____

Mother:	Not helpful (1)	Somewhat helpful (2)	Very helpful (3)
Father:	Not helpful (1)	Somewhat helpful (2)	Very helpful (3)

Comments:

_____

_____

Session 2, Date: _____

Mother:	Not helpful (1)	Somewhat helpful (2)	Very helpful (3)
Father:	Not helpful (1)	Somewhat helpful (2)	Very helpful (3)

Comments:

_____

_____

Session 3, Date: _____

Mother:	Not helpful (1)	Somewhat helpful (2)	Very helpful (3)
Father:	Not helpful (1)	Somewhat helpful (2)	Very helpful (3)

Comments:

_____

_____

PHASE I
FOR YPP COUNSELOR USE

Total number of sessions: _____

Please check the completed phase-specific program activities listed below:

- ☐ Explained program goals.
- ☐ Reviewed the boundaries of confidentiality.
- ☐ Written consent for program participation obtained.
- ☐ Assessement and case formulation complete.

Helpfulness scores

MOB total: _____
FOB total: _____
Couple score [(MOB total + FOB total) / 2]:_____

Counselor notes regarding fidelity:

_____

_____

_____

_____

_____

_____

_____

_____

PHASE 2
<u>FOR PARTICIPANT USE</u>

Please rate how this session helped you and your partner work together to take care of your baby. Please respond honestly. We want to use your feedback to make the program better for you and others.

Session 1, Date: _____

Mother:	Not helpful (1)	Somewhat helpful (2)	Very helpful (3)
Father:	Not helpful (1)	Somewhat helpful (2)	Very helpful (3)

Comments:

_____

_____

Session 2, Date: _____

Mother:	Not helpful (1)	Somewhat helpful (2)	Very helpful (3)
Father:	Not helpful (1)	Somewhat helpful (2)	Very helpful (3)

Comments:

_____

_____

Session 3, Date: _____

Mother:	Not helpful (1)	Somewhat helpful (2)	Very helpful (3)
Father:	Not helpful (1)	Somewhat helpful (2)	Very helpful (3)

Comments:

_____

_____

PHASE 2
FOR COUNSELOR USE

Total number of sessions: _____

Please check the completed phase-specific program activities listed below:

- ☐ MOB and FOB identified their personal goals based upon exploration of personal strengths and weaknesses.
- ☐ The couple identified their co-parenting relationship goals based upon relationship strengths and weaknesses.
- ☐ Counselor linked the couple's strengths and weaknesses to issues related to co-parenting.
- ☐ Counselor and couple agreed on which interpersonal relationship skills to work on first.

Helpfulness scores

MOB total: _____

FOB total: _____

Couple score [(MOB total + FOB total) / 2]:_____

Counselor notes regarding fidelity:

_____

_____

_____

_____

_____

_____

PHASE 3
<u>FOR PARTICIPANT USE</u>

Please rate how this session helped you and your partner work together to take care of your baby. Please respond honestly. We want to use your feedback to make the program better for you and others.

Session 1, Date: _____

	Mother:	Not helpful (1)	Somewhat helpful (2)	Very helpful (3)
	Father:	Not helpful (1)	Somewhat helpful (2)	Very helpful (3)

Comments:

_____

_____

Session 2, Date: _____

	Mother:	Not helpful (1)	Somewhat helpful (2)	Very helpful (3)
	Father:	Not helpful (1)	Somewhat helpful (2)	Very helpful (3)

Comments:

_____

_____

Session 3, Date: _____

	Mother:	Not helpful (1)	Somewhat helpful (2)	Very helpful (3)
	Father:	Not helpful (1)	Somewhat helpful (2)	Very helpful (3)

Comments:

_____

_____

Session 4, Date: _____

Mother:	Not helpful (1)	Somewhat helpful (2)	Very helpful (3)
Father:	Not helpful (1)	Somewhat helpful (2)	Very helpful (3)

Comments:

_____

_____

Session 5, Date: _____

Mother:	Not helpful (1)	Somewhat helpful (2)	Very helpful (3)
Father:	Not helpful (1)	Somewhat helpful (2)	Very helpful (3)

Comments:

_____

_____

Session 6, Date: _____

Mother:	Not helpful (1)	Somewhat helpful (2)	Very helpful (3)
Father:	Not helpful (1)	Somewhat helpful (2)	Very helpful (3)

Comments:

_____

_____

PHASE 3
FOR COUNSELOR USE

Total number of sessions: _____

Please check the completed phase-specific program activities listed below:

- ☐ The counselor and couple worked on at least three of the following interpersonal communication skills:
    - ☐ expressing needs and feelings
    - ☐ reflective listening
    - ☐ support skills
    - ☐ problem solving
    - ☐ stress reduction
    - ☐ acceptance
    - ☐ conflict de-escalation
    - ☐ communicating about family planning
    - ☐ minimizing negativity.

Helpfulness scores

MOB total: _____

FOB total: _____

Couple score [(MOB total + FOB total) / 2]:_____

Counselor notes regarding fidelity:

_____

_____

_____

_____

_____

PHASE 4
FOR PARTICIPANT USE

Please rate how this session helped you and your partner work together to take care of your baby. Please respond honestly. We want to use your feedback to make the program better for you and others.

Session 1, Date: _____

Mother:	Not helpful (1)	Somewhat helpful (2)	Very helpful (3)
Father:	Not helpful (1)	Somewhat helpful (2)	Very helpful (3)

Comments:

_____

_____

Session 2, Date: _____

Mother:	Not helpful (1)	Somewhat helpful (2)	Very helpful (3)
Father:	Not helpful (1)	Somewhat helpful (2)	Very helpful (3)

Comments:

_____

_____

Session 3, Date: _____

Mother:	Not helpful (1)	Somewhat helpful (2)	Very helpful (3)
Father:	Not helpful (1)	Somewhat helpful (2)	Very helpful (3)

Comments:

_____

_____

Session 4, Date: _____

Mother:	Not helpful (1)	Somewhat helpful (2)	Very helpful (3)
Father:	Not helpful (1)	Somewhat helpful (2)	Very helpful (3)

Comments:

_____

PHASE 4
FOR COUNSELOR USE

Total number of sessions: _____

Please check the completed phase-specific program activities listed below:

- ☐ The couple discussed changing roles, needs, and interpersonal boundaries with family.
- ☐ The couple discussed changing roles, needs, and interpersonal boundaries with friends.
- ☐ The couple discussed changing roles, needs, and interpersonal boundaries with each other.

Helpfulness scores

MOB total: _____

FOB total: _____

Couple score [(MOB total + FOB total) / 2]:_____

Counselor notes regarding fidelity:

_____

_____

_____

_____

_____

_____

PHASE 5
FOR PARTICIPANT USE

Please rate how this session helped you and your partner work together to take care of your baby. Please respond honestly. We want to use your feedback to make the program better for you and others.

Session 1, Date: _____

Mother:	Not helpful (1)	Somewhat helpful (2)	Very helpful (3)
Father:	Not helpful (1)	Somewhat helpful (2)	Very helpful (3)

Comments:

_____

_____

Session 2, Date: _____

Mother:	Not helpful (1)	Somewhat helpful (2)	Very helpful (3)
Father:	Not helpful (1)	Somewhat helpful (2)	Very helpful (3)

Comments:

_____

_____

Session 3, Date: _____

Mother:	Not helpful (1)	Somewhat helpful (2)	Very helpful (3)
Father:	Not helpful (1)	Somewhat helpful (2)	Very helpful (3)

Comments:

_____

_____

Total number of sessions: _____

Please check the completed phase-specific program activities listed below:

☐ The counselor and couple summarized progress and accomplishments to-date.

☐ The couple can identify future resources for family support and parenting.

Helpfulness scores

MOB total: _____

FOB total: _____

Couple score [(MOB total + FOB total) / 2]:_____

Counselor notes regarding fidelity:

_____

_____

_____

_____

_____

_____

PHASE 6
FOR PARTICIPANT USE

Please rate how this session helped you and your partner work together to take care of your baby. Please respond honestly. We want to use your feedback to make the program better for you and others:

Session 1, Date: _____

Mother:	Not helpful (1)	Somewhat helpful (2)	Very helpful (3)
Father:	Not helpful (1)	Somewhat helpful (2)	Very helpful (3)

Comments:

_____

_____

Session 2, Date: _____

Mother:	Not helpful (1)	Somewhat helpful (2)	Very helpful (3)
Father:	Not helpful (1)	Somewhat helpful (2)	Very helpful (3)

Comments:

_____

_____

Session 3, Date: _____

Mother:	Not helpful (1)	Somewhat helpful (2)	Very helpful (3)
Father:	Not helpful (1)	Somewhat helpful (2)	Very helpful (3)

Comments:

_____

_____

PHASE 6
FOR COUNSELOR USE

Total number of sessions: _____

Please check the completed phase-specific program activities listed below:

- ☐ Counselor and couple reconnected, reviewed current co-parenting status, and identified pressing relationship/co-parenting needs
- ☐ Used previously developed communication skills to address current co-parenting needs and goals.
- ☐ Identified immediate needs for parenting support/education.
- ☐ Introduced new communication skills if necessary; applied new skills to immediate needs.
- ☐ Counselor provided closure in the therapeutic relationship with the couples by reviewing progress, accomplishments and future goals; presented a certificate of completion.

Helpfulness scores

MOB total: _____

FOB total: _____

Couple score [(MOB total + FOB total) / 2]: _____

Counselor notes regarding fidelity:

_____

_____

_____

_____

_____

_____

PHASE 1 FIDELITY SCORE

Program activities score: _____
Dose score: _____
Helpfulness couple score: _____
(Program activities + Dose + Helpfulness) * (.10) = _____
                                        (Weighted phase 1 score)

PHASE 2 FIDELITY SCORE

Program activities score: _____
Dose score: _____
Helpfulness couple score: _____
(Program activities + Dose + Helpfulness) * (.20) = _____
                                        (Weighted phase 2 score)

PHASE 3 FIDELITY SCORE

Program activities score: _____
Dose score: _____
Helpfulness couple score: _____
(Program activities + Dose + Helpfulness) * (.30) = _____
                                        (Weighted phase 3 score)

PHASE 4 FIDELITY SCORE

Program activities score: _____
Dose score: _____
Helpfulness couple score: _____
(Program activities + Dose + Helpfulness) * (.20) = _____
(Weighted phase 4 score)

PHASE 5 FIDELITY SCORE

Program activities score: _____
Dose score: _____
Helpfulness couple score: _____
(Program activities + Dose + Helpfulness) * (.15) = _____
(Weighted phase 5 score)

PHASE 6 FIDELITY SCORE

Program activities score: _____
Dose score: _____
Helpfulness couple score: _____
(Program activities + Dose + Helpfulness) * (.05) = _____
(Weighted phase 6 score)

OVERALL FIDELITY SCORE:

_____ + _____ + _____ + _____ + _____ + _____ = _____
Phase 1   Phase 2   Phase 3   Phase 4   Phase 5   Phase 6   Overall score

BIBLIOGRAPHY

Adedokun, O. A., Childress, A. L., & Burgess, W. D. (2011). Testing conceptual frameworks of nonexperimental program evaluation designs using structural equation modeling. *American Journal of Evaluation, 32*(4), 480–493.

Abidin, R. R., Lovejoy, M. C., Weis, R. R., O'Hare, E. E., & Rubin, E. C. (1999). Parenting Stress Index—Short Form. *Psychological Assessment,* **11**, 534545

Alegría, M., Canino, G., Ríos, R., Vera, M., Calderón, J., Rusch, D., & Ortega, A. (2002). Inequalities in use of specialty mental health services among Latinos, African Americans, and non-Latino Whites. *Psychiatric Services, 53*(12), 1547–1555.

Altarriba, J., & Bauer, L. M. (1998). Counseling the Hispanic client: Cuban Americans, Mexican Americans, and Puerto Ricans. *Journal of Counseling & Development, 76*(4), 389–396.

Amato, P. R. (2001). Children of divorce in the 1990s: an update of the Amato and Keith (1991) meta-analysis. *Journal of Family Psychology, 15*(3), 355.

Amato, P. R. (2005). The impact of family formation change on the cognitive, social, and emotional well-being of the next generation. *Future of Children 15*(2), 75–96.

Amato, P. R., Landale, N. S., Havasevich, T. C., Booth, A., Eggebeen, D. J., Schoen, R., et al. (2008). Precursors of young women's family formation pathways. *Journal of Marriage and Family, 70*(5), 1271–1286.

American Psychological Association Task Force on Evidence-Based Practice for Children and Adolescents. (2008). *Disseminating evidence-based practice for children and adolescents: A systems approach to enhancing care.* Washington, DC: American Psychological Association.

Anderson Juarez, J., Marvel, K., Bresinski, K. L., Glazner, C., Towbin, M. M., & Lawton, S. (2006). Bridging the gap: A curriculum to teach residents cultural humility. *Family Medicine, 38*(2), 97–102.

Arcinue, F., & Prince, J. L. (2009). Counseling teen fathers: A developmentally sensitive strength-based approach. In C. Z. Oren, & D. C. Oren (Eds.), *Counseling fathers.* (pp. 231251). New York: Routledge/Taylor & Francis Group.

Arnett, J. J. (2001). Conceptions of the transition to adulthood: Perspectives from adolescence through midlife. *Journal of Adult Development, 8*(2), 133–143.

Austin, M. P., & Leader, L. (2000). Maternal stress and obstetric and infant outcomes: Epidemiological findings and neuroendocrine mechanisms. *Australia and New Zealand Journal of Obstetrics and Gynaecology, 40*(3), 331–337.

Baer, R. A. (2003). Mindfulness training as a clinical intervention: A conceptual and empirical review. *Clinical Psychology: Science and Practice, 10*, 125–143.

Bell, K. L., & Calkins, S. D. (2000). Relationships as inputs and outputs of emotion regulation. *Psychological Inquiry, 11*(3), 160–209.

Bellg, A. J., Borrelli, B., Resnick, B., Hecht, J., Minicucci, D. S., Ory, M., et al. (2004). Enhancing treatment fidelity in health behavior change studies: Best practices and recommendations from the NIH behavior change consortium. *Healthy Psychology, 23*(5), 443–451.

Belsky, J. (1984). The determinants of parenting: A process model. *Child Development, 55*, 83–96.

Belsky, J., & Pensky, E. (1988). Marital change across the transition to parenthood. *Marriage and Family Review, 12*, 133–156.

Benish, S., Quintana, S., & Wampold, B. (2011). Culturally adapted psychotherapy and the legitimacy of myth: A direct-comparison meta-analysis. *Journal of Counseling Psychology, 58*(3), 279–289.

Bernal, G. (2006). Intervention development and cultural adaptation research with diverse families. *Family Process, 45*(2), 143–151.

Bernal, G., & Domenech Rodríguez, M. M. (2012). *Cultural adaptations: Tools for evidence-based practice with diverse populations.* Washington, DC: American Psychological Association.

Bernal, G., Jiménez-Chafey, M. I., & Rodríguez, M. (2009). Cultural adaptation of treatments: A resource for considering culture in evidence-based practice. *Professional Psychology: Research & Practice, 40*(4), 361–368.

Bolland, J. M., Bryant, C. M., Lian, B. E., McCallum, D. M., Vazsonyi, A. T., & Barth, J. M. (2007). Development and risk behavior among African American, Caucasian, and mixed-race adolescents living in high poverty inner-city neighborhoods. *American Journal Of Community Psychology, 40*(3/4), 230–249.

Borders, A. B, Grobman, W., Amsden, L., & Holl J. (2007). Chronic stress and low birth weight neonates in a low-income population of women. *Obstetrics & Gynecology, 109*(2), 331–338.

Borrelli, B., Sepinwall, D., Ernst, D., Bellg, A. J., Czajkowski, S., Breger, R., et al. (2005). A new tool to assess treatment fidelity and evaluation of treatment fidelity across 10 years of health behavior research. *Journal of Consulting and Clinical Psychology, 73*(5), 852–860.

Boyan, S., & Temini, A. M. (2004). *The psychotherapist as parent coordinator in high-conflict divorce: Strategies and techniques.* New York: Routledge.

Bradford, K. (2010). Screening couples for intimate partner violence. *Journal of Family Psychotherapy, 21*(1), 76–82.

Breen, A. V., & McLean, K. C. (2010). Constructing resilience: Adolescent motherhood and the process of self-transformation. In K. C. McLean, & M. Pasupathi (Eds.), *Narrative development in adolescence: Creating the storied self* (pp. 151–168). New York: Springer.

Bronfrenbrenner, U. (1979). *The ecology of human development.* Cambridge, MA: Harvard University Press.

Brown, B., & Prinstein, M. J. (2011). *Encyclopedia of adolescence, Vols 1–3: Normative processes in development; Interpersonal and sociocultural factors; Psychopathology and non-normative processes.* San Diego: Elsevier.

Brown, S. L. (2012). Poverty status and the effects of family structure on child well-being. In V. Maholmes, & R. B. King (Eds.), *The Oxford handbook of poverty and child development* (pp. 54–67). New York: Oxford University Press.

Burton, L. (1990). Teenage childbearing as an alternative life-course strategy in multigenerational Black families. *Human Nature, 12,* 123–143.

Carlson, E. B. (2001). Psychometric study of a brief screen for PTSD: Assessing the impact of multiple traumatic events. *Assessment, **8***(4), 431441.

Carlson, M. J., & Magnuson, K. A. (2011). Low-income fathers' influence on children. *Annals of the American Academy of Political and Social Science, 635,* 95.

Carlson, M., & McLanahan, S. (2006). Strengthening unmarried families: Could enhancing couple relationships also improve parenting? *Social Service Review, 80*(2), 297–321.

Carlson, M., McLanahan, S., & Brooks-Gunn, J. (2008). Coparenting and nonresident fathers' involvement with young children after a nonmarital birth. *Demography, 45*(2), 461–488.

Caspi, Y., Carlson, E. B., & Klein, E. (2007). Validation of a screening instrument for posttraumatic stress disorder in a community sample of Bedouin men serving in the Israeli Defense Forces. *Journal Of Traumatic Stress, **20***(4), 517527.

Castro, F., Barrera, M. R., & Steiker, L. (2010). Issues and challenges in the design of culturally adapted evidence-based interventions. *Annual Review of Clinical Psychology, 6,* 213–239.

Cheadle, J. (2010). Patterns of nonresident father contact. *Demography, 47*(1), 206.

Christensen, A., & Jacobson, N. S. (2000). *Reconcilable differences.* New York: Guilford Press.

Coard, S. I., Nitz, K. & Felice, M. E. (2000). Repeat pregnancy among urban adolescents: Sociodemographic, family, and health factors. *Adolescence, 35*(137), 193–200.

Cohen, S., Kamarck, T., & Mermelstein, R. (1983). A global measure of perceived stress. *Journal of Health and Social Behavior, 24,* 386–396.

Cohen S., & Wills, T A. (1985). Stress, social support, and the buffering hypothesis. *Psychological Bulletin, 98,* 310–357.

Collins, W. A. (April 2002). *More than myth: The developmental significance of romantic relationships during adolescence.* Presidential Address delivered to the Society for Research on Adolescence, New Orleans.

Comas-Diaz, L., & Jacobsen, F. M. (1991). Ethnocultural transference and counter transference in the therapeutic dyad. *American Journal of Orthopsychiatry, 61*(3), 392–402.

Condon, J. T., & Corkindale, C. J. (1998). The assessment of parent-to-infant attachment: Development of a self-report questionnaire. *Journal Of Reproductive & Infant Psychology, **16***(1), 57.

Condon, J. T., Corkindale, C., & Boyce, P. (2008). Assessment of postnatal paternal-infant attachment: development of a questionnaire instrument. *Journal of Reproductive & Infant Psychology, **26***(3), 195210.

Cowan, P., Cowan, C., & Knox, V. (2010). Marriage and fatherhood programs. *The Future of Children* [Online serial], *20*(2), 205–230.

Cowan, P. A., & Cowan, C. P. (1988). Changes in marriage during the transition to parenthood: Must we blame the baby? In: G. Y. Michaels, & W. A. Goldberg (Eds.), *The transition to parenthood: Current theory and research* (pp. 114–154). New York: Cambridge University Press.

Cowan, C. P., & Cowan, P. A. (1995). Interventions to ease the transition to parenthood: Why they are needed and what they can do. *Family Relations: Journal of Applied Family & Child Studies, 44*, 412–423.

Cowan, P. A., & Cowan, C. P. (2002). Interventions as tests of family systems theories: Marital and family relationships in children's development and psychopathology. *Development and Psychopathology, 14*, 731–759.

Cowan, P., Cowan, C., & Knox, V. (2010). Marriage and fatherhood programs. *Future of Children, 20*(2), 205–230.

Cowan, P. A., Cowan, C. P., Schulz, M. S., & Heming, G. (1994). Prebirth to preschool family factors in children's adaptation to kindergarten. In R. D. Parke, & S. G. Sheppard (Eds.). *Exploring family relationships with other social contexts. Family research consortium: Advances in family research* (pp. 75–114). Hillsdale, NJ: Erlbaum.

Cross, W., Grant, B., & Ventuneac, A. (2012). Black identity and well-being: Untangling race and ethnicity. In J. M. Sullivan, & A. M. Esmail (Eds.), *African American identity: Racial and cultural dimensions of the Black experience* (pp. 125–146). Lanham, MD: Lexington Books.

Cultural and Linguistic Access Standards, United States Department of Health and Human Services, Office of Minority Health (July 1, 2013). Retrieved from: http://minorityhealth. hhs.gov/templates/browse.aspx?lvl=2&lvlID=152013.

De Weerth, C., Hees, Y., & Buitelaar, J. K. (2003). Prenatal maternal cortisol and infant behavior during the first 5 months. *Early Human Development*, 139–151.

DeNavas-Walt, C., Proctor, B., & Smith, J. (September 2012). *Income, poverty, and health insurance coverage in the United States: 2011.* Retrieved from: http://www.census.gov.

Dole, N., Savitz, A., Hertz-Picciotto, I., Siega-Riz, A. M., McMahon, M. J., & Buekens, P. (2003). Maternal stress and preterm birth. *American Journal of Epidemiology, 157*, 14–24.

Domenech-Rodríguez, M., & Wieling, E. (2005). Developing culturally appropriate, evidence-based treatments for interventions with ethnic minority populations. In M. Rastogi, & E. Wieling (Eds.), *Voices of color: First-person accounts of ethnic minority therapists* (pp. 313–333). Thousand Oaks, CA: Sage.

Dubowitz, H., Black, M. M., Cox, C. E., Kerr, M. A., Litrownik, A. J., Radhakrishna, A., et al. (2001). Father involvement and children's functioning at age 6 years: A multisite study. *Child Maltreatment, 6*(4), 300.

Easterbrooks, M., Barrett, L., Brady, A., & Davis, C. (2007). Complexities in research on fathering: Illustrations from the Tufts study of young fathers. *Applied Developmental Science, 11*(4), 214–220.

Eckenrode, J., Campa, M., Luckey, D., Henderson, C., Cole, R., Kitzman, H., et al. (2010). Long-term effects of prenatal and infancy nurse home visitation on the life course of youths: 19-year follow-up of a randomized trial. *Archives of Pediatrics & Adolescent Medicine, 164*(1), 9–15.

Englund, M. M., Kuo, S., Puig, J., & Collins, W. (2011). Early roots of adult competence: The significance of close relationships from infancy to early adulthood. *International Journal of Behavioral Development, 35*(6), 490–496.

Erikson, E. (1980). *Identity and the life cycle.* New York: Norton.

Fagan, J. (2008). Randomized study of a prebirth coparenting intervention with adolescent and young fathers. *Family Relations, 57*(3), 309–323.

Fagan, J., & Palkovitz, R. (2007). Unmarried, nonresident fathers' involvement with their infants: A risk and resilience perspective. *Journal of Family Psychology, 21*, 479–489.

Fagot, B. L., Pears, K. C., Capaldi, D. M., Crosby, L., & Leve, C. S. (1998). Becoming an adolescent father: Precursors and parenting. *Developmental Psychology, 34*(6), 1209–1219.

Feinberg, M., Brown, L., & Kan, M. (2012). A multi-domain self-report measure of coparenting. *Parenting: Science and Practice, 12*, 1–21.

Feinberg, M. E. (2003). The internal structure and ecological context of coparenting: A framework for research and intervention. *Parenting: Science and Practice*, 3(2), 95–131.

Feinberg, M. E., Brown, L. D., & Kan, M. L. (2012). A multi-domain self-report measure of coparenting. *Parenting: Science and Practice*, *12*(1), 1–21.

Feinberg, M. E., & Kan, M. L. (2008). Establishing family foundations: Intervention effects on coparenting, parent/infant well-being, and parent-child relations. *Journal of Family Psychology*, *22*(2), 253–263.

Feinberg, M. E., & Sakuma, K. (2011). Co-parenting interventions for expecting parents. In J. P. McHale, & K. M. Lindahl (Eds.), *Coparenting: A conceptual and clinical examination of family systems.* (pp. 171190). Washington, DC: American Psychological Association.

Feit, M. D., Wodarski, J. S., & Paschal, A. M. (2006). *Voices of African American teen fathers: "I'm doing what I got to do."* New York: Routledge.

Florsheim, P., Burrow-Sanchaz, J., Minami, T., Heavin, S., McArthur, L., & Hudak, C. (2012). The Young Parenthood Program: A randomized trial of a counseling program for pregnant adolescents and their coparenting partners. *American Journal of Public Health, 102, 10, 18861892.*

Florsheim, P., McArthur, L., Hudak, C., Heavin, S., & Burrow-Sanchez, J. (2011). The Young Parenthood Program: Preventing intimate partner violence between adolescent mothers and young fathers. *Journal of Couple and Relationship Therapy*, *10*, 117–134.

Florsheim, P., & Moore, D. (2012). Young fathers and the transition to parenthood: An interpersonal analysis of paternal outcomes. In P. Kerig, M. Shultz, & S. Hauser (Eds.), *Adolescence and beyond: family processes and development.* (pp. 200223). New York: Oxford University Press.

Florsheim, P., & Ngu, L. (2006). Differential outcomes among adolescent fathers: Understanding fatherhood as a transformative process. In L. Kowaleski-Jones, & N. Wolfinger (Eds.), *Fragile families and the marriage agenda* (pp. 226–248). New York: Springer.

Florsheim, P., & Smith, A. (2005). Expectant adolescent couple interactions and subsequent parenting behaviors. *Infant and Mental Health Journal*, *26*(6), 504–520

Florsheim, P., Sumida, E., McCann, C. Winstanley, M., Fukui, R. Seefeldt, T., et al. (2003). Adjustment to parenthood among young African American and Latino couples: Relational predictors of risk for parental dysfunction. *Journal of Family Psychology, 17,* 65–79.

Fontana, D., & Slack, I. (1997). *Teaching meditation to children: A practical guide to the use and benefits of meditation techniques.* Boston: Element.

Fowler, J. (2012). Suicide risk assessment in clinical practice: Pragmatic guidelines for imperfect assessments. *Psychotherapy*, *49*(1), 81–90

Fox, R. A., Brenner, V. V., & Fox, R. A. (1998). Parent Behavior Checklist. *Journal of Genetic Psychology, 159,* 251256.

Frewin, K., Tuffin, K., & Rouch, G. (2007). Managing identity: Adolescent fathers talk about the transition to parenthood. *New Zealand Journal of Psychology*, *36*(3), 161–167.

Furman, W., & Shaffer, L. (2003). The role of romantic relationships in adolescent development. In P. Florsheim, & P. Florsheim (Eds.), *Adolescent romantic relations and sexual behavior: Theory, research and practical implications* (pp. 3–22). Mahwah, NJ: Erlbaum.

Furman, W., & Simon, V. A. (2006). Actor and partner effects of adolescents' romantic working models and styles on interactions with romantic partners. *Child Development, 77*(3), 588–604.

Furstenberg, F. F. (2011). The recent transformation of the American Family: Witnesssing and exploring social change. In M. J Carlson and P. England (Eds.) *Social class and changing families in an unequal America.* (pp 192220). Sanford, CA. Stanford University Press.

Furstenberg, F. F. (2007). *Destinies of the disadvantaged: The politics of teenage childbearing.* New York: Russell Sage.

Gaskin-Butler, E. T., Markievitz, M., Swenson, C., & McHale, J. (2012). Prenatal representations of coparenting among unmarried first-time African American mothers. *Family Process, 51*(3), 360–375.

Gearing, R., El-Bassel, N., Ghesquiere, A., Baldwin, S., Gillies, J., & Ngeow, E. (2011). Major ingredients of fidelity: A review and scientific guide to improving quality of intervention research implementation. *Clinical Psychology Review*, *31*(1), 79–88.

Geller, J. D., & Farber, B. A. (1993). Factors influencing the process of internalization in psychotherapy. *Psychotherapy Research, 3*, 166–180.

Gjerdingen, D. K., & Yawn, B. P. (2007). Postpartum depression screening: Importance, methods, barriers, and recommendations for practice. *The Journal of the American Board of Family Medicine, 20*(3), 280–288.

Goldfinger, K., & Pomerantz, A. M. (2010). *Psychological assessment and report writing.* Thousand Oaks, CA: Sage.

Goodman, R. (2001). Psychometric properties of the Strengths and Difficulties Questionnaire (SDQ). *Journal of the American Academy of Child and Adolescent Psychiatry, 40*, 1337–1345.

Gottman, J. (1999). *The marriage clinic: a scientifically based marital therapy.* New York: Norton.

Gottman, J., Gottman, J., & Shapiro, A. (2010). *Strengthening couple relationships for optimal child development: Lessons from research and intervention.* Washington, DC: American Psychological Association.

Gottman, J. M. & Gottman, J. S. (1999). The marriage survival kit: A research-based marital therapy. In R. Berger, & M. T. Hannah (Eds.). *Preventive approaches in couples therapy* (pp. 304–330). Philadelphia: Brunner/Mazel.

Griner, D., & Smith, T. (2006). Culturally adapted mental health intervention: A meta-analytic review. *Psychotherapy (Chicago), 43*(4), 531–548.

Grych, J. H. (2002). Marital relationships and parenting. In M. Bornstein (Ed). *Handbook of parenting*: Vol. 4: *Social conditions and applied parenting* (2nd ed.) (pp. 203–225). Mahwah, NJ: Erlbaum.

Grych, J. H., & Fincham, F. D. (2001). *Interparental conflict and child development: Theory, research, and applications.* New York: Cambridge University Press.

Guidelines on Multicultural Education, Training, Research, Practice, and Organizational Change for Psychologists, American Psychological Association, APA, 2002.

Gurman, A. S. (2008). *Clinical handbook of couple therapy.* New York: Guildford Press.

Harknett, K., & McLanahan, S. S. (2004). Racial and ethnic differences in marriage after the birth of a child. *American Sociological Review, 69*(6), 790–811

Harris, M., & Franklin, C. (2012). Taking charge: A solution-focused intervention for pregnant and parenting adolescents. In C. Franklin, T. S. Trepper, W. J. Gingerich, & E. E. McCollum (Eds.), *Solution-focused brief therapy: A handbook of evidence-based practice* (pp. 247–263). New York: Oxford University Press.

Harter, S. (1990). Self and identity development. In S. Feldman, & G. R. Elliott (Eds.), *At the threshold: The developing adolescent* (pp. 352–387). Cambridge, MA: Harvard University Press.

Hatton, H., Conger, R., Larsen-Rife, D., & Ontai, L. (2010). *Strengthening couple relationships for optimal child development: Lessons from research and intervention* (pp. 115–129). Washington, DC: American Psychological Association.

Hawkins, A. J., & Fackrell, T. A. (2010). Does relationship and marriage education for lower-income couples work? A meta-analytic study of emerging research. *Journal of Couple & Relationship Therapy, 9*(2), 181–191.

Hawkins, A. J., Stanley, S. M., Cowan, P. A., Fincham, F. D., Beach, S. H., Cowan, C. P., et al. (2013). A more optimistic perspective on government-supported marriage and relationship education programs for lower income couples. *American Psychologist, 68*(2), 110–111.

Hays, D. G. (2013). *Assessment in counseling: A guide to the use of psychological assessment procedures, 5th ed.* Alexandria, VA: American Counseling Association.

Helms, J. E. (1994). The conceptualization of racial identity and other "racial" constructs. In E. J. Trickett, R. J. Watts, & D. Birman (Eds.), *Human diversity: Perspectives on people in context* (pp. 285–311). San Francisco: Jossey-Bass.

Henley, K., & Pasley, K. (2005). Conditions affecting the association between father identity and father involvement. *Fathering, 3*(1), 59–80.

Howell, H. B., & Yonkers, K. (2006). Baby got the blues: Treating depressed pregnant and postpartum teens. In R. L. Spitzer, M. B. First, J. W. Williams, & M. Gibbon (Eds.), *DSM-IV-TR® casebook: Experts tell how they treated their own patients*, Vol. 2 (pp. 190–198). Arlington, VA: American Psychiatric Publishing.

Hrdy, S. (2009). *Mothers and others: The evolutionary origins of mutual understanding.* Cambridge, MA: Harvard University Press.

Huizink, A. C., Robles De Medina, P. G., Mulder, E. J. H, Visser, G. H. A., & Buitelaar, J. K. (2002). Psychological measures of prenatal stress as predictors of infant temperament. *Journal of the American Academy of Child and Adolescent Psychiatry, 41*(9), 1078–1085.

Hwang, W. (2012). Integrating top-down and bottom-up approaches to culturally adapting psychotherapy: Application to Chinese Americans. In G. Bernal, & M. M. Domenech Rodríguez (Eds.), *Cultural adaptations: Tools for evidence-based practice with diverse populations* (pp. 179–198). Washington, DC: American Psychological Association.

Israel, B., Eng, E., Schulz, A. J., & Parker, E. A. (Eds.). (2005). *Methods in community based participatory research in health.* San Francisco: Jossey-Bass.

Jacobson, N., & Christensen, A. (1996). *Integrative couple therapy: Promoting acceptance and change.* New York: Norton.

James, R. K., & Gilliland, B. E. (2013). *Crisis intervention strategies, 7th ed.* Belmont, CA: Brooks/Cole.

Johnson, M. D. (2013). Optimistic or quixotic? More data on marriage and relationship education programs for lower income couples. *American Psychologist, 68*(2), 111–112.

Kabat-Zinn, J. (1990). *Full catastrophe living: Using the wisdom of your mind to face stress, pain and illness.* New York: Dell.

Kabat-Zinn, J. (2003). Mindfulness-based interventions in context: Past, present, and future. *Clinical Psychology: Science and Practice, 10,* 144–156.

Karver, M., Shirk, S., Handelsman, J. B., Fields, S., Crisp, H., Gudmundsen, G., et al. (2008). Relationship process in youth psychotherapy: Measuring alliance, alliance building behaviors and client involvement. *Journal of Emotional and Behavioral Disorders, 16*(1), 15–28.

Katz, A. (1993). *Self-help in America: A social movement perspective.* New York: Twayne.

Kiecolt-Glaser, J. K., & Newton T. L. (2001). Marriage and health: His and hers. *Psychological Bulletin, 127* (4), 472–503.

Kiselica, M. S. (2011). *When boys become parents: Adolescent fatherhood in America.* Piscataway, NJ: Rutgers University Press.

Knight, J. R., Sherritt, L., Harris, S., Gates, E. C., & Chang, G. (2003). Validity of brief alcohol screening tests among adolescents: A comparison of the AUDIT, POSIT, CAGE, and CRAFFT. *Alcoholism: Clinical and Experimental Research, 27*(1), 67–73.

Kroger, J. (2012). The status of identity: Developments in identity status research. In P. K. Kerig, M. S. Schulz, & S. T. Hauser (Eds.), *Adolescence and beyond: Family processes and development* (pp. 64–83). New York: Oxford University Press.

Lamb, M. E. (Ed.) (2010). *The role of the father in child development, 5th ed.* Hoboken, NJ: Wiley.

Lau, A. S. (2006). Making the case for selective and directed cultural adaptations of evidence-based treatments: Examples from parent training. *Clinical Psychology: Science & Practice, 13*(4), 295–310.

Lau, A. S. (2012). Reflections on adapting parent training for Chinese immigrants: Blind alleys, thoroughfares, and test drives. In G. Bernal, & M. M. Domenech Rodríguez (Eds.), *Cultural adaptations: Tools for evidence-based practice with diverse populations* (pp. 133–156). Washington, DC: American Psychological Association.

Lau, A. S., Fung, J. J., Ho, L. Y., Liu, L. L., & Gudiño, O. G. (2011). Parent training with high-risk immigrant Chinese families: A pilot group randomized trial yielding practice-based evidence. *Behavior Therapy, 42*(3), 413–426.

Lerman, R. (1993). A national profile of young unwed fathers. In R. Lerman, & P. Ooms (Eds.), *Young unwed fathers: Changing roles and emerging policies* (pp. 27–51). Philadelphia: Temple University Press.

Lerner, R. M., Alberts, A. E., Jelicic, H., & Smith, L. M. (2006). Young people are resources to be developed: promoting positive youth development through adult-youth relations and community assets. In E. Clary, J. E. Rhodes, E. Clary, & J. E. Rhodes (Eds)., *Mobilizing adults for positive youth development: Strategies for closing the gap between beliefs and behaviors* (pp. 19–39). New York: Springer Science.

Levy, K., Meehan, K., Kelly, K., Reynoso, J., Weber, M., Clarkin, J., et al. (2006). Change in attachment patterns and reflective function in a randomized control trial of transference-focused psychotherapy for borderline personality disorder. *Journal of Consulting and Clinical Psychology, 74*(6), 1027–1040.

Liebenberg, L., Ungar, M., & Leblanc, J. (2013). The CYRM-12: A brief measure of resilience. *Canadian Journal of Public Health, 104*(2), e131–135.

MacLanahan, S. S., & Sandefur, G. (1994). *Growing up with a single parent: what hurts, what helps.* Cambridge, MA: Harvard University Press.

Maker, C., & Ogden, J. (2003). The miscarriage experience: More than just a trigger to psychological morbidity? *Psychology and Health, 18*(3), 403–415.

Mazzucchelli, T. G., & Sanders, M. R. (2010). Facilitating practitioner flexibility within an empirically supported intervention: Lessons from a system of parenting support. *Clinical Psychology: Science and Practice, 17*(3), 238–252.

McHale, J., Waller, M. R., & Pearon, J. (2012). Coparenting interventions for fragile families: What do we know and where do we need to go next? *Family Process, 51*(3), 284–306.

McHale, J. P., & Lindall, K. M. (Eds.) (2011). *Coparenting: A conceptual and clinical examination of family systems.* Washington, DC: American Psychological Association.

McHugh, R., Murray, H. W., & Barlow, D. H. (2009). Balancing fidelity and adaptation in the dissemination of empirically-supported treatments: The promise of transdiagnostic interventions. *Behaviour Research and Therapy, 47*(11), 946–953.

McLanahan, S., & Beck, A. N. (2010). Parental relationships in fragile families. *Future of Children, 20*(2), 17–37.

McLanahan, S., Garfinkel, I., Reichman, N. E., & Teitler, J. O. (2001). Unwed parents or fragile families: Implications for welfare and child support policy. In L. L. Wu & B. Wolfe (Eds.), *Out of wedlock: Causes and consequences of nonmarital fertility* (pp. 202–228). New York: Russell Sage.

Messinger, A. M., Davidson, L. L., & Rickert, V. I. (2010). IPV among adolescent reproductive health patients: The role of relationship communication. *Journal of Interpersonal Violence, 26*(9), 1851–1867.

Mikulincer, M., Florian, V., Cowan, P. A., & Pape Cowan, C. (2002). Attachment security in couple relationships: A systematic model and its implications for family dynamics. *Family Process, 41*(3), 405–434.

Milbrath, C., Ohlson, B., & Eyre, S. L. (2009). Analyzing cultural models in adolescent accounts of romantic relationships. *Journal of Research on Adolescence, 19*(2), 313–351.

Millar, A., Simeone, R. S., & Carnevale, J. T. (2001). Logic models: A systems tool for performance management. *Evaluation and Program Planning, 24*, 73–81.

Miller-Johnson, S., Winn, D. M., Coie, J., Maumary-Gremaud, A., Hyman, C., Terry, R., & Lochman, J. (1999). Motherhood during the teen years: A developmental perspective on risk factors for childbearing. *Development and Psychopathology, 11*, 85–100.

Milner, J. S. (1994). Assessing physical child abuse risk: The child abuse potential inventory. Clinical Psychology Review, *14*(6), 547583.

Moynihan, D. P., Smeeding, T. M., & Rainwater, L. (2004). *The future of the family.* New York: Russell Sage.

Munro, A., & Bloor, M. (2010). Process evaluation: The new miracle ingredient in public health research? *Qualitative Research, 10*(6), 699–713.

Murray, C. (2012). *Coming apart: The state of white America 19602010.* New York: Crown.

Naar-King, S., & Suarez, M. (2011). *Motivational interviewing with adolescents and young adults.* New York: Guilford Press.

Newman, M. L., & Roberts, N. A. (2013). *Health and social relationships: The good, the bad, and the complicated.* Washington, DC: American Psychological Association.

Ngu, L., & Florsheim, P. (2011). The development of relational competence among young high-risk fathers across the transition to parenthood. *Family Process, 50*, 184–202.

Nicolas, G., & Schwartz, B. (2012). Culture first: Lessons learned about the importance of the cultural adaptation of cognitive behavior treatment interventions for Black Caribbean youth. In G. Bernal, & M. M. Domenech Rodríguez (Eds.), *Cultural adaptations: Tools for evidence-based practice with diverse populations* (pp. 71–90). Washington, DC: American Psychological Association.

Norcross, J. C. (2010). The therapeutic relationship. In B. L. Duncan, S. D. Miller, B. E. Wampold, & M. A. Hubble (Eds.), *Heart & soul of change in psychotherapy*, 2nd ed. Washington, DC: American Psychological Association.

Nydegger, R. (2006). Postpartum depression: more than the 'baby blues'? In T. G. Plante (Ed.), *Mental disorders of the new millennium: Biology and function*, Vol 3. (pp. 1–23). Westport, CT: Praeger.

O'Connor, M. L. (1997). By six months postpartum, many teenagers are not using a method effectively. *Family Planning Perspectives, 29*(6), 289–290.

Office of the Surgeon General (US); Center for Mental Health Services (US); National Institute of Mental Health (US) (August 2001). Mental health: culture, race, and ethnicity. A supplement to Mental health: a report of the surgeon general. Rockville, MD: Substance Abuse and Mental Health Services Administration (US). Retrieved from: http://www.ncbi.nlm.nih.gov/books/NBK44243/.

Olmstead, S. B., Furtis, T. G., & Pasley, K. (2009). Exploration of married and divorced, nonresident men's perceptions and organization of their father role identity. *Fathering, 7*(3), 249–268.

Osofsky, J. D. (2005). Professional training in infant mental health: Introductory overview. *Infants & Young Children, 18*(4), 266–268. doi:10.1097/00001163-200510000-00003.

Owen, J., & Hilsenroth, M. J. (2011). Interaction between alliance and technique in predicting patient outcome during psychodynamic psychotherapy. *Journal of Nervous and Mental Disease, 199*(6), 384–389.

Parra-Cardona, J., & Busby, D. M. (2006). Exploring relationship functioning in premarital Caucasian and Latino/a couples: Recognizing and valuing cultural differences. *Journal of Comparative Family Studies, 37*(3), 345–359.

Parra-Cardona, J. R., Wampler, R. S., & Sharp, E. A. (2006). "Wanting to be a good father": Experiences of adolescent fathers of Mexican decent in a teen fathers program. *Journal of Marital and Family Therapy, 32*(2), 215–231.

Paulson, J. F., & Bazemore, S. D. (2010). Prenatal and postpartum depression in fathers and its association with maternal depression: a meta-analysis. *JAMA, 303*(19), 1961–1969.

Pedersen, P. B., Crethar, H. C., & Carlson, J. (2008). *Inclusive cultural empathy: Making relationships central in counseling and psychotherapy, 1st ed.* Washington, DC: American Psychological Association.

Pleck, J. H. (2010). Paternal involvement: Revised conceptualization and theoretical linkages with child outcomes. In M. E. Lamb (Ed.), *The role of the father in child development*, 5th ed. (pp. 58–93). Hoboken, NJ: Wiley.

Popenoe, D. (2005). *The state of our unions 2005: The social health of marriage in America.* National Marriage Project. New Brunswick, NJ: Rutgers.

Popenoe, D., & Whitehead, B. D. (2002). *Should we live together? What young adults need to know about cohabitation before marriage: A comprehensive review of recent research.* Charlottesville, VA: National Marriage Project.

Principles of Community Engagement (2nd ed.). Clinical and Translational Science Awards Consortium, Community Engagement Key Function Committee Task.

Rapp, C. A., & Goscha, R. J. (2004). The principles of effective case management of mental health services. *Psychiatric Rehabilitation Journal, 27*(4), 319–333.

Resnicow, K., Baranowski, T., Ahluwalia, J., & Braithwaite, R. (1999). Cultural sensitivity in public health: defined and demystified. *Ethnicity & Disease, 9*(1), 10–21.

Ridge, N. W., Warren, J. S., Burlingame, G. M., Wells, M. G., & Tumblin, K. M. (2009). Reliability and validity of the youth outcome questionnaire self-report. *Journal of Clinical Psychology, 65*(10), 1115–1126.

Roberts, A. R., & Ottens, A. J. (2005). The seven-stage crisis intervention model: A roadmap to goal attainment, problem solving, and crisis resolution. *Brief Treatment and Crisis Intervention, 5*(4), 329–339.

Robles, T. F., Slatcher, R. B., Trombello, J. M., & McGinn, M. M. (2013). Marital quality and health: A meta-analytic review. *Psychological Bulletin*, March 25 [epub ahead of print].

Roisman, G. I., Padrón, E., Sroufe, L., & Egeland, B. (2002). Earned-secure attachment status in retrospect and prospect. *Child Development, 73*(4), 1204–1219.

Rossi, P., Lipsey, M. W., & Freeman, H. E. (2004). *Evaluation. A systematic approach*, 7th ed. Thousand Oaks, CA: Sage.

Rowlands, I. J., & Lee, C. (2010). "The silence was deafening": Social service and health support after miscarriage. *Journal of Reproductive and Infant Psychology, 28*(3), 274–286.

Rumbaut, R. G. (2005). *Ethnicity and causal mechanisms* (pp. 301–334). New York: Cambridge University Press.

Santelli, J., & Kirby D. (2010). State policy effects on teen fertility and evidence-based policies. *Journal of Adolescent Health, 46*(6), 515–516.

Scharte, M., & Bolte, G. (2013). Increased health risks of children with single mothers: The impact of socio-economic and environmental factors. *European Journal of Public Health, 23*(3), 469–475.

Schoenwald, S. K., Garland, A. F., Chapman, J. E., Frazier, S. L., Sheidow, A. J., & Southam-Gerow, M. A. (2011). Toward the effective and efficient measurement of implementation fidelity. *Administration and Policy in Mental Health and Mental Health Services Research, 38*(1), 32–43.

Schulz, M., Cowan, C., & Cowan, P. (2006). Promoting healthy beginnings: A randomized controlled trial of a preventive intervention to preserve marital quality during the transition to parenthood. *Journal of Consulting and Clinical Psychology, 74*(1), 20–31

Shade, K., Kools, S., Weiss, S. J., & Pinderhughes, H. (2011). A conceptual model of incarcerated adolescent fatherhood: Adolescent identity development and the concept of intersectionality. *Journal of Child and Adolescent Psychiatric Nursing, 24*, 98–104.

Shadish, W. R., Cook, T. D., & Leviton, L. C. (1991). *Foundations of program evaluation: Theories of practice*. Thousand Oaks, CA: Sage.

Shattuck, R., & Kreider, R. (May 2013). *Social and economic characteristics of currently unmarried women with a recent birth: 2011*. Retrieved from http://www.census.gov.

Shirk, S. R., & Karver, M. (2003). Prediction of treatment outcome from relationship variables in child and adolescent therapy: A meta-analytic review. *Journal of Consulting and Clinical Psychology, 71*(3), 452–464.

Shumaker, S. A., & Brownell, A. (1984), Toward a theory of social support: Closing conceptual gaps. *Journal of Social Issues, 40*, 11–36.

Simmons, C. A., & Lehmann, P. (2013). *Tools for strengths-based assessment and evaluation*. New York: Springer.

Simpson, J. A., Rholes, W., Campbell, L., & Wilson, C. L. (2003). Changes in attachment orientations across the transitions to parenthood. *Journal of Experimental Social Psychology, 39*(4), 317–331.

Smeeding, T. M., Garfinkel, I., & Mincy, R. B. (2011). Young disadvantaged men: Fathers, families, poverty, and policy. *Annals of the American Academy of Political and Social Science, 635*(1), 6–21.

Smith, T. B., & Silva, L. (2011). Ethnic identity and personal well-being of people of color: A meta-analysis. *Journal of Counseling Psychology, 58*(1), 42–60.

Solmeyer, A. R., Feinberg, M. E., Coffman, D. L., & Jones, D. E. (2013). The effects of the family foundations prevention program on coparenting and child adjustment: A mediation analysis. *Prevention Science, Feb 13, 2013*.

Stanley, S. M., Blumberg, S. L., & Markman, H. J. (1999). Helping couples fight for their marriages: The PREP approach. In R. Berger, & M. T. Hannah (Eds.), *Preventive approaches in couples therapy*, pp. 279–303. Philadelphia: Brunner/Mazel.

Stewart, D. E., Robertson, E., Dennis, C-L., Grace, S. L., & Wallington, T. (2003). *Postpartum depression: Literature review of risk factors and interventions*. Retrieved from: http://www.who.int.

Stoddard, S. A., Henly, S. J., Sieving, R. E., & Bolland, J. (2011). Social connections, trajectories of hopelessness, and serious violence in impoverished urban youth. *Journal of Youth and Adolescence, 40*(3), 278–295.

Sue, D., Ivey, A. E., & Pedersen, P. B. (1996). *A theory of multicultural counseling and therapy*. Belmont, CA: Thomson.

Sussman, L. K. (2004). The role of culture in definitions, interpretations, and management of illness. In U. P. Gielen, J. M. Fish, & J. G. Draguns (Eds.), *Handbook of culture, therapy, and healing* (pp. 37–65). Mahwah, NJ: Erlbaum.

Swanson, K. M., Chen, H., Graham, C., Wojnar, D. M., & Petras, A. (2009). Resolution of depression and grief during the first year after miscarriage: A randomized controlled clinical trial of couples-focused interventions. *Journal of Women's Health, 18*(8), 1245–1257.

Szapocznik, J., & Kurtines, W. (1993). Family psychology and cultural diversity: Opportunities for theory, research, and application. *American Psychologist, 48*, 400–407. [Reprinted in N.

Goldberger, & J. Veroff. (1995). *Essential papers in psychology and culture*. New York: NYU Press.]

Tach, L., & Edin, K. (2011). Relationship contexts of young disadvantaged men. *Annals of the American Academy of Political & Social Science, 635*, 76–94.

Tervalon, M., & Murray-Garcia, J. (1998). Cultural humility versus cultural competence: A critical distinction in defining physician training outcomes in multicultural education. *Journal of Healthcare for the Poor and Underserved, 9*(2), 117–125.

Thomas, L., Donovan, D., Sigo, R., Austin, L., & Marlatt, G. (2009). The community pulling together: a tribal community-university partnership project to reduce substance abuse and promote good health in a reservation tribal community. *Journal of Ethnicity in Substance Abuse, 8*(3), 283–300.

Tocce, K. M., Sheeder, J. L., & Teal, S. B. (2012). Rapid repeat pregnancy in adolescents: do immediate postpartum contraceptive implants make a difference? *American Journal of Obstetrics and Gynecology, 206*(6), 481.e1–481.e7.

Tucker, A. R., & Blythe, B. (2008). Attention to treatment fidelity in social work outcomes: A review of the literature from the 1990s. *Social Work Research, 32*(3), 185–190.

Tuerk, E., McCart, M. R., & Henggeler, S. W. (2012). Collaboration in family therapy. *Journal of Clinical Psychology, 68*(2), 168–178.

Tuffin, K., Rouch, G., & Frewin, K. (2010). Constructing adolescent fatherhood: responsibilities and intergenerational repair. *Culture, Health, and Sexuality, 12*(5), 485–498.

Ungar, M. (2010). What is resilience across cultures and contexts? Advances to the theory of positive development among individuals and families under stress. *Journal of Family Psychotherapy, 21*(1), 1–16.

Ungar, M., & Liebenberg, L. (2011). Assessing resilience across cultures using mixed-methods: Construction of the child and youth resilience measure-28. *Journal of Mixed-Methods Research, 5*(2), 126–149.

Ungar, M., Liebenberg, L., Boothroyd, R., Kwond, W. M., Lee, T. Y., Leblanc, J., & Makhnach, A. (2008). The study of youth resilience across cultures: Lessons from a pilot study of measurement development. *Research in Human Development, 5*, 166–180.

Vallejo, G. G., Fernández, J. R., & Secades, R. R. (2004). Application of a mixed model approach for assessment of interventions and evaluation of programs. *Psychological Reports, 95*(3), 1095–1118.

Vance, J. C., Boyle, F. M., Najman, J. M., & Thearle, M. J. (2002). Couple distress after sudden infant or perinatal death: A 30-month follow up. *Journal of Paediatric Child Health, 38*, 368–372.

Wampold, B. E., Mondin, G. W., Moody, M., Stich, F., Benson, K., & Ahn, H. (1997). A meta-analysis of outcome studies comparing bona fide psychotherapies: Empiricially, "all must have prizes." *Psychological Bulletin, 122*(3), 203–215.

Weinfield, N. S., Sroufe, L., Egeland, B., & Carlson, E. (2008). Individual differences in infant-caregiver attachment: Conceptual and empirical aspects of security. In J. Cassidy, P. R. Shaver (Eds.), *Handbook of attachment: Theory, research, and clinical applications*, 2nd ed. (pp. 78–101). New York: Guilford Press.

Wertsch, J. V. (1985). *Vygotsky and the social formation of mind*. Cambridge, MA: Harvard University Press.

Wolfe, D., Scott, K., Reitzel-Jaffe, D., Wekerle, C., Grasley, C., & Straatman, A. (2001). Development and validation of the Conflict in Adolescent Dating Relationships Inventory. *Psychological Assessment, 13*(2), 277–293.

Wrenn, C. G. (1985). Afterword: The culturally encapsulated counselor revisited. In P. Pedersen (Ed.), *Handbook of cross-cultural counseling and therapy* (pp. 323–330). Westport, CT: Greenwood.

INDEX